ESPAÑA Y PORTUGAL

Copyright by C. S. HAMMOND & CO., N.Y.

ESCALA

KILÓMETROS
0 50 100 150 200

MILLAS
0 50 100 150 200

Capitales ....
Límites Internacionales ....

FRANCIA

ANDORRA

Mar Mediterráneo

Longitud Oeste de Greenwich

ISLAS BALEARES

Menorca
Mallorca
Palma
Ibiza

Barcelona
Tarragona

CATALUÑA

ARAGÓN

Río Ebro

Zaragoza

NAVARRA

VIZCAYA
San Sebastián
Bilbao

Golfo de Gascuña

Covadonga
Oviedo
ASTURIAS

León

Burgos

Valladolid

Zamora

Salamanca

CASTILLA LA VIEJA

Río Duero

Segovia
Escorial
Avila
Madrid

CASTILLA LA NUEVA

Cuenca

Valencia

Alicante

Murcia
Cartagena

La Mancha

Toledo

Río Tajo

Río Guadiana

EXTREMADURA

Badajoz

ANDALUCIA

Guadalquivir

Córdoba
Río Genil
Granada
Almería

Sevilla
Itálica

Málaga

Gibraltar
(Brit.)

Tarifa

Cádiz

Estr. de Gibraltar

ESPAÑA

GALICIA

La Coruña
Cabo Finisterre
Santiago
Vigo
Río Miño

Río Duero

Oporto

Lisboa

PORTUGAL

Océano Atlántico

Basic
Conversational Spanish

Basic
Conversational
Spanish

GREGORY G. LaGRONE
University of Texas

HOLT, RINEHART AND WINSTON   NEW YORK

Preface

This book is designed to facilitate a conversational approach to Spanish. Each lesson opens with a short model text in Spanish, dealing with topics of everyday life. The model texts, which form the basis for the oral and written exercises, combine narration or description with dialogue, and contain examples of all that is new, in vocabulary and constructions. The aim throughout is threefold: (1) to supply a reasonable amount of ready-made conversational material, (2) to help develop fluency through appropriate drills, and (3) to emphasize original, independent use of the language.

The twenty-five lessons follow a natural sequence of ideas, paralleled by a gradual progression in syntactical difficulty. It is to be hoped that this premeditated plan is as unobtrusive as possible. The five review lessons offer an opportunity to pause and take stock, by presenting, on facing pages, a summary of usage and a test exercise. The Appendix contains reference lists of verb forms, and the English-Spanish vocabulary supplements the index, since the first appearance of words and phrases is noted by lesson number.

The vocabulary and constructions correlate rather closely with the frequency counts, not only because these were consulted, but because simple, everyday Spanish must necessarily have such a correlation. On the other hand, it is all too easy to use high-frequency words and constructions to express low-frequency ideas. In this respect, the frequencies, as recorded for native speakers, sometimes differ radically from those of English-speaking persons who are learning the language. If a text of this kind were to adhere strictly to the frequency counts, it would not even include the name of the language being studied. By the same token there are some high-frequency words which do not fit readily into conversational material of this kind.

Those who are familiar with my earlier texts will, I believe, find here certain improvements in methods and materials which make for a more usable book. My goals have been: (1) a practical approach to pronunciation, (2) an even distribution of syntactical matter, (3) unity of ideas and vocabulary in the model texts, (4) close linking of texts, explanations, and exercises, (5) uniformity in length and difficulty of the lessons, (6) simplicity in the drill exercises, (7) emphasis on the expression of ideas in the other exercises, and (8) a manageable mechanical arrangement, in format and paging.

For helping me keep my "basic" Spanish as natural as possible, within its inevitable limits, I have become indebted on several occasions to Professor and Mrs. Ramón Martínez López and to Mrs. Victoria Romera-Navarro. For contributing the same service to the English portions, and for other assistance with the work, I am indebted to my wife, Margaret Allyn LaGrone. To Professor Ernest F. Haden I am indebted for help with a number of linguistic problems. The introduction to pronunciation is a product of our collaboration. Finally, I wish to express my appreciation to the many users of my earlier works whose generous suggestions for improvements have been freely incorporated in this book.

G. G. L.

Contents

Introduction

The ability to pronounce the thirty-odd sounds of Spanish in varying sequences forms the basis of a good pronunciation of the language. To imitate new sounds, most people, after early childhood, need to be aware of the position of the tongue, lips, etc., and to think in terms of stress, linking, and intonation patterns.

1. Individual Sounds. In Spanish there are five basic vowel sounds, and these vary only slightly according to position or stress. The position of the speech organs for producing these sounds is shown here.*

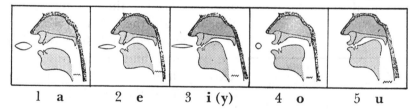

1 a   2 e   3 i (y)   4 o   5 u

The nearest English equivalents would be: *ah, eh, ēē, oh, ōō.* To make the Spanish sounds, assume extreme and fixed positions, noting particularly the position of the lips. Keep the sounds brief and clear, avoiding the English tendency to relax at the end, producing an extra sound as an "off-glide."

For pronouncing combinations of vowels, it is helpful to practice going from one position to the other without interrupting the voice and without obscuring any of the sounds.

ae	ai, ay	ao	au
ea	ei, ey	eo	eu
oa	oi, oy	oc	ou

---

* These drawings are reproduced from Professor Haden's *How to Pronounce Spanish* (Henry Holt and Co.), which gives a fuller introduction to pronunciation.

Note the following pairs of voiced consonants.

Nos. 6, 8, 10: Usually the air passage is not quite closed. Practice them with vowel sounds, shifting the stress (**ába, abá,** etc.). In making **b, v** (No. 6) avoid rounding the lips (as in English *w*) or using the teeth (as in English *v*).

6 **b, v**   7 **b, v**

aba	ebe	ibi	obo	ubu
ava	eve	ivi	ovo	uvu
ada	ede	idi	odo	udu
aga	egue	igui	ogo	ugu

8 **d**   9 **d**

Nos. 7, 9, 11: After a pause (or after a consonant with the same point of articulation), the air passage is closed. Begin the voicing (vibration of the vocal cords) before opening the passage, and avoid aspiration (extra puff or *h*-sound). Note that for **d** (No. 9) the tip of the tongue is against the upper teeth.

10 **g**   11 **g**
gu + *e, i*   **gu** + *e, i*

ba	be	bi	bo	bu
va	ve	vi	vo	vu
da	de	di	do	du
ga	gue	gui	go	gu

Four of these positions are used for voiceless consonants.

No. 12: The tongue position varies considerably according to the vowel that follows. Note that the sound is like No. 10 except that there is no voicing.

12 **j**
g + *e, i*

ja	je, ge	ji, gi	jo	ju
aja	eje, ege	iji, igi	ojo	uju

13 p   14 t

Nos. 13, 14, 15: Avoid aspiration (extra puff or *h*-sound). Note that for **t** the tip of the tongue is against the upper teeth. The letter *k* is used in very few words.

15 c, k
qu + *e, i*

pa	pe	pi	po	pu
ta	te	ti	to	tu
ca	que	qui	co	cu
ka	ke	ki	ko	ku
apa	epe	ipi	opo	upu
ata	ete	iti	oto	utu
aca	eque	iqui	oco	ucu

No. 16: In Spain the standard **s** is made with the tip of the tongue, and is briefer and less tense than English *s*. A variant **s**, like that of English, is used in parts of Spain and most of Spanish America. In these same regions the **s**-sound is also used for **z, c** + *e, i* (No. 17). The sound usually becomes voiced when followed by a voiced consonant.

16 s

sa	se	si	so	su	esde

No. 17: In Spain the standard sound for **z, c** + *e, i* is a voiceless *th*-sound made with the tongue visibly between the teeth, and with strong exhalation of the breath. The sound usually becomes voiced when followed by a voiced consonant.

17 z
c + *e, i*

za	ce	ci	zo	zu	azgo
aza	ece	ici	ozo	uzu	uzgo

No. 18: The sound resembles English *ch* (as in *cheek)*, but is briefer and with lip position determined by the neighboring vowels.

18 ch

cha	che	chi	cho	chu
acha	eche	ichi	ocho	uchu

19 y (i)

No. 19: In most regions the y-sound is pronounced with the passage more nearly closed than in English, and in emphatic speech, with the passage completely closed after a pause (or after a consonant with the same point of articulation). In many regions the y-sound is also used for **ll** (No. 20).

ya, ia	ye, ie	yo, io	yu, iu
aya	eye	oyo	uyu

20 ll

No. 20: The sound for **ll** (except where the simple y-sound is used) is a palatalized *l:* an *"l"* pronounced with the tongue in position for *y.*

lla	lle	llo	llu
alla	elle	ollo	ullu

21 ñ

No. 21: The ñ-sound is a palatalized *n:* an *"n"* pronounced with the tongue in position for *y.*

aña	eñe	iñi	oño	uñu

22 l

No. 22: Note that for l the back of the tongue is not rounded as in English. Often the tongue is in position for a following consonant (**c** + *e, i,* **ch, d, ll, ñ, t, y, z**). After l the passage is closed for **d** or **y.**

ala	ele	ili	olo	ulu
bla	cla	fla	gla	pla
alce	alza	elche	oldo	ultu

23 r

No. 23: The sound is a single tap. Keep the tip of the tongue flexible. Avoid moving the jaws or rounding the lips (as in English *r*).

ara	ere	iri	oro	uru
bra	cra	fra	gra	pra
tra	tre	tri	tro	tru

No. 24: The sound is a trilled **r** (two or more taps). Keep the tip of the tongue flexible, even while practicing with extra force. The single letter *r* is trilled at the beginning of a word, or after *l, n, s;* the letter *rr* is always trilled. In *s* + *r* the *s* may be pronounced with the tongue in position for *r*.

24	**r, rr**	ra	re	ri	ro	ru
		arra	erre	irri	orro	urru
		elra	enre	isra	onra	unre

| 25 | **h** (always silent) | ah | eh | hi | oh | hu |

| 26 | **f** (as in English) | fa | fe | fi | fo | fu |

27 **x** + *vowel* (like **gs** or **ks**); **x** + *consonant* (like **s** or **ks**)

exa	exo	axi	exi	oxi
exce	expo	expli	exte	extra

28 **m, n** The nasals are as in English, except that before another consonant they are pronounced with the tongue or lips in position for that consonant. After a nasal the passage is closed for **b, d, g** + *a, o, u,* **gu** + *e, i,* **v, y.**

amba	once	anca	enfe	ongo
invi	onza	engue	onja	ingue

2. Alphabet.

LETTERS	SOUNDS		LETTERS	SOUNDS		LETTERS	SOUNDS
a	*a*	1	j	*jota*	12	r, rr	*erre*	23-24
b	*be*	6-7	k	*ka*	15	s	*ese*	16
c	*ce*	15-17	l	*ele*	22	t	*te*	14
ch	*che*	18	ll	*elle*	20	u	*u*	5
d	*de*	8-9	m	*eme*	28	v	*ve*	6-7
e	*e*	2	n	*ene*	28	w	*ve doble*	foreign
f	*efe*	26	ñ	*eñe*	21		*(doble u)*	words
g	*ge*	10-12	o	*o*	4	x	*equis*	27
h	*hache*	25	p	*pe*	13	y	*ye*	3, 19
i	*i*	3, 19	q	*cu*	15	z	*zeta*	16-17

3. Syllables.

(a) Spanish words have as many syllables as they have vowel sounds. Note, however, that unaccented **i** or **u** combines with a preceding or following vowel to form a diphthong.

sa-lu-dos	lue-go	gra-cias	Lui-sa
Fe-li-pe	bue-no	fa-mi-lia	ciu-dad

(b) A single consonant (including **ch, ll, rr**) goes with the vowel that follows it.

to-dos	no-che	e-lla	o-cu-rrir
ma-ña-na	mu-cha-cho	ca-lle	re-co-rrer

(c) The last of a group of consonants, or a consonant + **l** or **r**, goes with the following vowel.

vis-ta	tar-de	Pa-blo	siem-pre
cla-se	bas-tan-te	e-jem-plo	nues-tro

4. Stress and Spelling.

(a) Most words ending in a vowel or **n** or **s** are stressed on the *next to the last* syllable. Most words ending in a consonant other than **n** or **s** are stressed on the *last* syllable.

has-ta	*ha*-blan	us-*ted*	es-*tar*
des-pe-*di*-da	re-*cuer*-dos	Mi-*guel*	es-*toy*

(b) All other words of more than one syllable are spelled with an accent mark over the stressed vowel.

a-*sí*	es-*tán*	a-*diós*	*fá*-cil
sim-*pá*-ti-co	a-le-*mán*	e-*xá*-me-nes	di-*fí*-cil

5. Written Accent. The written accent, besides indicating stressed syllables (see §4), has two additional uses.

(a) It is placed over any stressed **i** or **u** that comes before or after an **a**, **e**, or **o**.

dí-as	Ma-rí-a	mí-o	le-í-a

(b) It is used to distinguish between words otherwise spelled alike. One of each such pair—the one more often stressed in a sentence—has an accent mark over the stressed vowel. Compare:

como, *as*	que, *that*	tu, *your*	el, *the*
cómo, *how*	qué, *what*	tú, *you*	él, *he*

6. Phrasing. In Spanish the important unit of speech is the phrase (a group of syllables spoken without a pause). Normally several phrases are linked together into a larger grouping. The words within such a group are usually spoken as if they formed a single word, except that (1) initial **r** of words remains trilled, and (2) "strong" vowels (**a, e, o**), as well as "weak" vowels (**i, u**), may link between words to form diphthongs or triphthongs. Examples:

GROUP	NOTES ON PRONUNCIATION
Buenos días. (bue-nos-di-as)	**s** (voiced before voiced consonant); **d** (air passage not closed)
¿Cómo está usted? (co-moes-taus-ted)	**o** + **e, a** + **u** (final vowel + initial vowel in one syllable)
Bien, gracias, ¿y usted? (bien-gra-cias-yus-ted)	**n** + **g** (nasal in position for following consonant); **y** + **u** (in one syllable)
La familia está bien. (la-fa-mi-liaes-ta-bien)	**ia** + **e** (final diphthong + initial vowel in one syllable); **b** (air passage not closed)
Todos están bien. (to-do-ses-tam-bien)	**s** + **e** (final consonant + initial vowel); **n** (**m**) + **b** (nasal in position for following consonant)

7. Intonation. There are many variations in intonation according to the circumstances under which each sentence is spoken. These variations usually occur, however, within certain typical patterns, which should be noted and practiced.

No. 1: The pitch rises up to the first stressed syllable, and drops to its lowest note after the last stressed syllable. If the first or last syllable is stressed, there is a rise or fall within the syllable.

1

María es mejicana.

Todos están *bien*.

No. 2: There is usually a higher pitch at the end of each group within a statement.

2

Felipe, Pablo y *yo* / somos norteamericanos.
Entiendo el espa*ñol*, / pero no lo hablo.

No. 3: In questions the most typical pattern has the highest pitch on the first stressed syllable, then a falling intonation followed by a rise after the last stressed syllable, or on the last syllable if stressed.

3

¿Habla español María?
¿Cómo está usted?

Basic
Conversational Spanish

1 Saludos y despedidas

Buenos días. Buenas tardes. Buenas noches.
Adiós. Hasta luego. Hasta la vista. Hasta mañana.

(Felipe y Pablo.)

FELIPE. Buenos días, Pablo.
PABLO. Buenos días. ¿Cómo está usted? 5
FELIPE. Muy bien, gracias, ¿y usted?
PABLO. Estoy bien, gracias.

(María y Luisa.)

MARÍA. Buenas tardes, Luisa. ¿Cómo estás?
LUISA. Bien, gracias, ¿y tú? 10
MARÍA. Muy bien. ¿Cómo está la familia?
LUISA. Está bien, gracias.
MARÍA. Recuerdos a todos.
LUISA. Gracias. Hasta luego.
MARÍA. Adiós. Hasta la vista. 15

(Pablo y Miguel.)

PABLO. ¡Hola! Buenas noches, Miguel. ¿Qué tal?
MIGUEL. Bien, ¿y tú?
PABLO. Así así, gracias.
MIGUEL. La familia, ¿bien? 20
PABLO. Todos están bien, gracias.
MIGUEL. Hasta mañana, ¿eh?
PABLO. Hasta mañana.

VOCABULARY

a to
adiós good-by
así así fair, so-so
bien well, fine, all right
buenas noches good evening, hello; good night
buenas tardes good afternoon, hello
buenos días good morning, hello
¿cómo? how?
las despedidas farewells, goodbys
¿eh? eh?, eh what?, right?
está (you) are *(polite);* (it) is
están (they) are
estar to be
estás (you) are *(familiar)*
estoy I am
la familia family
Felipe Philip
gracias thanks, thank you
hasta until

¡hola! hey!, hi!, hello!
la *f. sing.* the
luego soon, then; hasta luego so long, see you later
Luisa Louise
mañana tomorrow; hasta mañana see you tomorrow
María Mary
Miguel Michael
muy very, quite
Pablo Paul
¿qué tal? how goes it?
los recuerdos regards, greetings; recuerdos a todos remember me to everybody
los saludos greetings
todos *pl.* all, everybody
tú you *(familiar)*
usted you *(polite)*
la vista sight, view, meeting; hasta la vista so long, good-by
y and

GRAMMATICAL EXPLANATIONS

1. **Inverted Punctuation Marks (¿ and ¡).** In Spanish an inverted punctuation mark is used at the beginning of a question or exclamation, in addition to the regular mark at the end (¿...?, ¡...!). The beginning of the question or exclamation is not necessarily the beginning of the sentence.

¡Hola! ¿Qué tal?   *Hello! How goes it?*
Estoy bien, gracias, ¿y usted?   *I'm fine, thank you, and you?*

2. **Accent Marks.** *(Cf. Introduction,* §§4-5.) Note the use of accent marks according to certain rules of spelling, which concern syllables (**así, está, están, estás, adiós**), weak vowels (**días, María**), and words (**cómo, qué, tú**).

3. Gender of Nouns. Spanish nouns are masculine or feminine; none are neuter. It is best to learn the gender by associating the proper form of the definite article ("the") with the nouns.

4. Forms of the Definite Article.

	SINGULAR	PLURAL
MASCULINE	el $\Big\}$ *the*	los $\Big\}$ *the*
FEMININE	la	las

5. Familiar and Polite Forms of Address. In Spanish there are two sets of forms for *you, your, to you,* etc.: (1) the "familiar" forms (the traditional *second-person* forms), which are used primarily among members of the family or among intimate friends, and (2) the "polite" forms (all *third-person* forms), which are used in more formal speech.

The polite third-person forms derived from the use of **vuestra merced,** *your grace* (now contracted to **usted,** *you),* which required the third-person forms of the verb, the object pronouns, the possessives, etc. In most of Spanish America the third-person plural forms are used as familiar, as well as polite, forms of address.

6. Subject Pronouns.

PERSON	SINGULAR	PLURAL
1ST	yo, *I*	nosotros (masc.) $\Big\}$ *we* nosotras (fem.)
2ND	tú, *you* (familiar)	vosotros (masc.) $\Big\}$ *you* (familiar) vosotras (fem.)
3RD	usted, *you* (polite) él, *he* ella, *she*	ustedes, *you* (polite) ellos (masc.) $\Big\}$ *they* ellas (fem.)

(a) **Usted** and **ustedes** may be abbreviated to **V.** and **VV.,** **Vd.** and **Vds.,** or **Ud.** and **Uds.**

(b) The subject pronouns are used mainly for stress (that is, to express or imply a contrast between different subjects). **Usted** and **ustedes** are also used for politeness, but are not normally repeated within a sentence or a series of short sentences.

7. Verb. Present indicative of **estar,** *to be.*

PERSON	SINGULAR	PLURAL
1ST	**estoy,** *I am*	**estamos,** *we are*
2ND	**estás,** *you are* (familiar)	**estáis,** *you are* (familiar)
3RD	**está** $\begin{cases} you\ are\ \text{(polite)} \\ he,\ she,\ \text{or}\ it\ is \end{cases}$	**están** $\begin{cases} you\ are\ \text{(polite)} \\ they\ are \end{cases}$

EXERCISES

A. STRUCTURE PRACTICE. *(Use the models as guides for the exercises, by selecting one item from each column.)*

1. Estoy
Estamos $\Big\}$ bien,
La familia está muy bien, $\Big\}$ gracias.
así así,

*Answer.** 1. ¿Cómo está usted? 2. ¿Cómo están ustedes? 3. ¿Cómo está la familia?

Translate.† 1. I'm so-so, thank you. 2. We're fine, thank you. 3. The family is quite well, thank you.

2. Todos
Pablo y Miguel $\Big\}$ están $\Big\{$ bien,
María y Luisa muy bien, $\Big\}$ gracias.
así así,

Answer. 1. ¿Cómo están todos? 2. ¿Cómo están Pablo y Miguel? 3. ¿Cómo están María y Luisa?

---

* In the first drills on new material, it is helpful to express the ideas in complete sentences, though in actual conversation this would often seem unnatural.

† Translation should be the transfer of ideas, not individual words, from one language to another. Word by word translations are rarely correct and often have no meaning.

Translate. 1. Everybody is fine, thank you. 2. Mary and Louise are quite well, thank you. 3. Paul and Michael are so-so, thank you.

3. Adiós.   ⎫   ⎧ todos.
     Hasta luego.   ⎬ Recuerdos a   ⎨ la familia.
     Hasta mañana.   ⎭   ⎩ Felipe.

Give appropriate replies. 1. Adiós. 2. Hasta luego. 3. Hasta mañana.

Translate. 1. Good-by. Remember me to the family. 2. See you later. Remember me to Philip. 3. See you tomorrow. Remember me to everybody.

B. DRILL EXERCISES.

1. *Use the proper form of* **estar** *with each subject pronoun.* (*Example:* yo—yo estoy.) 1. nosotros. 2. usted. 3. ustedes. 4. ella. 5. ellos.

2. *Use an appropriate subject pronoun with each form of* **estar.** (*Example:* estoy—yo estoy.) 1. estamos. 2. está. 3. están. 4. estás. 5. estáis.

3. *Ask how each person or group is.* (*Example:* Pablo— ¿Cómo está Pablo?) 1. Pablo y Miguel. 2. María. 3. María y Luisa. 4. Felipe. 5. Felipe y Pablo.

4. *Answer without using a subject noun or pronoun.* (*Example:* ¿Cómo está usted? — Estoy bien, gracias.) 1. ¿Cómo están ustedes? 2. ¿Cómo está la familia? 3. ¿Cómo está Miguel? 4. ¿Cómo está Luisa? 5. ¿Cómo están María y Pablo?

C. QUESTIONS. (*Give appropriate replies based on your own ideas rather than on any particular statements in* *the text.)** 1. ¿Cómo está usted? 2. La familia, ¿bien? 3. ¿Cómo está Miguel? 4. ¿Cómo está Luisa? 5. ¿Cómo están Pablo y Felipe? 6. Buenos días. ¿Qué tal? 7. ¿Están ustedes bien? 8. ¿Cómo está la familia? 9. ¿Todos están bien? 10. Hasta mañana, ¿eh?

D. TRANSLATION. *(Express these ideas in Spanish.)* 1. Good afternoon. How are you? 2. How's the family? 3. And how is Mary? 4. She is fine, thank you. 5. Hello (Good evening), Philip. How goes it? 6. So-so, and you? 7. I'm fine, thank you. 8. Remember me to the family. 9. How are they? 10. They are all well (All are well). 11. How are you *(plural)?* 12. We're fine, thank you. 13. Good-by. See you later. 14. So long. 15. See you tomorrow.

E. CONVERSATION AND COMPOSITION. Topic: An exchange of greetings and farewells. *(In so far as possible, adapt the materials of the text to your own circumstances, first orally and then in writing.)*

---

* After the material has been practiced sufficiently in drill exercises, it is best to try to anticipate its use in real situations, where the replies repeat fewer of the elements of the question and are not limited to giving the exact information requested.

2 | Lenguas

Hablo español un poco. También hablo algo el francés. Entiendo el italiano, pero no lo hablo. También entiendo un poco el alemán.

(Miguel, Elena y Felipe.)

MIGUEL.   ¿Habla usted español, señorita?   5
ELENA.   Sí, señor, lo hablo un poco . . . en la clase de español.
FELIPE.   Lo hablamos poco y mal.
MIGUEL.   No, señor, lo hablan ustedes muy bien. ¿Hablan también el francés?   10
ELENA.   Lo hablamos algo.
FELIPE.   Tú lo hablas bastante bien. Yo lo hablo muy poco . . . ¿Qué lenguas habla usted?
MIGUEL.   Hablo el español y el francés, y también un poco el portugués.   15
ELENA.   ¿No habla usted el inglés?
MIGUEL.   No, señorita. Lo entiendo bastante bien, pero no lo hablo.
ELENA.   Lo habla Luisa, ¿verdad?
MIGUEL.   Sí, Luisa lo habla bastante bien.   20
FELIPE.   ¿Hablan ustedes en español con Isabel?
MIGUEL.   Sí, siempre hablamos en español.
ELENA.   ¿Qué lenguas habla Isabel?
MIGUEL.   Habla sólo el inglés y el español. También entiende un poco el alemán y el ruso.   25

[8]

VOCABULARY

el **alemán** German *(language)*
algo *adv.* some, somewhat, a
  little
bastante *adv.* enough; rather,
  fairly
la **clase** class, course; **clase de**
  español Spanish class
con with
de of
Elena Helen
en in, at
entender to understand
entiende (she) understands
entiendo I understand
el **español** Spanish *(language)*
el **francés** French *(language)*
habla (you) speak, (she)
  speaks; **¿habla usted?** do
  you speak?
hablamos we speak
hablan (you, *pl.*) speak
hablar to speak, to talk
hablas (you) speak
hablo (I) speak

el **inglés** English *(language)*
Isabel Elizabeth
el **italiano** Italian *(language)*
las **lenguas** languages
lo *obj. pron., m. sing.* it; **lo**
  hablo I speak it
mal badly, poorly
no no, not; **no lo hablo** I
  don't speak it
pero but
poco *adv.* little
el **portugués** Portuguese *(lan-*
  guage)
¿qué? what? which?
el **ruso** Russian
señor sir; **señora** ma'am;
  señorita Miss
sí yes; **sí, señor** yes (sir)
siempre always
sólo *adv.* only
también also, too
un poco *adv.* a little
la **verdad** truth; **¿verdad?** true?
  (= doesn't she, *etc.*)

GRAMMATICAL EXPLANATIONS

1. Idiomatic Form. ¿Verdad?, *true?, isn't it so?,* is used to
ask for confirmation of a statement (affirmative or negative).

Usted habla inglés, ¿verdad?	*You speak English, don't you?*
Miguel no lo habla, ¿verdad?	*Michael doesn't speak it, does he?*
Todos están bien, ¿verdad?	*They are all well, aren't they?*

2. Small Letters for Words of Nationality, etc. As in English, the names of persons or places are capitalized, but the
derived forms (for example, names of languages or nationality)
are not capitalized.

Entiende el **francés** y el **ruso.**	*He understands French and Rus-sian.*

3. Definite Article with Names of Languages. The definite article is regularly used with names of languages, except after **de,** *of,* **en,** *in,* and certain verbs (like **hablar,** *to speak).*

Entienden **el portugués.**	*They understand Portuguese.*
Todos hablamos **inglés.**	*We all speak English.*
Está en la clase de **español.**	*He is in the Spanish class.*
Siempre hablan **en italiano.**	*They always speak in Italian.*

Even after **de, en,** or **hablar,** the article is used when the idea is not partitive ("some") but general ("all"). This usually involves stress (either contrast with some other language or use of an adverb of manner with **hablar).**

Hablo **el francés** y **el alemán.**	*I speak French and German.*
Hablan muy bien **el español.**	*They speak Spanish very well.*

4. Word Order in Statements. There are some basic differences between Spanish and English word order.

(a) The negative word **no,** *not,* and also the object pronouns *(him, her, it,* etc.) normally precede the verb.

Elena **no lo** habla.	*Helen does not speak it.*

(b) A long or stressed subject may follow the verb.

No lo hablan **Pablo y Felipe.**	*Paul and Philip do not speak it.*

(c) An adverb may come between the verb and noun object.

Todos hablan **bien** el español.	*They all speak Spanish well.*

5. Word Order in Questions. The basic pattern is an inversion of subject and verb (normal order for *pronouns)* or subject and predicate (normal order for *nouns).*

¿Habla **usted** portugués?	*Do you speak Portuguese?*
¿Habla italiano **Isabel?**	*Does Elizabeth speak Italian?*

(a) As in English, interrogative words or phrases come first.

¿**Cómo** está usted?	*How are you?*
¿**Qué lenguas** habla usted?	*What languages do you speak?*

(b) Note that often there is no inversion in Spanish because of the omission of subject pronouns. As in English, this form can be used even when the subject is expressed.

¿Hablan francés?	*Do they speak French?*
¿Luisa habla inglés?	*Louise speaks English?*

(c) Long or stressed elements tend to come at the end of the sentence.

¿Habla español **usted?**	*Do you speak Spanish?* (Subject pronoun stressed)
¿Habla María **el alemán?**	*Does Mary speak German?* (Object stressed)
¿Habla María **el** francés **y el** inglés?	*Does Mary speak French and English?* (Long predicate)

6. Meanings of the Present Indicative. The meaning depends on the context and the construction. Compare:

habla	*(he) speaks* or *(he) is speaking*
¿habla?	*does (he) speak?* or *is (he) speaking?*
no habla	*(he) does not speak* or *(he) is not speaking*

7. Verbs. Present indicative of **entender,** *to understand,* and **hablar,** *to speak, to talk.*

Entender		**Hablar**	
entiendo	entendemos	hablo	hablamos
entiendes	entendéis	hablas	habláis
entiende	entienden	habla	hablan

EXERCISES

A. STRUCTURE PRACTICE.*

1. Sí, señor, ⎫
   Sí, señora, ⎬ lo ⎰ hablo ⎱ un poco.
   Sí, señorita, ⎭   ⎱ hablamos ⎰
                          ⎱ hablan ⎰

Answer. 1. ¿Habla usted español? 2. ¿Hablan ustedes alemán? 3. ¿Hablan francés María y Luisa?

---

* For suggested procedure, see Lesson 1.

Translate. 1. Yes (sir), they speak it a little. 2. Yes (ma'am), I speak it a little. 3. Yes (Miss), we speak it a little.

2. No, señor,   ⎫   ⎧ hablo.
   No, señora,   ⎬   no lo   ⎨ hablamos.
   No, señorita,   ⎭   ⎩ hablan.

Answer. 1. ¿Habla usted italiano? 2. ¿Hablan ustedes portugués? 3. ¿Hablan ruso Pablo y Felipe?

Translate. 1. No (ma'am), they don't speak it. 2. No, (Miss), I don't speak it. 3. No (sir), we don't speak it.

3. Entiendo   ⎫   el español   ⎫   un poco.
   Entendemos   ⎬   el italiano   ⎬   muy poco.
   Entiende   ⎭   el portugués   ⎭   bastante bien.

Answer. 1. ¿Entiende usted el español? 2. ¿Entienden ustedes el italiano? 3. ¿Entiende Miguel el portugués?

Translate. 1. We understand Spanish a little. 2. He understands Italian rather well. 3. I understand Portuguese very little.

B. Drill Exercises.

1. *Add a subject pronoun for stress. (Example:* No lo hablo. — No lo hablo yo.) 1. No lo entiendo. 2. No lo hablamos. 3. No lo entendemos. 4. No lo hablas. 5. No lo entendéis.

2. *Ask whether each person or group speaks Spanish. (Example:* Pablo — ¿Habla español Pablo?) 1. Pablo y Elena. 2. Miguel. 3. Miguel y Luisa. 4. Felipe. 5. Felipe y María.

3. *State that each person or group understands Spanish. (Example:* Elena — Elena entiende el español.) 1. Elena y yo. 2. María. 3. María y yo. 4. Pablo. 5. Pablo y yo.

C. QUESTIONS.* 1. ¿Habla usted español? 2. ¿Lo entiende bastante bien? 3. ¿Habla usted en español con Luisa? 4. ¿Entiende usted el francés? 5. ¿Lo habla un poco? 6. ¿Qué lenguas entiende usted? 7. ¿Qué lenguas entiende María? 8. ¿Habla usted en inglés con María? 9. Miguel habla español, ¿verdad? 10. ¿Habla también el inglés? 11. ¿Entiende algo el portugués? 12. ¿Qué lenguas habla Miguel? 13. ¿Hablan francés María y Elena? 14. ¿Lo hablan en la clase de francés? 15. Isabel entiende el ruso, ¿verdad? 16. ¿Entiende también el alemán? 17. ¿Lo entiende Felipe? 18. ¿Lo entiende usted? 19. ¿Entienden ustedes el italiano? 20. ¿Qué lengua habla usted con Felipe?

D. TRANSLATION. 1. You speak Spanish, don't you? 2. I speak it a little. 3. We speak it in the Spanish class. 4. We speak it very badly. 5. No (sir), you speak it very well. 6. What languages do *you* speak? 7. I only speak Spanish and French. 8. I also understand Italian and Portuguese a little. 9. Don't you speak English? 10. No (Miss), I understand it a little, but I don't speak it. 11. Mary and Louise speak it, don't they? 12. They speak it quite well. 13. You speak in Spanish with Elizabeth, don't you? 14. Yes, we always speak in Spanish. 15. What languages does Elizabeth speak? 16. She only speaks English and Spanish. 17. Doesn't she speak German? 18. She understands German and Russian a little. 19. Does Mary understand German? 20. She understands it rather well.

E. CONVERSATION AND COMPOSITION.* Topic: Languages that you or your friends speak or understand.

---

* For suggested procedure, see Lesson 1.

3 Nacionalidad

Soy norteamericano. Hablo sólo el inglés. Estudio el
español, pero lo hablo muy poco. El español no es fácil.
Es bastante difícil, pero es interesante. A veces hablo
español con Miguel y Luisa. Miguel es español. Luisa
es mejicana. Los dos son muy simpáticos.   5

(Miguel, Elena y José.)

MIGUEL. ¿Son norteamericanos los señores Martín?
ELENA. No, él es francés; ella es alemana.
MIGUEL. Hablan muy bien el inglés, ¿verdad?
JOSÉ. Sí, lo hablan muy bien, casi sin acento.   10
MIGUEL. ¿Es norteamericano Eduardo?
JOSÉ. No, es inglés.
MIGUEL. Es un muchacho muy simpático.
ELENA. Usted es español, ¿verdad?
MIGUEL. Sí, señorita, soy de España.   15
JOSÉ. ¿De dónde son los señores Pérez?
MIGUEL. Él es mejicano; ella es española.
ELENA. ¿Quiénes son los señores Pérez?
MIGUEL. El señor Pérez es profesor de español. Enseña
aquí en la Universidad.   20
ELENA. ¿Hablan inglés los dos?
MIGUEL. Don Antonio lo habla bastante bien, pero doña
Inés lo habla muy poco.
JOSÉ. ¿Cómo es la señora Pérez?
MIGUEL. Es bonita y simpática.   25

VOCABULARY

el **acento** accent; **sin acento** without an accent
alemán, alemana *adj.* or *noun* German
Antonio Anthony
aquí here
bonito, -a pretty
casi almost
de from
difícil difficult, hard
don *m.*, **doña** *f.*, *titles of respect used with first names*
¿dónde? where?; **¿de dónde son?** where are (they) from?
dos two; **los dos** both
Eduardo Edward
enseña he teaches
enseñar to teach
es (you) are, (he, she, it) is; **¿cómo es?** what is (she) like?
España *f.* Spain
español, española *adj.* or *noun* Spanish, Spaniard
estudiar to study
estudio I am studying
fácil easy
francés, francesa French, Frenchman, *etc.*

Inés Agnes
inglés, inglesa English, Englishman, *etc.*
interesante interesting
José Joseph
mejicano, -a *adj.* or *noun* Mexican
el **muchacho** boy, fellow; la **muchacha** girl
la **nacionalidad** nationality
norteamericano, -a *adj.* or *noun* American
el **profesor**, la **profesora** professor *or* teacher
¿quién? (*pl.* **¿quiénes?**) who?
el **señor** gentleman, Mr.; la **señora** lady, wife, Mrs.; la **señorita** young lady, Miss; los **señores** lady and gentleman, Mr. and Mrs.
ser to be
simpático, -a likable, nice, pleasant
sin without
son (they) are
soy I am
un, una a *or* an
la **universidad** university
la **vez** time; **a veces** at times, sometimes

GRAMMATICAL EXPLANATIONS

1. Definite Article with Titles. The definite article is regularly used with titles (except **don** and **doña**) in speaking *about* a person (but not *to* the person).

El profesor Pérez es mejicano.
Professor Pérez is Mexican.
La señora Pérez es española.
Mrs. Pérez is Spanish.
Don Antonio y **doña** Inés son simpáticos.
Don Antonio and Doña Inés are likable.

In direct address the article is omitted (and usually the surname also). For politeness **señor** or **señora** may precede another title.

¿Es usted español, **Sr. Pérez?**	*Are you Spanish, Mr. Pérez?*
¿Cómo está usted, **señora** *(or*	*How are you, Mrs. Pérez?*
Sra. Pérez)?	
Buenos días, **señor (profesor).**	*Good morning, sir.*

Note that titles are written with small letters except when abbreviated (**señor, Sr.; señora, Sra.; señorita, Srta.; señores, Sres.; don, D.; doña, D.ª**).

2. Forms of the Indefinite Article.

	SINGULAR	PLURAL
MASCULINE	**un** ⎫ *a, an*	**unos** ⎫ *some, a few*
FEMININE	**una** ⎭	**unas** ⎭

3. Predicate Nouns Used as Adjectives. Predicate nouns (or phrases) which serve to classify (by nationality, profession, religion, etc.) are used adjectively, without the indefinite article.

Miguel es **español.**	*Michael is a Spaniard (= Spanish).*
¿Es profesor D. Antonio?—Sí, es profesor de español.	*Is Don Antonio a teacher?—Yes, he is a Spanish teacher.*

The addition of a qualifying adjective usually eliminates this adjectival use of the noun, and the article is used. Note that the indefinite article is always more stressed than in English.

Es **un** profesor simpático.	*He is a likable professor.*

4. Position of Descriptive Adjectives. Descriptive adjectives usually follow the nouns that they modify.

Es una lengua **difícil.**	*It is a difficult language.*
José es un muchacho **simpático.**	*Joseph is a likable fellow.*
María y Luisa son muchachas muy **bonitas.**	*Mary and Louise are very pretty girls.*

5. Gender and Number of Nouns and Adjectives.

(a) **Endings.** For either nouns or adjectives the most usual endings in the singular are **-o** (masculine) and **-a** (feminine). Other adjectives (except words of nationality) rarely change in the feminine. To form the plural, add s if the singular ends in a vowel (for example, **simpático, simpáticos; interesante, interesantes**); add **es** if it ends in a consonant (**difícil, difíciles**).

Because of the conventions of Spanish spelling (see Introduction, §§1, 4), words of two or more syllables whose singular ends in **n** or **s** must add or drop an accent mark when **es** is added for the plural (**alemán, alemanes; inglés, ingleses**); and words ending in **z** have a spelling change, **z > c**, in the plural (**vez, veces**).

(b) **Agreement.** Adjectives agree in gender and number with the nouns (or pronouns) that they modify. The masculine plural is used to include two or more forms of different gender.

Luisa es **mejicana**, ¿verdad?	*Louise is Mexican, isn't she?*
Las dos son **españolas.**	*Both (girls) are Spanish.*
Felipe y Elena no son **alemanes.**	*Philip and Helen are not German.*
¿Son (ellos) **norteamericanos?**	*Are they American?*

6. Meanings of *ser* and *estar.*

Both **ser** and **estar** mean *to be.* **Ser** expresses an essential *characteristic;* it tells *what* the person or thing is. **Estar** expresses an incidental *condition;* it tells *how* or *where* the person or thing is.

No **soy** francés. **Soy** norteamericano.	*I'm not French. I'm an American.*
¿De dónde **es** Miguel?—**Es** de España.	*Where is Michael from?—He is from Spain (= is Spanish).*
¿Dónde **está** Pablo?—**Está** en la Universidad.	*Where is Paul?—He is at the University.*
¿Cómo **es** María?—**Es** bonita y simpática.	*What is Mary like?—She is pretty and likable.*
¿Cómo **está** Elena?—**Está** bien, gracias.	*How is Helen?—She is well, thank you.*

7. Verbs. Present indicative of **enseñar,** *to teach,* **estudiar,** *to study,* and **ser,** *to be.*

Enseñar		Estudiar		Ser	
enseño	enseñamos	estudio	estudiamos	soy	somos
enseñas	enseñáis	estudias	estudiáis	eres	sois
enseña	enseñan	estudia	estudian	es	son

EXERCISES

A. STRUCTURE PRACTICE.

1. Don Antonio ⎫ ⎧ simpático.
El profesor Pérez ⎬ **es** ⎨ mejicano.
El señor Martín ⎭ ⎩ profesor de español.

Answer. 1. ¿Cómo es don Antonio? 2. ¿De dónde es el profesor Pérez? 3. ¿Quién es el señor Martín?

Translate. 1. Mr. Martin is likable. 2. Don Antonio is a Spanish teacher. 3. Professor Pérez is a Mexican.

2. María y Luisa ⎫ ⎧ bonitas.
Las dos muchachas ⎬ **son** ⎨ mejicanas.
Las dos señoras ⎭ ⎩ simpáticas.

Answer. 1. ¿Cómo son María y Luisa? 2. ¿De dónde son las dos muchachas? 3. ¿Cómo son las dos señoras?

Translate. 1. The two ladies are Mexican. 2. Mary and Louise are likable. 3. The two girls are pretty.

3. El español ⎫ ⎧ fácil.
El alemán ⎬ **es una lengua** ⎨ difícil.
El francés ⎭ ⎩ interesante.

Answer. 1. ¿Es fácil el español? 2. ¿Es difícil el alemán? 3. ¿Es interesante el francés?

Translate. 1. Spanish is an easy language. 2. French is a difficult language. 3. German is an interesting language.

B. Drill Exercises.

1. *Use the indefinite article instead of the definite. (Example:* la familia — una familia.) 1. la clase. 2. el profesor. 3. la señora. 4. las señoritas. 5. los señores.

2. *Change to the plural. (Example:* muchacho simpático — muchachos simpáticos.) 1. señora simpática. 2. muchacha bonita. 3. profesor simpático. 4. muchacho español. 5. muchacha mejicana.

3. *Add an appropriate subject pronoun for stress. (Example:* Soy norteamericano. — Yo soy norteamericano.) 1. Somos norteamericanos. 2. Es español. 3. Es mejicana. 4. Son simpáticas. 5. Son ingleses.

4. *Change to the negative. (Example:* Lo estudio. — No lo estudio.) 1. Lo enseño. 2. Lo enseñamos. 3. Lo estudian. 4. Lo estudias. 5. Lo estudiáis.

C. Questions. 1. ¿Es usted norteamericano (norteamericana)? 2. ¿Estudia usted el español? 3. ¿Es fácil el español? 4. ¿Es interesante? 5. ¿Habla usted en español con Miguel y Luisa? 6. ¿Son mejicanos Miguel y Luisa? 7. ¿De dónde son los señores Pérez? 8. ¿Dónde enseña el profesor Pérez? 9. ¿Qué enseña? 10. ¿Cómo es la señora Pérez? 11. ¿Habla inglés don Antonio? 12. ¿Lo habla doña Inés? 13. ¿Quién es el señor Martín? 14. ¿De dónde son los señores Martín? 15. ¿Hablan bien el inglés los dos? 16. ¿Son norteamericanos José y Elena? 17. ¿Es bonita Elena? 18. ¿Cómo es José? 19. Eduardo es inglés, ¿verdad? 20. ¿Habla bien el inglés?

D. Translation. 1. We are Americans. 2. We are studying Spanish here at the University. 3. It is not an easy language. 4. It is rather difficult, but it is interesting.

5. You speak Spanish very well, almost without an accent.
6. At times I speak Spanish with Michael and Louise.
7. Both are Mexicans, aren't they?   8. She is a Mexican;
he is a Spaniard.   9. Louise is a very pretty girl.   10. Are
Mr. and Mrs. Pérez Spanish?   11. She is Spanish; he is
Mexican.   12. Who is Mr. Pérez?   13. Don Antonio is a
Spanish teacher.   14. He teaches here at the University.
15. What is Mrs. Pérez like?   16. She is very pleasant.
17. Where are Mr. and Mrs. Martin from?   18. He is
French; she is German.   19. Edward is English, isn't he?
20. He is a very likable fellow.

E. CONVERSATION AND COMPOSITION. Topic: Nationality of several people that you know.

NOUNS AND ADJECTIVES

(Reference List of Forms in Lessons 1–3)

NOUNS*

MASCULINE		FEMININE	
acento	Miguel	alemana	María
alemán†	muchacho	clase	mejicana
Antonio	norteamericano	despedida	muchacha
Eduardo	Pablo	Elena	nacionalidad
español	portugués†	España	norteamericana
Felipe	profesor	española	profesora
francés†	recuerdo	familia	señora
inglés†	ruso	francesa	señorita
italiano	saludo	Inés	universidad
José	señor	inglesa	verdad
mejicano		Isabel	vez *(pl.* veces)
		lengua	vista
		Luisa	

ADJECTIVES*

MASCULINE	FEMININE	MASCULINE	FEMININE
alemán†	alemana	inglés†	inglesa
bonito	bonita	interesante	interesante
difícil	difícil	mejicano	mejicana
español	española	norteamericano	norteamericana
fácil	fácil	simpático	simpática
francés†	francesa		

* For plural: vowel + **s**, consonant + **es**.

† Note loss of accent mark in the plural:

alemán, alemanes	inglés, ingleses
francés, franceses	portugués, portugueses

[21]

Clases

Este año tengo cinco clases. Estudio inglés, español, historia, filosofía y química. El inglés es bastante fácil. El español es un poco más difícil. La historia y la filosofía son asignaturas interesantes, y no son tan difíciles como la química. Todas mis clases son bastante interesantes. 5

(Elena y Pablo.)

ELENA. Nuestra clase de español es fácil e interesante, ¿verdad?

PABLO. Sí, bastante. La lengua no es fácil, pero el profesor no es muy exigente. 10

ELENA. Dicen que a veces sí es exigente. ¿Cuántas clases tiene usted este año?

PABLO. Tengo cinco: español, física, química, matemáticas y zoología. 15

ELENA. ¡Cuántas ciencias! ¿Por qué no estudia usted asignaturas más fáciles?

PABLO. Porque son menos interesantes. ¿Qué clases tiene usted?

ELENA. Inglés, francés, español, historia y sociología. 20

PABLO. ¡Cuántas lenguas! Sus clases son más difíciles que las mías.

ELENA. No, las de usted son mucho más difíciles.

PABLO. Para algunos las lenguas son difíciles.

ELENA. Y para otros son más difíciles las ciencias. 25

VOCABULARY

alguno, -a someone; *pl.* some
el **año** year
la **asignatura** course, subject
la **ciencia** science
cinco five
como as
¿cuánto, -a? how much?; *pl.* how many?
¡cuánto, -a! how much!; *pl.* how many!, what a lot (of)!
decir to say, to tell
dicen they say
e and *(used before i- or hi-)*
este, esta this; **estos, estas** these
exigente demanding, strict
la **filosofía** philosophy
la **física** physics
la **historia** history
más more; **más . . . que** more . . . than; **más fácil** easier; **más difícil** harder
las **matemáticas** mathematics
menos less

mi *adj.* my
mío, -a *adj.* mine; **las mías** *pron., f. pl.* mine
mucho *adv.* much, very much, a lot, a great deal
nuestro, -a *adj.* our
otro, -a other, another
para *prep.* for
porque because
¿por qué? why?
que *conj.* that; *after a comparative* than
la **química** chemistry
sí es is *(emphatic)*
la **sociología** sociology
su *adj.* your
tan as, so; **tan . . . como** as . . . as
tener to have
tengo I have
tiene (you) have
todo, -a all
usted *obj. of prep.* you; **las de usted** *pron., f. pl.* yours
la **zoología** zoology

GRAMMATICAL EXPLANATIONS

1. Definite Article with General Nouns. The definite article is usually required with nouns used in a general or abstract sense.

La química no es fácil.   *Chemistry is not easy.*
Las ciencias son interesantes.   *Sciences are interesting.*

The article is not used when the meaning is partitive (often the case after **estudiar, de,** or **en**) or when a list is given.

Estudiamos **filosofía.**   *We're studying philosophy.*
Mi clase **de historia** es fácil.   *My history class is easy.*
Tengo cuatro clases: **inglés, francés, historia y física.**   *I have four classes: English, French, history, and physics.*

2. Adjective Phrases. In Spanish, prepositional phrases correspond to the English adjectival use of nouns.

Mi clase **de química** es difícil.	*My chemistry class is difficult.*
Nuestro profesor **de física** es muy exigente.	*Our physics professor is very strict.*

3. Emphatic Affirmative. The affirmative word **sí** may precede the verb to emphasize an affirmative idea. Sometimes the verb is omitted, leaving **sí** standing for the clause.

No hablan francés, pero **sí hablan** español.	*They don't speak French, but they do speak Spanish.*
No siempre es exigente, pero a veces **sí** (= **sí** es exigente).	*He's not always strict, but sometimes he is (= is strict).*

4. Possessive Case of Nouns. Possession is indicated by the use of the preposition **de,** *of.*

Las clases **de Pablo** son bastante difíciles.	*Paul's classes are rather difficult.*
Las clases **del profesor Pérez** son muy interesantes.	*Professor Pérez' classes are very interesting.*

The name of the thing possessed may be omitted, converting the article into an unstressed pronoun.

Las clases de Elena son más fáciles que **las de Pablo** (= las clases de Pablo).	*Helen's classes are easier than Paul's (= those of Paul or Paul's classes).*

5. Unstressed Possessive Adjectives.

ONE POSSESSOR		TWO OR MORE POSSESSORS	
mi, mis	*my*	**nuestro, -a, -os, -as**	*our*
tu, tus	*your*	**vuestro, -a, -os, -as**	*your*
su, sus	{*your, his,* *her, its*	**su, sus**	{*your* *their*

These unstressed forms precede the nouns that they modify, and agree with them in gender and number.

Nuestra clase.	*Our class. (Fem. sing.)*
Mis clases.	*My classes. (Fem. plur.)*
Su profesor.	*Your (or His, Her, Their) teacher.*

6. Stressed Possessive Adjectives and Pronouns.

ONE POSSESSOR		TWO OR MORE POSSESSORS	
mío, -a, -os, -as	*mine*	nuestro, -a, -os, -as	*ours*
tuyo, -a, -os, -as	*yours*	vuestro, -a, -os, -as	*yours*
suyo, -a, -os, -as	{ *yours, his,* *hers, its*	suyo, -a, -os, -as	{ *yours* *theirs*

(*a*) These forms are used in stressed positions (after the noun or as predicate adjectives). With the definite article, they serve as pronouns (standing for a noun + a possessive).

Es más exigente el profesor **nuestro.**	*Our teacher is stricter.* (Stressed possessive)
Estamos en una clase **suya.**	*We're in a class of his.*
Mi clase es más difícil que **la suya** (= la clase suya).	*My class is more difficult than yours* (= *your class*).

(*b*) For clarity of reference there are alternate third-person forms: **de** + **usted, él, ella, ustedes, ellos, ellas.**

¿Cómo son las clases **de usted?**	*What are your classes like?*
Las clases **de él** son más interesantes que **las de ella.**	*His classes are more interesting than hers.*

7. Verbs. Present indicative of **decir,** *to say, to tell,* and **tener,** *to have.*

Decir		Tener	
digo	decimos	tengo	tenemos
dices	decís	tienes	tenéis
dice	dicen	tiene	tienen

EXERCISES

A. Structure Practice.

1.
$$\left.\begin{array}{l} \text{Estudio} \\ \text{Estudiamos} \\ \text{Estudian} \end{array}\right\} \left.\begin{array}{l} \text{física} \\ \text{sociología} \\ \text{matemáticas} \end{array}\right\} \text{este año.}$$

Answer. 1. ¿Estudia usted física? 2. ¿Estudian ustedes sociología? 3. ¿Estudian matemáticas Pablo y Eduardo?

Translate. 1. They are studying physics this year. 2. I am studying sociology this year. 3. We are studying mathematics this year.

2. La historia ⎫
La filosofía ⎬ es una asignatura ⎧ fácil.
La química ⎭   ⎨ difícil.
                                      ⎩ interesante.

Answer. 1. ¿Es fácil su clase de historia? 2. ¿Es difícil su clase de filosofía? 3. ¿Es interesante su clase de química?

Translate. 1. Philosophy is an easy course. 2. History is an interesting course. 3. Chemistry is a difficult course.

3. Sus clases ⎫
Las suyas ⎬ son más fáciles que ⎧ las mías.
Las de Pablo ⎭   ⎨ las nuestras.
                                    ⎩ las de Elena.

Answer. 1. ¿Son fáciles las clases de Felipe? 2. ¿Son fáciles las clases de Elena? 3. ¿Son más fáciles que las de Pablo?

Translate. 1. His classes are easier than ours. 2. Hers are easier than Helen's. 3. Paul's are easier than mine.

B. Drill Exercises.

1. *Change the noun and adjective to the plural. (Example:* mi clase — mis clases.) 1. nuestra clase. 2. mi profesor. 3. nuestro profesor. 4. tu asignatura. 5. vuestra lengua.

2. *Give the form of the possessive pronoun corresponding to each of the following. (Example:* mi clase — la mía.) 1. nuestra clase. 2. mis clases. 3. sus asignaturas. 4. nuestro profesor. 5. la familia de él.

3. *Express without using the noun. (Example:* Mi clase es más fácil. — La mía es más fácil.) 1. Su clase es más difícil. 2. Nuestro profesor es más exigente. 3. Mis asig-

naturas son más fáciles. 4. Nuestra clase es más interesante. 5. Las clases de él son más difíciles.

4. *Reverse the order of the nouns or adjectives, chang-
ing* y *to* e *before* i- *or* hi-. *(Example:* inglés y español —
español e inglés.) 1. historia y química. 2. interesante y
fácil. 3. Isabel y María. 4. italiano y alemán. 5. ingleses
y franceses.

5. *Change first to the negative, then to the emphatic
affirmative. (Example:* La química es difícil. — La química
no es difícil. La química sí es difícil.) 1. El español es fácil.
2. La filosofía es interesante. 3. El profesor es exigente.
4. La muchacha es bonita. 5. Los profesores son simpáticos.

C. Questions. 1. ¿Cuántas clases tiene usted este año?
2. ¿Qué ciencias estudia usted? 3. ¿Qué lenguas estudia?
4. ¿Es difícil el español? 5. ¿Es más difícil que el alemán?
6. ¿Por qué no estudia usted el ruso? 7. ¿Cómo es su clase
de inglés? 8. ¿Es exigente el profesor? 9. ¿Son las lenguas tan difíciles como las ciencias? 10. ¿Para algunos son
más difíciles las ciencias? 11. ¿Tiene usted asignaturas más
difíciles que el español? 12. ¿Son interesantes todas sus
clases? 13. ¿Son fáciles? 14. ¿Son menos difíciles que las
de Elena? 15. ¿Son interesantes las asignaturas fáciles?
16. ¿Dicen que es difícil la física? 17. ¿Es la filosofía más
interesante que la historia? 18. ¿Es profesor de español el
señor Pérez? 19. ¿Dónde enseña? 20. ¿Qué enseña el
señor Martín?

D. Translation. 1. This year I have five classes.
2. I am studying English, French, Spanish, history, and
mathematics. 3. What a lot of (How many) languages!
4. For some, sciences are easier and more interesting.

5. What sciences are you studying?   6. I am studying physics, chemistry, and zoology.   7. Your classes are harder than mine.   8. Difficult courses are always interesting. 9. Easy courses are not so interesting.   10. Our Spanish class is very interesting, isn't it?   11. The professor is not very strict.   12. They say that at times he *is* strict.   13. Our history teacher is very strict, isn't he?   14. Yes, but his classes are interesting.   15. Helen says that French is as easy as Spanish.   16. Everybody says (All say) that Spanish is not difficult.   17. *I* say that it *is* difficult.   18. Is it as difficult as chemistry?   19. Paul's classes are more difficult than Helen's, aren't they?   20. *He* says that sciences are easier than languages.

E. CONVERSATION AND COMPOSITION. Topic: Some courses that you and your friends are taking.

POSSESSIVES

(Reference List of Forms; cf. Lesson 4, §§5–6)

	ONE POSSESSOR	TWO OR MORE POSSESSORS
UNSTRESSED ADJECTIVES *(Used before a noun)*	mi, mis tu, tus su, sus	nuestro, -a, -os, -as vuestro, -a, -os, -as su, sus
STRESSED ADJECTIVES *(Used after a noun or as predicate adjective)*	mío, -a, -os, -as tuyo, -a, -os, -as suyo, -a, -os, -as *or* { de usted de él de ella	nuestro, -a, -os, -as vuestro, -a, -os, -as suyo, -a, -os, -as *or* { de ustedes de ellos de ellas
PRONOUNS *(Used to stand for a noun + a possessive)*	el mío los míos la mía las mías el tuyo los tuyos la tuya las tuyas el suyo los suyos la suya las suyas *or* { el / la / los / las } de { usted / él / ella	el nuestro los nuestros la nuestra las nuestras el vuestro los vuestros la vuestra las vuestras el suyo los suyos la suya las suyas *or* { el / la / los / las } de { ustedes / ellos / ellas

5 | Amigos

Tengo varios amigos españoles y mejicanos. A veces hablo español con ellos. Miguel Gómez es un muchacho español que estudia ingeniería aquí en la Universidad. Somos buenos amigos. Nuestra amiga Luisa Rivera es una linda muchacha mejicana. No conozco muy bien a 5 María Guzmán. Es amiga de Luisa y de Miguel. Los tres van conmigo al cine algunas noches.

(María, Felipe y Luisa; después Miguel.)

MARÍA.   ¿Conocen ustedes al profesor Pérez?

FELIPE.   Yo no tengo el gusto.   10

LUISA.   ¿Es un señor bajo y moreno, ni viejo ni joven?

MARÍA.   Así es. Y muy amable.

LUISA.   Sí, lo conozco. Y su señora, ¿no es rubia, bonita, bastante joven?

MARÍA.   Eso dicen. A ella no la conozco. ¿Conocen 15 ustedes a su primo Juan Castillo?

FELIPE.   ¿Juanito, el primo del profesor Pérez? Le conozco muy bien. Es un buen amigo mío.

LUISA.   ¿Cómo es?

MARÍA.   Es alto, rubio y bastante guapo.   20

FELIPE.   Veo que aquí viene Miguel. ¡Hola! Buenas noches, Miguel.

MIGUEL.   Muy buenas . . . ¿Estamos listos?

FELIPE.   Sí, sí. Vamos en mi coche. Lo tengo muy cerca de aquí.   25

VOCABULARY

a *(lit.* "to") *used as the sign
of a personal noun object*
al (= a + el) to the; *see* a
algún, alguno, -a some
alto, -a tall
amable amiable, kind
el amigo, la amiga friend
así so, thus, like that
bajo, -a short *(of stature)*
buen, bueno, -a good
cerca *adv.* near, nearby;
cerca de *prep.* near
el cine cinema, movies
el coche car
conmigo with me
conocen (you, *pl.*) know
conocer to know, to be acquainted with
conozco I know
del (= de + el) of the
después later, afterwards
ella *obj. of prep.* her; a ella
. . . la her *(stressed)*
ellos *obj. of prep.* them
eso that *(idea or fact)*
guapo, -a handsome, good-
looking

el gusto pleasure
la ingeniería engineering
ir to go
joven young
Juan John; Juanito Johnny
la *obj. pron.* her
le *obj. pron.* him
lindo, -a pretty
listo, -a ready
lo *obj. pron.* him, it
moreno, -a dark, brunet,
brunette
ni . . . ni neither . . . nor
la noche evening, night
el primo, la prima cousin
que *rel. pron.* that, who
rubio, -a fair, blond, blonde
tres three
vamos we are going
van (they) go
varios, -as several
venir to come
veo I see
ver to see
viejo, -a old
viene (he) comes

GRAMMATICAL EXPLANATIONS

1. Contractions: *al* and *del*. There are two written contractions in Spanish: **al** (= a + el), *to the,* and **del** (= de + el),
of the (masculine singular).

2. Position of Descriptive Adjectives *(Continued).* Unstressed adjectives which express subjective attitudes precede
the nouns that they modify.

Luisa es una **linda** muchacha   *Louise is a pretty Mexican girl.*
mejicana.

3. **Shortened Forms of Adjectives.** A few adjectives have lost the final -o of the masculine singular when immediately preceding the noun modified.

Juan es un **buen** amigo mío.	*John is a good friend of mine.*
Hablan de **algún** amigo suyo.	*They're speaking of some friend of theirs.*

4. **Personal a.** When the noun object of a verb (direct or indirect) is a person or personified thing, it is regularly preceded by the preposition **a**. The verb **tener,** *to have,* however, rarely has this construction.

¿Conoce usted **a Juanito?**	*Do you know Johnny?*
No entienden **al profesor.**	*They don't understand the teacher.*
Tenemos muchos amigos aquí.	*We have many friends here.*

This personal **a** is not used before the regular direct or indirect object pronouns, but is used before most other pronouns (or adjectives used as pronouns) when referring to persons. For stress or clarity, a prepositional form is often used in addition to the regular object pronoun.

¿Los conoce usted?—No los co-nozco **a todos.**	*Do you know them?—I don't know them all.*
No la conozco **a ella.**	*I don't know her.*
¿**A quiénes** ven ustedes?	*Whom do you see?*
Mi familia conoce **a la suya.**	*My family knows theirs.*

5. **Prepositional Object Pronouns.** The personal pronouns used as objects of prepositions are the same as the subject pronouns, except for the first and second persons singular: **mí,** *me,* and **ti,** *you* (familiar).

¿Es para **mí** o para **ti?**	*Is it for me or for you* (familiar)?
Hablan de **ustedes.**	*They are talking about you.*
Voy al cine con **ellos.**	*I'm going to the movies with them.*

The forms **mí** and **ti** combine with the preposition **con,** *with,* to give the special forms **conmigo** and **contigo.**

No van **conmigo.** ¿Van **contigo?**	*They aren't going with me. Are they going with you?*

6. Direct and Indirect Object Pronouns. The direct and indirect object pronouns differ only in the third person singular and plural.

PERSON	SINGULAR	PLURAL
1ST	**me,** *me, (to) me*	**nos,** *us, (to) us*
2ND	**te,** *you, (to) you*	**os,** *you, (to) you*
3RD		
DIRECT:	**le** (masc.) *you, him* **lo** (masc. or neut.) *you, him, it* **la** (fem.) *you, her, it*	**los** (masc.) **las** (fem.) } *you, them*
INDIRECT:	**le** *(to) you, him, her, it*	**les** *(to)* you, them

(*a*) Variations in the use of the masculine direct object forms **le** and **lo** for persons are mainly regional. Neuter **lo** refers to ideas.

Todos **lo** dicen.   *Everybody says it.*

(*b*) For stress or clarity (and often in the case of **usted, ustedes,** for politeness), a prepositional form is used in addition to the regular object pronoun. If the verb is omitted, only the prepositional form remains.

No le entienden **a usted.**   *They don't understand you.*
Le conozco **a él,** pero **a ella** no   *I know him, but not her* (= *I* (= **a ella** no **la** conozco).   *don't know her*).

7. Verbs. Present indicative of **conocer,** *to know, to be acquainted with,* **ir,** *to go,* **venir,** *to come,* and **ver,** *to see.*

Conocer		Ir	
conozco	conocemos	voy	vamos
conoces	conocéis	vas	vais
conoce	conocen	va	van

Venir		Ver	
vengo	venimos	veo	vemos
vienes	venís	ves	veis
viene	vienen	ve	ven

EXERCISES

A. STRUCTURE PRACTICE.

1. Conozco ⎫   ⎧ Miguel.
       Conocemos ⎬ muy bien a ⎨ Luisa.
       Conocen ⎭   ⎩ María.

Answer. 1. ¿Conoce usted a Miguel Gómez? 2. ¿Conocen ustedes a Luisa Rivera? 3. ¿Conocen Miguel y Luisa a María Guzmán?

Translate. 1. I know Louise quite well. 2. We know Michael quite well. 3. They know Mary quite well.

2. Le ⎫ conozco   ⎫
       La ⎬ conocemos ⎬ muy bien.
       Los ⎭ conoce   ⎭

Answer. 1. ¿Conoce usted a Felipe? 2. ¿Conocen ustedes a Elena? 3. ¿Conoce Pablo a Miguel y a Luisa?

Translate. 1. I know them quite well. 2. We know him quite well. 3. He knows her quite well.

3. Elena ⎫   ⎧ conmigo.
       Pablo ⎬ va al cine ⎨ con nosotros.
       Miguel ⎭   ⎩ con ellas.

Answer. 1. ¿Quién va al cine con usted? 2. ¿Quién va al cine con ustedes? 3. ¿Quién va al cine con María y Luisa?

Translate. 1. Paul is going to the movies with them. 2. Michael is going to the movies with me. 3. Helen is going to the movies with us.

B. DRILL EXERCISES.

1. *Add an appropriate prepositional form for stress on the direct object pronoun. (Example:* Le veo. — Le veo a

él.)   1. La veo.   2. Las veo.   3. Los veo.   4. Me ven.
5. Nos ven.

2. *Change the direct object pronoun to the plural. (Example:* Le conozco. — Los conozco.)   1. La conozco.   2. Lo conozco.   3. Me conocen.   4. Te conocen.   5. Le conocen.

3. *Change the indirect object pronoun to the plural. (Example:* Le hablan. — Les hablan.)   1. Le enseñan.   2. Te hablan.   3. Te dicen eso.   4. Me enseñan.   5. Me dicen eso.

4. *Change the noun and its modifiers to the plural. (Example:* Conozco a un muchacho español. — Conozco a unos muchachos españoles.)   1. Conocemos a un muchacho mejicano.   2. Hablan con una señora francesca.   3. Aquí vienen con un buen amigo.   4. Veo a una linda muchacha. 5. Conocemos a una linda muchacha mejicana.

C. Questions.   1. ¿Tiene usted amigos españoles? 2. ¿Conoce usted a Miguel Gómez?   3. Miguel estudia ingeniería, ¿verdad?   4. ¿Entiende Miguel el inglés?   5. ¿Hablan ustedes en español?   6. ¿Quién es Luisa Rivera? 7. ¿Es amiga de usted?   8. ¿Son amigas María y Luisa? 9. ¿Conoce usted al señor Rivera?   10. ¿Cómo es? ¿Bajo, moreno, bastante joven?   11. ¿Conocen ustedes al primo del profesor Pérez?   12. ¿Cómo es Juanito? ¿Alto, rubio, guapo?   13. Ustedes son buenos amigos, ¿verdad?   14. ¿Va Juanito al cine con usted esta noche?   15. ¿Quiénes van con ustedes?   16. ¿Van también José y Elena?   17. ¿Es Elena una muchacha alta, rubia, bonita?   18. ¿Cómo es su prima? 19. José es bastante guapo, ¿verdad?   20. ¿Tiene usted su coche cerca de aquí?

D. Translation.   1. Do you know Mr. and Mrs. Pérez?   2. I don't have the pleasure.   3. Do you know them?

4. I know him, but not her.   5. Mr. Pérez is a very pleasant gentleman.   6. He is short, dark, neither young nor old. 7. They say that his wife is blonde, pretty, rather young. 8. Do you know their cousin Juan Castillo?   9. Johnny is a good friend of mine.   10. He is tall, blond, and rather good-looking.   11. I have several Spanish and Mexican friends.   12. Do you speak Spanish with them?   13. Sometimes we speak in Spanish.   14. María Guzmán is going to the movies with me tonight (this evening).   15. She is a pretty Mexican girl.   16. Here comes our friend Paul. 17. Hello, Paul! How goes it?   18. Good afternoon. How are you?   19. Are we ready?   20. I have my car quite near here.

E. CONVERSATION AND COMPOSITION. Topic: Some friends of yours.

PERSONAL PRONOUNS

(Reference List of Forms in Lessons 1 and 5)

		SUBJECT	INDIRECT OBJECT	DIRECT OBJECT	PREPOSITIONAL OBJECT
SINGULAR		yo	me	me	mí*
		tú	te	te	ti*
		usted	le	le, lo, la	usted
		él	le	le, lo	él
		ella	le	la	ella
PLURAL		nosotros, -as	nos	nos	nosotros, -as
		vosotros, -as	os	os	vosotros, -as
		ustedes	les	los, las	ustedes
		ellos	les	los	ellos
		ellas	les	las	ellas

* Con + mí = conmigo; con + ti = contigo.

GRAMMATICAL NOTES————

(Use the following grammatical notes as a guide for reviewing forms and usage. Then test your knowledge of them by using the corresponding Test Exercises on the opposite page.)

1. Definite Article.

Forms: **el, la, los, las** (Lesson 1: §4); **a + el = al, de + el = del** (5:1).

Usage: definite article used with names of languages—but not usually after **hablar, de,** or **en,** except when stressed after **hablar** (2:3); with titles—but not with **don, doña,** or with others when used in direct address (3:1); with nouns used in a general or abstract sense—but not when the meaning is partitive (as is often the case after **estudiar, de,** or **en)** or when a list is given (4:1).

2. Indefinite Article.

Forms: **un, una, unos, unas** (3:2).

Usage: indefinite article omitted before unqualified predicate nouns (or phrases) used adjectivally (3:3).

3. Nouns.

Forms: endings usually **-o,** masculine, and **-a,** feminine; plural: vowel + **s,** consonant + **es** (3:5).

Usage: **a** used before personal noun objects (5:4); **de** used to form possessive case of nouns (4:4) or adjective phrases (4:2); subject after predicate when stressed or in questions (2:4-5).

(Continued on page 40)

(Complete the Spanish sentences with the idea indicated. Check your answers by using the corresponding Grammatical Notes on the opposite page.)

1. Definite Article.

1. *(the)* Adiós. Recuerdos a _____ familia.
2. *(to the)* No lo dicen _____ profesor.
3. *(English)* Entienden muy bien _____.
4. *(Spanish)* Usted habla _____, ¿verdad?
5. *(in French)* Siempre hablamos _____.
6. *(Mrs.)* María es amiga de _____ Martín.
7. *(Professor)* _____ Pérez es amigo nuestro.
8. *(sciences)* Para algunos _____ son fáciles.
9. *(history)* ¿Estudian ustedes _____ este año?

2. Indefinite Article.

1. *(a)* El alemán es _____ lengua difícil.
2. *(an American)* Eduardo no es _____.
3. *(a teacher)* Don Antonio es _____ muy simpático.

3. Nouns.

1. *(girl)* Luisa es una _____ muy bonita.
2. *(teachers)* Todos mis _____ son simpáticos.
3. *(Michael)* Conocemos muy bien _____.
4. *(Helen's)* Las clases _____ son interesantes.
5. *(chemistry)* Nuestra clase _____ es muy difícil.

(Continued on page 41)

[39]

GRAMMATICAL NOTES, CONTINUED

4. Personal Pronouns.

Forms: subject (1:6), prepositional (5:5), direct and in-indirect object (5:6). List on p. 37.

Usage: familiar and polite forms for *you* (1:5); subject pronouns, except **usted, ustedes,** used mainly for stress (1:6); subject pronouns after verb in questions (2:5); direct or indirect object pronouns before verb (2:4); prepositional forms added for stress on direct or indirect object pronouns, or used alone when verb is omitted (5:6).

5. Adjectives.

Forms: endings usually **-o,** masculine, and **-a,** feminine; plural: vowel + **s,** consonant + **es** (3:5); shortened forms **buen** and **algún** before masculine singular noun (5:3).

Usage: descriptive adjectives usually after the noun (3:4), but before the noun when merely expressing a subjective attitude (5:2).

6. Possessive Adjectives and Pronouns.

Forms: familiar and polite forms for *your* (1:5); gender and number according to noun modified (4:5-6). List on p. 29.

Usage: unstressed adjectives (**mi, mis,** etc.) before the noun (4:5); stressed adjectives (**mío, -a, -os, -as,** etc.) after the noun or as predicate adjectives, or, with the article (**el mío, la mía,** etc.), as pronouns (4:6).

7. Verbs.

Verbs used: **estar** (Lesson 1), **entender, hablar** (2), **enseñar, estudiar, ser** (3), **decir, tener** (4), **conocer, ir, venir, ver** (5).

Usage: familiar and polite forms for *you* (1:5); **no** before verb for negative (2:4); **sí** before verb for emphatic affirmative (4:3); meanings of present indicative according to context (2:6); **ser** used to express an essential characteristic, **estar** to express condition or location (3:6).

TEST EXERCISES, CONTINUED

4. Personal Pronouns.

1. *(you)* ¿Qué lenguas estudia _____?
2. *(with them)* Hablo español _____.
3. *(with me)* Esta noche van _____ al cine.
4. *(her)* Yo _____ veo en la clase de francés.
5. *(me)* José _____ dice que el profesor es exigente.
6. *(them)* ¿Quién _____ enseña el alemán?
7. *(speak it)* Yo también _____ un poco.
8. *(her)* Le conozco a él pero _____ no.

5. Adjectives.

1. *(good-looking)* Felipe es bastante _____.
2. *(blonde)* Las dos muchachas son _____.
3. *(French)* ¿Son _____ Eduardo e Isabel?
4. *(good)* Pablo es un _____ amigo mío.
5. *(Spanish friends)* Tengo varios _____.
6. *(pretty girl)* María es una _____ mejicana.

6. Possessive Adjectives and Pronouns.

1. *(My)* _____ amigos son muy amables.
2. *(Our)* _____ amiga Luisa va con nosotros.
3. *(of his)* María y Luisa son amigas _____.
4. *(mine)* Su familia conoce a _____.
5. *(theirs)* Nuestro profesor es más exigente que _____.
6. *(hers)* Las clases de él son más fáciles que _____.

7. Verbs.

1. *(are)* Buenos días. ¿Cómo _____ ustedes?
2. *(do you have)* ¿Dónde _____ tu coche?
3. *(doesn't speak)* Elena _____ el portugués.
4. *(She does speak)* _____ el francés.
5. *(come)* Veo que aquí _____ nuestros amigos.
6. *(is)* Isabel _____ bonita y simpática.
7. *(are)* Todos _____ listos, ¿verdad?
8. *(is)* Juanito _____ en la universidad.

6 Familia

En mi familia somos cinco: mis padres, mis dos hermanos y yo. Mi hermano es mayor que yo y mi hermana menor. Mi hermano tiene veintiún años. Se llama José. Mi hermana tiene diez y siete años. Se llama Elena. Mi padre, que es abogado, tiene unos cincuenta años. Mi 5 madre tiene unos cuarenta y cinco años. Tengo otros parientes que viven en esta ciudad: dos de mis abuelos, tres tíos y cinco primos.

(María y Felipe.)

MARÍA. Usted tiene dos hermanos, ¿verdad? 10

FELIPE. Sí. José y Elena.

MARÍA. ¿Son mayores o menores que usted?

FELIPE. José es mayor, Elena es menor. ¿Cuántos hermanos tiene usted?

MARÍA. No tengo hermanos. Soy hija única. 15

FELIPE. ¿Qué parientes tiene usted en esta ciudad?

MARÍA. Un tío soltero llamado Jorge González, hermano de mi madre, y una prima casada, Josefina Solís de Castro, que tiene dos hijos.

FELIPE. El esposo de su prima, ¿se llama Pedro Castro? 20

MARÍA. Sí. Es abogado. ¿Lo conoce usted?

FELIPE. Es amigo de mi padre, Daniel Lamar. ¿Qué edad tienen los sobrinos de usted?

MARÍA. El mayor tiene siete u ocho años. La menor es una niñita de unos seis meses. 25

VOCABULARY

el **abogado** lawyer
el **abuelo** grandfather; la **abuela** grandmother; los **abuelos** grandparents
casado, -a married
cincuenta fifty
la **ciudad** city
cuarenta y cinco forty-five
diez y siete seventeen
la **edad** age; ¿qué edad tienen? how old are (they)?
el **esposo** husband; la **esposa** wife
el **hermano** brother; la **hermana** sister; los **hermanos** brother(s) and sister(s)
el **hijo** son; la **hija** daughter; los **hijos** children
Jorge George
llama see **llamar**
llamado, -a named
llamar to call; **llamarse** to call oneself, to be named; **se llama** (his, her) name is
la **madre** mother
mayor older or oldest
menor younger or youngest

el **mes** month; **de unos seis meses** about 6 months old
el **niño** boy, child; la **niña** girl; la **niñita** little girl
o or
ocho eight
el **padre** father; *pl.* parents
el **pariente**, la **parienta** relative
Pedro Peter
se oneself, himself, herself
seis six
siete seven
el **sobrino** nephew *or* cousin's son; la **sobrina** niece; los **sobrinos** niece(s) and nephew(s)
soltero, -a unmarried, single
el **tío** uncle; la **tía** aunt; los **tíos** uncle(s) and aunt(s)
u or *(used before* **o-** *or* **ho-**)
único, -a sole, only
unos, -as some, about
veintiún, veintiuno, -a twenty-one; **tiene veintiún años** (he) is 21 years old
viven (they) live
vivir to live

GRAMMATICAL EXPLANATIONS

1. Idiomatic Forms.

(a) **Ser**, *to be,* used with expressions of number.

En mi familia **somos cinco**.　　*There are five of us in my family.*

(b) **Tener...años**, etc., *to be...(years) old,* etc.

¿Qué edad tiene su padre?　　*What is your father's age?*
Mi hermano **tiene veinte años**.　　*My brother is twenty years old.*
¿Cuántos años tiene la hija?　　*How old is the daughter?*
Es una niñita **de seis meses**.　　*She's a little girl six months old.*

2. Noun Object without Indefinite Article. In Spanish, particularly in negative or interrogative constructions, the indefinite article is not used before nouns that refer to types rather than individuals.

No tengo **hermana.**	*I don't have a sister.*
¿Tiene usted **hermanos?**	*Have you any brothers and sisters?*

3. Cardinal Numerals, 1-100.

1	uno, -a	11	once	21	veintiuno, -a
2	dos	12	doce	22	veintidós
3	tres	13	trece	23	veintitrés
4	cuatro	14	catorce	24	veinticuatro
5	cinco	15	quince	25	veinticinco
6	seis	16	diez y seis	26	veintiséis
7	siete	17	diez y siete	27	veintisiete
8	ocho	18	diez y ocho	28	veintiocho
9	nueve	19	diez y nueve	29	veintinueve
10	diez	20	veinte	30	treinta

31	treinta y uno, -a		60	sesenta
32	treinta y dos		70	setenta
40	cuarenta		80	ochenta
41	cuarenta y uno, -a		90	noventa
50	cincuenta		100	ciento

(a) The forms **uno, -a, veintiuno, -a,** etc. agree in gender with the words that they modify. When they come before a masculine noun (or before another numeral), they are shortened to **un, veintiún,** etc.

José tiene **veintiún** años.	*Joseph is twenty-one years old.*

(b) When the word **ciento,** *a hundred, one hundred,* comes immediately before the word that it modifies, it is shortened to **cien.**

Su abuelo tiene **cien** años.	*His grandfather is a hundred years old.*

4. Reflexive Pronouns. The first and second person object pronouns may be used reflexively.

Yo **me** conozco bien.	*I know myself well.*
Nos decimos que es fácil.	*We tell ourselves that it's easy.*

For the third person there are special reflexive forms: **se** (direct or indirect object) and **sí** (prepositional object), meaning *yourself, himself, herself, oneself, yourselves, themselves.* The form **sí** (like **mí** and **ti**) combines with the preposition **con** to give a special form: **consigo.**

¿Se llaman ellos amigos?	*Do they call themselves friends?*
Juanito habla de sí.	*Johnny is speaking of himself.*
No lo tienen **consigo.**	*They don't have it with them.*

For emphasis on a direct or indirect object, a prepositional form is added, often intensified by **mismo, -a,** *same, selfsame.* Since the plural forms sometimes have a reciprocal meaning ("each other," "one another"), the use of **mismos, -as** may be necessary for clarity.

Se enseña a sí mismo.	*He teaches himself.*
Todos se conocen.	*They all know one another. (Or: They all know themselves.)*
Se conocen a sí mismos.	*They know themselves.*

5. Reflexive Verbs. Many Spanish verbs have come to have special meanings when used reflexively. For example, the verb **llamar,** *to call,* when used reflexively, **llamarse,** *to call oneself,* usually means *to be named.* Ambiguity is sometimes avoided by the use of the stressed form, which restores the literal meaning.

¿Cómo se llama usted?	*What is your name?*
Me llamo Felipe.	*My name is Philip.*
Mis hermanos **se llaman** José y Elena.	*My brother and sister are named Joseph and Helen.*
Se llama Juanito **a sí mismo,** ¿verdad?	*He calls himself Johnny, doesn't he?*

6. Verbs. Present indicative of **llamarse,** *"to call oneself,"* *to be named,* and **vivir,** *to live.*

Llamarse		Vivir	
me llamo	nos llamamos	vivo	vivimos
te llamas	os llamáis	vives	vivís
se llama	se llaman	vive	viven

EXERCISES

A. STRUCTURE PRACTICE.

1. Mi hermano ⎫   ⎧ José.
   Mi primo   ⎬ se llama ⎨ Juan.
   Nuestro tío ⎭   ⎩ Jorge.

Answer. 1. ¿Cómo se llama su hermano? 2. ¿Cómo se llama su primo? 3. ¿Cómo se llama el tío de ustedes?

Translate. 1. My cousin is named George. 2. My brother is named John. 3. Our uncle is named Joseph.

2. Me llamo   ⎫ Felipe.
   Se llama   ⎬ Elena.
   Los (Las) dos se llaman ⎭ Juan.

Answer. 1. ¿Cómo se llama usted? 2. ¿Cómo se llama su hermana? 3. ¿Cómo se llaman sus primos?

Translate. 1. My name is John. 2. Her name is Helen. 3. Both are named Philip.

3. Tengo ⎫ diez y nueve ⎫
   Tiene ⎬ veintiún   ⎬ años.
   Tienen ⎭ veinticinco ⎭

Answer. 1. ¿Cuántos años tiene usted? 2. ¿Cuántos años tiene su hermano? 3. ¿Qué edad tienen sus primas?

Translate. 1. I am twenty-one years old. 2. He is twenty-five years old. 3. They are nineteen years old.

B. DRILL EXERCISES.

1. *Use the proper reflexive pronoun with each verb form.* (*Example:* llamo — me llamo.) 1. llama. 2. llamamos. 3. llaman. 4. llamas. 5. llamáis.

2. *Add an appropriate subject pronoun for stress.* (*Example:* Me llamo Felipe. — Yo me llamo Felipe.) 1. Nos

llamamos Pablo y José.   2. Se llama Isabel.   3. Se llaman
María y Luisa.   4. Nos llamamos Elena y María.   5. Se
llaman Miguel y Luisa.

3. *Count in Spanish from one to twenty, and by tens
from ten to a hundred.*

4. *Read in Spanish.* 1. 25.   2. 38.   3. 42.   4. 54.   5. 66.
6. 77.   7. 89.   8. 91 años.   9. 21 muchachas.   10. 100 muchachos.

C. QUESTIONS.   1. ¿Cómo se llama usted?   2. ¿Cuántos son ustedes en su familia?   3. ¿Cuántos hermanos tiene
usted?   4. ¿Cómo se llaman?   5. ¿Son mayores o menores
que usted?   6. ¿Cuántos años tiene usted?   7. ¿Vive su
familia en esta ciudad?   8. ¿Dónde viven sus abuelos?
9. ¿Qué edad tienen sus padres?   10. ¿Qué otros parientes
tiene usted?   11. ¿Cuántos tíos tiene usted?   12. ¿Son casa-
dos?   13. ¿Cuántos hijos tienen?   14. ¿Cómo se llaman sus
primos?   15. ¿Tienen hijos sus hermanos o sus primos?
16. ¿Qué edad tienen sus sobrinos?   17. ¿Cómo se llaman?
18. ¿Es hija única María Guzmán?   19. ¿Qué parientes
tiene?   20. ¿Cómo se llama el esposo de su prima Josefina?

D. TRANSLATION.   1. What is your name?   2. My
name is Edward.   3. How old are you?   4. I am nineteen
years old.   5. How many are there in your family?   6. There
are six of us in my family.   7. How old are your brothers
and sisters?   8. My older brother is twenty-one years old.
9. One of my sisters is fifteen years old.   10. My youngest
sister is thirteen years old.   11. How many brothers and
sisters do you have?   12. What are their names?   13. Mary
doesn't have any brothers and sisters, does she?   14. No,
she is an only child.   15. Her cousin Josephine has two
children.   16. The older is about seven or eight years old.

17. Her cousin's daughter (Her niece) is a little girl six months old. 18. Josephine's husband is a lawyer. 19. Does Mary have any other relatives in this city? 20. She has a bachelor uncle named George.

E. CONVERSATION AND COMPOSITION. Topic: Your relatives.

FAMILY RELATIONS

(Cf. Lessons 5 and 6)

mis abuelos
(padres de
mi padre)

mis abuelos
(padres de
mi madre)

mis tíos
(hermanos de
mi padre)

mi padre___mi madre

mis tíos
(hermanos de
mi madre)

mis primos
(hijos de
mis tíos)

mis hermanos y YO

mis primos
(hijos de
mis tíos)

mis sobrinos
(hijos de
mis primos)

mis sobrinos
(hijos de
mis hermanos)

mis sobrinos
(hijos de
mis primos)

7 Vida de todos los días

Hago casi las mismas cosas todos los días. Me levanto a las siete de la mañana. Me desayuno a las siete y media. Salgo de casa a las nueve menos cuarto. Llego a la Universidad a las nueve en punto. Vuelvo a casa a las tres, y estudio toda la tarde. Como, o ceno, a eso de las siete. 5 Por la noche estudio un poco, leo el periódico o charlo con mis amigos. Me acuesto temprano, a las diez o a las diez y media.

(Elena, Felipe y José.)

ELENA. ¿Qué hora es? 10
FELIPE. Por mi reloj es la una y media. ¿Qué hora tienes tú, José?
JOSÉ. Las dos menos veinticinco minutos.
FELIPE. ¿A qué hora llegan tus amigas?
ELENA. A eso de las dos y cuarto. 15
JOSÉ. Yo estoy un poco cansado esta tarde. Me levanto muy temprano y tengo tres clases por la mañana.
FELIPE. Sí, te levantas a las siete y media.
ELENA. ¡Y no tienes clases por la tarde!
JOSÉ. Estudio toda la tarde. 20
ELENA. ¿Toda la tarde?
FELIPE. ¿Cuándo haces eso?
JOSÉ. A veces tomo café, leo el periódico y charlo con mis amigos.
FELIPE. Y a veces duermes toda la tarde. 25

VOCABULARY

a at; **a eso de** at about
acostarse (ue) to go to bed; **me acuesto** I go to bed
el **café** coffee
cansado, -a tired
la **casa** house; home
cenar to eat supper; **ceno** I eat supper
comer to eat (dinner); **como** I eat dinner
la **cosa** thing
¿cuándo? when?
el **cuarto** quarter (of an hour); **a las nueve menos cuarto** at a quarter to nine
charlar to chat, to talk; **charlo** I chat
desayunarse to eat breakfast; **me desayuno** I eat breakfast
el **día** day; **todos los días** every day
dormir (ue) to sleep; **duermes** you sleep
hacer to do, to make; **hago** I do; **haces** you do
la **hora** hour; time (of day)
leer to read; **leo** I read

levantarse to get up; **me levanto** I get up; **te levantas** you get up
llegar to arrive; **llego** I arrive; **llegan** (they) arrive
la **mañana** morning; **a las siete de la mañana** at seven in the morning, at 7 A. M.
medio, -a half; **las siete y media** half past seven
el **minuto** minute
mismo, -a same
el **periódico** newspaper
por in, during, through; by
el **punto** point, dot; **en punto** on the dot, sharp
el **reloj** watch
salir to leave, to go out; **salgo de casa** I leave home
la **tarde** afternoon
temprano early
tomar to take; to have (food or drink); **tomo** I take
la **vida** life; **vida de todos los días** daily routine
volver (ue) to return, to go back; **vuelvo a casa** I return home

GRAMMATICAL EXPLANATIONS

1. Idiomatic Forms.

(a) **Casa**, *house, home.* In prepositional phrases the word **casa**, *house*, is used without an article to mean *home.*

Vuelvo **a casa** (= a mi casa).   *I return home.*

(b) **Salir (de)**, *to leave (from), to go out (of).* If the place that one leaves is mentioned, the preposition **de** is used.

Salgo de casa a las nueve.   *I leave home at nine.*

2. Time of Day.

(a) **Hours.** The word **hora,** *hour,* is used in questions, but is omitted in statements. Note that after one o'clock, the plural is used.

¿Qué hora es?	*What time is it?*
Es la una.	*It is one o'clock.*
Son las dos.	*It is two o'clock.*
¿A qué hora?	*At what time?*
A la una.	*At one o'clock.*
A las dos.	*At two o'clock.*
A eso de las tres.	*At about three o'clock.*

(b) **Minutes.** After the half hour, minutes (or quarter hours) are usually subtracted. The word **minutos,** *minutes,* is usually omitted, as in English.

Es la una **y diez** (minutos).	*It is ten (minutes) after one.*
Son las dos **menos veinte.**	*It is twenty of two (or 1:40).*
A la una y **media.**	*At half past one (or 1:30).*
A las cinco menos **cuarto.**	*At a quarter to five (or 4:45).*

(c) **Morning, afternoon, etc.** After a specific hour, **de,** *of,* is used; otherwise, **por,** *in, during* (sometimes **en,** *in*).

A las cinco **de** la tarde.	*At five in the afternoon.*
Tengo clases **por** la mañana.	*I have classes in the morning.*

3. Present Indicative of Regular Verbs. The present indicative can usually be formed as follows: remove the ending of the infinitive (**-ar, -er, -ir**); to this "stem" add the endings of the present indicative.

-ar VERBS		-er VERBS		-ir VERBS	
tom-ar, *to take*		**com-er,** *to eat*		**viv-ir,** *to live*	
I take (am taking, do take), you take, etc.		*I eat (am eating, do eat), you eat,* etc.		*I live (am living, do live), you live,* etc.	
tomo	tomamos	como	comemos	vivo	vivimos
tomas	tomáis	comes	coméis	vives	vivís
toma	toman	come	comen	vive	viven

The endings for **-er** and **-ir** verbs are identical except in four forms, of which three appear here: the infinitive (**comer,** vivir) and the first and second persons plural of the present indicative (com**emos**, viv**imos**; com**éis**, viv**ís**).

The regular verbs used so far in this text are: **cenar, comer, charlar, desayunarse, enseñar, estudiar, hablar, leer, levantarse, llamarse, llegar, tomar, vivir.**

4. Present Indicative of Irregular Verbs.

(a) **Radical-Changing Verbs.** The most common type of irregularity is a change in the stem vowel when stressed (**o > ue, e > ie,** or **e > i**). Examples:

Dormir (ue)		Entender (ie)	
duermo	dormimos	entiendo	entendemos
duermes	dormís	entiendes	entendéis
duerme	duermen	entiende	entienden

Other verbs of this type are **acostarse (ue)** and **volver (ue)**.

(b) **Verbs Irregular only in the First Person Singular.**

conocer: **conozco**	salir: **salgo**
hacer: **hago**	ver: **veo**

(c) **Other Irregular Verbs.** Those used so far in this text are: **estar** (Lesson 1), **ser** (Lesson 3), **decir, tener** (Lesson 4), **ir, venir** (Lesson 5).*

EXERCISES

A. Structure Practice.

1. Es la una ⎫ y cuarto.
    Son las dos ⎬ y media.
    Son las tres ⎭ menos diez.

Answer. 1. ¿Es la una y cuarto?   2. ¿Qué hora es? 3. ¿Qué hora tiene usted?

Translate. 1. It's half past one.   2. It's ten of two.   3. It's a quarter past three.

---

* For Tables and Reference List, see p. 200 ff.

2. Me levanto ⎫   a las siete y media.
     Me desayuno ⎬   a eso de las ocho.
     Salgo de casa ⎭   a las nueve menos cuarto.

Answer. 1. ¿A qué hora se levanta usted?   2. ¿A qué hora se desayuna?   3. ¿A qué hora sale de casa?

Translate. 1. I get up at seven thirty.   2. I leave home about eight o'clock.   3. I have breakfast at a quarter to nine.

3. Vuelvo ⎫   a las tres ⎫
     Volvemos ⎬ a casa ⎨ a las cuatro ⎬ de la tarde.
     Vuelve ⎭   a las cinco ⎭

Answer. 1. ¿A qué hora vuelve usted a casa?   2. ¿A qué hora vuelven ustedes a casa?   3. ¿A qué hora vuelve a casa su hermano?

Translate. 1. I return home at four o'clock in the afternoon.   2. He returns home at three o'clock in the afternoon.   3. We return home at five o'clock in the afternoon.

B. Drill Exercises.

1. *Tell the time in Spanish. (Example:* 1:15 — Es la una y cuarto.) 1. 2:30.   2. 7:15.   3. 9:20.   4. 10:50.   5. 12:45.

2. *Change the time to a quarter of an hour later. (Example:* A la una y media. — A las dos menos cuarto.) 1. A las tres y cuarto.   2. A las cuatro y media.   3. A las seis en punto.   4. A las ocho y diez.   5. A la una menos cinco.

3. *Give the first person singular present indicative of each verb. (Example:* tomar — tomo.) 1. cenar.   2. llegar.   3. comer.   4. leer.   5. vivir.

4. *Give the first person plural present indicative of each verb. (Example:* tomar — tomamos.) 1. hablar.   2. charlar.   3. estudiar.   4. comer.   5. vivir.

5. *Change from the third person singular to the third person plural. (Example:* entiende — entienden.) 1. vuelve. 2. duerme. 3. viene. 4. dice. 5. se acuesta.

C. Questions. 1. ¿Qué hora es? 2. ¿Qué hora tienen ustedes? 3. ¿Se levanta usted temprano? 4. ¿A qué hora se desayuna usted? 5. ¿A qué hora sale usted de casa? 6. ¿A qué hora llega a la Universidad? 7. ¿Vive usted cerca de aquí? 8. ¿Tiene usted clases por la tarde? 9. ¿A qué hora vuelve usted a casa? 10. ¿Está usted cansado (cansada) por la tarde? 11. ¿Cuántas horas duerme usted? 12. ¿Qué hace usted por la tarde? 13. ¿Lee usted el periódico todos los días? 14. ¿Estudia usted a veces toda la tarde? 15. ¿Cuándo toma usted café? 16. ¿Estudia usted por la noche? 17. ¿Cuándo charla usted con sus amigos? 18. ¿Cena usted temprano? 19. ¿Qué hace usted por la noche? 20. ¿A qué hora llegan sus amigos esta noche?

D. Translation. 1. We get up early. 2. We eat breakfast at a quarter past eight. 3. I leave home at eight thirty. 4. I arrive at the University at nine on the dot. 5. We live near here. 6. I have three classes in the morning. 7. I don't have any classes in the afternoon. 8. At what time do you return home? 9. Sometimes I study all afternoon. 10. This afternoon I'm a little tired. 11. What time is it? 12. It's a quarter after one. 13. What time do you have? 14. By my watch it's a quarter of two. 15. I have coffee at three in the afternoon. 16. We eat supper about six thirty. 17. I read the paper every evening. 18. We always study a little in the evening. 19. We also chat with our friends. 20. This evening we are going to the movies at eight.

E. Conversation and Composition. Topic: Your daily routine.

8 El tiempo

Hoy hace buen tiempo. No hace calor. No hace frío.
Hace sol. No llueve. Hace un tiempo muy agradable.
Pero a veces hace aquí un tiempo bastante desagradable.
Llueve mucho. También nieva mucho. En el invierno
hace mucho frío. En el verano hace mucho calor. Hace 5
buen tiempo en la primavera y en el otoño. Hace mal
tiempo en el verano y en el invierno.

(Elena, José y Felipe.)

ELENA. ¿Qué tiempo hace esta mañana?
JOSÉ. No lo sé. Malo, sin duda. 10
FELIPE. Hace frío, está nublado y hay mucha humedad.
JOSÉ. Cuando hace tan mal tiempo, siempre cojo un
   resfriado.
ELENA. ¿Tienes frío ahora?
JOSÉ. No, no tengo mucho frío. 15
FELIPE. El pobre Juanito ya tiene un resfriado.
ELENA. ¡Pobre muchacho! Lo siento mucho.
FELIPE. El clima de nuestra ciudad no es ideal.
ELENA. No sé . . . No es tan malo. Tenemos unos meses
   muy agradables. 20
JOSÉ. ¿Cuáles, por ejemplo?
ELENA. Marzo y abril . . .
JOSÉ. En marzo hace viento y en abril llueve mucho.
ELENA. Septiembre y octubre . . .
JOSÉ. A veces hace calor y a veces hace frío. 25

VOCABULARY

abril *m.* April
agradable agreeable, pleasant
ahora now
el **calor** warmth, heat; **hace calor** it is warm, it is hot
el **clima** climate
coger (j) to catch; **cojo** I catch
¿**cuál**? *pron.* which (one)?
cuando when
desagradable disagreeable, unpleasant
la **duda** doubt; **sin duda** without doubt, no doubt
el **ejemplo** example; **por ejemplo** for example
el **frío** cold; **hace frío** it is cold; ¿**tienes frío**? are you cold?
hay there is, there are
hoy today
la **humedad** humidity; **hay mucha humedad** it is very humid
ideal ideal
el **invierno** winter
llover (ue) to rain
mal, malo, -a bad

marzo *m.* March
mucho, -a much; *pl.* many; **hace mucho frío** it is very cold
nevar (ie) to snow
nublado, -a cloudy
octubre *m.* October
el **otoño** fall, autumn
pobre poor
la **primavera** spring
el **resfriado** cold *(illness)*; **coger un resfriado** to catch (a) cold
saber to know *(a fact)*; **no (lo) sé** I don't know
sentir (ie) to feel, to regret; **lo siento mucho** I'm very sorry
septiembre *m.* September
el **sol** sun, sunshine; **hace sol** it is sunny
el **tiempo** weather; **hace buen tiempo** the weather is fine; ¿**qué tiempo hace**? how is the weather?
el **verano** summer
el **viento** wind; **hace viento** it is windy
ya already

GRAMMATICAL EXPLANATIONS

1. Idiomatic Forms.

(a) **Tener (mucho) calor,** *to be (very) warm* or *hot;* **tener (mucho) frío,** *to be (very) cold* (referring to persons).

No tengo calor. Tengo frío.	*I'm not warm. I'm cold.*
¿Tienen ustedes frío ahora?	*Are you cold now?*
Tenemos mucho frío.	*We're very cold.*

Hace frío = it's cold outside

(b) **Sentir(lo),** *to regret (it), to be sorry.* The verb **sentir,** like the English verb *to regret,* must have an object expressed.

Lo sentimos mucho.	*We're very sorry. (Or: We regret it very much.)*

(c) **Saber(lo),** *to know (it).* The verb **saber,** *to know,* usually has an object expressed. The omission of the object in certain instances makes the statement less specific or definite.

¿Qué tiempo hace?—No **lo** sé.	*How's the weather?—I don't know.*
No sé...No es tan malo.	*I don't know...It's not so bad.*

2. Definite Article with Proper Nouns when Modified. The definite article is regularly used with the names of persons or places when modified, except in exclamations or in direct address (speaking *to* the person).

El pobre Juanito tiene un resfriado.	*Poor Johnny has a cold.*
¡**Pobre** Juanito!	*Poor Johnny!*

3. Meanings of *pobre*. The word **pobre,** *poor,* when in an unstressed position (before the noun) has a figurative meaning, *unfortunate.* In a stressed position (after the noun or as a predicate adjective) it has its literal meaning, *needy.*

El **pobre muchacho** siempre coge un resfriado.	*The poor boy always catches cold.*
Juan es un **muchacho pobre.**	*John is a poor (= needy) boy.*

4. Months of the Year. The names of the months of the year are masculine. They are not capitalized.

enero	*January*	julio	*July*
febrero	*February*	agosto	*August*
marzo	*March*	septiembre	*September*
abril	*April*	octubre	*October*
mayo	*May*	noviembre	*November*
junio	*June*	diciembre	*December*

5. The Weather. In many expressions concerning the weather, the verbs **hace,** *it makes,* and **hay,** *there is,* are used with a noun object, which may be modified by an adjective.

¿Qué tiempo **hace?**	*How's the weather?*
Hace buen tiempo.	*The weather is fine.*
Hace (mucho) calor.	*It is (very) warm.*
Hace (mucho) frío.	*It is (very) cold.*
Hace (mucho) viento.	*It is (very) windy.*
Hace *(or* **Hay)** sol.	*It is sunny.*
Hay (mucha) humedad.	*It is (very) humid.*

(a) When an adjective follows the noun, the indefinite article is used.

Hace un tiempo agradable.   *The weather is pleasant.*

(b) The verb **estar,** *to be,* is used with adjectives, and there are a few special verbs, like **llover,** *to rain,* and **nevar,** *to snow.*

Está nublado.	*It is cloudy.*
Llueve ahora.	*It is raining now.*
Nieva mucho.	*It snows a lot.*

6. Verbs.

(a) **Radical-Changing:** llover (ue), nevar (ie), sentir (ie).

(b) **Irregular in the First Person Singular:** saber: **sé.**

(c) **Orthographic-Changing Verbs.** Because of the conventions of Spanish spelling, some verbs require spelling changes in certain forms. In the present indicative such changes occur in the final consonant of the stem of certain **-er** and **-ir** verbs when before **-o (qu > c, gu > g, c > z, g > j).** Example: **coger (g > j): cojo.**

EXERCISES

A. STRUCTURE PRACTICE.

1. Hoy   ⎫   ⎧ sol.
    A veces   ⎬ hace   ⎨ calor.
    Siempre   ⎭   ⎩ buen tiempo.

Answer. 1. ¿Qué tiempo hace hoy?   2. ¿Hace calor a veces?   3. ¿Hace buen tiempo siempre?

Translate. 1. Today the weather is good.   2. It is always sunny.   3. At times it is warm.

2. En marzo   ⎫   ⎧ viento.
    En julio   ⎬ hace mucho   ⎨ calor.
    En diciembre   ⎭   ⎩ frío.

Answer. 1. ¿Qué tiempo hace en marzo? 2. ¿Qué tiempo hace en julio?   3. ¿Qué tiempo hace en diciembre?

Translate. 1. In December it is very cold.   2. In March it is very windy.   3. In July it is very warm.

3. En la primavera   ⎫   ⎧ muy bueno.
    En el otoño   ⎬ hace un tiempo   ⎨ agradable.
    En el invierno   ⎭   ⎩ desagradable.

Answer.   1. ¿Qué tiempo hace en la primavera? 2. ¿Qué tiempo hace en el otoño?   3. ¿Qué tiempo hace en el invierno?

Translate. 1. In the fall the weather is very good.   2. In the spring the weather is pleasant.   3. In the winter the weather is unpleasant.

B. Drill Exercises.

1. *Give the six forms of the present indicative.* 1. Tengo frío.   2. Lo siento.   3. Ya lo se.

2. *Use **hace** with each noun or phrase.* (*Example:* frío— Hace frío.) 1. calor.   2. viento.   3. sol.   4. buen tiempo. 5. un tiempo agradable.

3. *Use **mucho, -a** with the noun object.* (*Example:* Hace calor. — Hace mucho calor.) 1. Hace frío.   2. Tengo calor. 3. Hay humedad.   4. Tenemos frío.   5. No hace calor.

C. Questions. 1. ¿Qué tiempo hace?   2. ¿Hay mucha humedad? 3. ¿Hace frío? 4. ¿Está nublado ahora? 5. No

llueve, ¿verdad?   6. ¿Hace sol?   7. ¿Hace mal tiempo?
8. ¿Hace un tiempo bastante agradable?   9. ¿Tiene usted
calor?   10. ¿Coge usted un resfriado cuando hace frío?
11. ¿Es bueno el clima de nuestra ciudad?   12. ¿Hace buen
tiempo en la primavera?   13. ¿En qué mes hace más viento?
14. ¿En qué mes llueve mucho?   15. ¿Qué meses son muy
agradables?   16. ¿Qué meses son bastante desagradables?
17. ¿Hace mucho calor en el verano?   18. ¿Llueve mucho
en el invierno?   19. ¿Nieva mucho?   20. ¿Qué tiempo hace
en el otoño?

D. TRANSLATION. 1. How's the weather today?   2. The
weather is fine now.   3. It is sunny.   4. It's not cloudy.
5. Sometimes the weather here is very pleasant.   6. But
our city's climate is not ideal.   7. It rains a lot in the spring
and in the winter.   8. It's very hot in the summer.   9. It's
also very humid.   10. It's very windy in March and in
April.   11. The weather is pleasant in the fall.   12. It's
rather cold in January and in February.   13. Does it snow
a lot?   14. Are you cold now?   15. I'm not warm.   16. Do
you have a cold?   17. I always catch cold when the weather
is bad.   18. Poor Michael has a cold, doesn't he?   19. I'm
very sorry.   20. Why do we always talk about the weather?

E. CONVERSATION AND COMPOSITION. Topic: The
weather in your home town.

by seasons

9 Diversiones

Mis diversiones favoritas son los deportes, el cine, la radio y la televisión. Los deportes que me gustan más son el futbol, el beisbol y el tenis. No juego al futbol, pero voy a casi todos los partidos. Voy al cine cuando hay una película buena. Los mejores programas de radio 5 y de televisión no empiezan hasta las ocho de la noche. No me interesan mucho los programas de la mañana y de la tarde.

(Felipe, José y Elena.)

FELIPE. ¿A qué hora empieza el programa de la orquesta 10 sinfónica?

JOSÉ. No lo sé. ¿Piensas escucharlo?

FELIPE. Sí. Ya sabes que me gusta la música clásica.

ELENA. Creo que empieza a las tres.

JOSÉ. A mí me gusta más la música de baile. 15

ELENA. Yo prefiero mirar la televisión.

JOSÉ. Yo también, cuando los programas son buenos.

ELENA. Hay varios muy buenos el domingo por la tarde.

JOSÉ. Me parecen mejores los programas deportivos los martes por la noche. 20

FELIPE. Sí, a tí te gustan los deportes. ¿Piensas ir al partido de la semana que viene?

JOSÉ. ¡Ya lo creo! Va a ser muy buen partido.

ELENA. ¿Puede ganar nuestro equipo?

JOSÉ. Creo que sí. Juega muy bien este año. 25

VOCABULARY

el **baile** dance
el **beisbol** baseball
clásico, -a classical
creer to believe, to think; **creo que sí** I think so; **¡ya lo creo!** yes, indeed!, I should say so!
el **deporte** sport
deportivo, -a *adj.* sports
la **diversión** entertainment, pastime
el **domingo** Sunday
empezar (ie) to begin
el **equipo** team
escuchar to listen (to); **escucharlo** to listen to it
favorito, -a favorite
el **futbol** football
ganar to earn, to win
gustar to please; **me gusta** (it) pleases me, I like (it); **me gustan más** I like (them) better *or* best
interesar to interest
ir a (+ *inf.*) to be going to (*do something*)

jugar (ue) to play (*a game*); **jugar al futbol** to play football
el **martes** Tuesday
más more *or* most
mejor better *or* best
mirar to look (at), to watch
la **música** music
la **orquesta** orchestra; **orquesta sinfónica** symphony orchestra
parecer to seem   *me parece* "*it seems to me*"
el **partido** game
la **película** film, picture, movie
pensar (ie) to think; to intend
poder (ue) to be able (can, may)
preferir (ie) to prefer
el **programa** program
la **radio** radio
la **semana** week; **la semana que viene** next week
la **televisión** television
el **tenis** tennis

GRAMMATICAL EXPLANATIONS

1. Idiomatic Forms.

(a) **Ir a** (+ infinitive), *to be going to* (do something). **As** in English, this form is often used for the future.

Nuestro equipo **va a ganar.**   *Our team is going to win.*

(b) **Pensar** (+ infinitive), *to intend to* (do something).

Pensamos ir al partido.   *We intend to go to the game.*

(c) **Creer que sí,** *to think so;* **creer que no,** *to think not.*

¿Podemos ganar?—**Creo que sí.**   *Can we win?—I think so.*

(d) **Jugar a,** *to play* (a game).

¿**Juega** usted **al futbol?**   *Do you play football?*

2. Definite Article with Names of Entertainments. The names of games and other entertainments are usually used in a general sense, and require the definite article. The article is omitted in adjectival phrases.

Me gusta **el cine** más que la televisión. — *I like the movies better than television.*

¿Qué programas **de radio** y **de televisión** le gustan más? — *Which radio and television programs do you like best?*

3. Days of the Week. The names of the days of the week are masculine. They are not capitalized.

el **lunes**	*Monday*	el **viernes**	*Friday*
el **martes**	*Tuesday*	el **sábado**	*Saturday*
el **miércoles**	*Wednesday*	el **domingo**	*Sunday*
el **jueves**	*Thursday*		

The definite article is regularly used except after the verb **ser,** *to be.* No preposition is used except in adjectival phrases.

Hay buenos programas **el domingo** por la tarde. — *There are good programs on Sunday afternoon.*

Hoy es **miércoles.** — *Today is Wednesday.*

¿Va usted al partido **del sábado?** — *Are you going to the game on Saturday (= Saturday's game)?*

4. Object Pronouns with the Infinitive. Object pronouns follow the infinitive and are attached to it. If the infinitive is part of a verb phrase which is considered as a *unit,* the pronoun may precede the whole phrase.

Pensamos **escucharlo.** — *We intend to listen to it.*

Vamos a **verlos** (*or* **Los** vamos a ver) esta tarde. — *We're going to (= We shall) see them this afternoon.*

5. Verbs Used Mainly in the Third Person. Some verbs are used mainly in the third person, often with a thing as subject and a person as indirect object. The same ideas are usually expressed in English with the person as the subject.

Los programas me **parecen** interesantes.	*The programs seem interesting to me.*
Nos **gusta** la música clásica.	*We like classical music. (Lit. Classical music pleases us.)*
¿Le **interesan** a usted los programas deportivos?	*Are you interested in the sports programs? (Or: Do the sports programs interest you?)*

(*a*) Because of length or stress, the subject (the thing that pleases, interests, etc.) often follows the verb.

Me gustan **estos programas**.	*I like these programs.*

(*b*) A noun object, whether before or after the verb, is repeated as an object pronoun.

A José le gustan mucho.	*Joseph likes them a lot.*
No le gustan a **Felipe**.	*Philip doesn't like them.*

6. Verbs.

(*a*) **Regular:** creer, escuchar, ganar, gustar, interesar, mirar.

(*b*) **Radical-Changing:** empezar (ie), jugar (ue), pensar (ie), poder (ue), preferir (ie).

(*c*) **Irregular in the First Person Singular:** parecer: **parezco.**

EXERCISES

A. STRUCTURE PRACTICE.

1. Me ⎫   ⎧ el cine.
    Nos ⎬ gusta mucho ⎨ la radio.
    Le ⎭   ⎩ el futbol.

Answer. 1. ¿Le gusta el cine?   2. ¿Les gusta la radio? 3. ¿Le gusta a José el futbol?

Translate. 1. We like football a lot.   2. I like the radio a lot.   3. He likes the movies a lot.

2.   Me ⎫
         Nos ⎬ gustan los programas ⎰ del lunes.
         Le ⎭   ⎱ del martes.
                                         del miércoles.

Answer. 1. ¿Qué programas le gustan a usted?   2. ¿Qué programas les gustan a ustedes?   3. ¿Qué programas le gustan a Elena?

Translate. 1. I like the programs on Tuesday.   2. She likes the programs on Monday.   3. We like the programs on Wednesday.

3.   Me ⎫ gustan   ⎫ los deportes.
         Nos ⎬ interesan más   ⎬ los programas de radio.
         Le ⎭ parecen mejores ⎭ los programas de televisión.

Answer. 1. ¿Qué diversiones le gustan a usted?   2. ¿Qué programas les interesan más a ustedes?   3. ¿Qué programas le parecen mejores a José?

Translate. 1. I like the radio programs.   2. The television programs seem better to us.   3. He's more interested in sports.

B. Drill Exercises.

1. *Add an appropriate prepositional form to stress or clarify the object pronoun. (Example:* Me gusta. — Me gusta a mí.) 1. Me interesa.   2. Le gusta.   3. Les interesa. 4. Te gusta.   5. Nos parece bien.

2. *Use* **Le gusta** *or* **Les gusta** *with each object, according to whether it is singular or plural. (Example:* a mis hermanos — Les gusta a mis hermanos.) 1. a mi hermana. 2. a mis padres.   3. a mi tío.   4. a mis primos.   5. a José y a Elena.

3. *Use* **Me gusta** *or* **Me gustan** *with each subject, according to whether it is singular or plural. (Example:* los deportes — Me gustan los deportes.) 1. el programa. 2. los programas. 3. los bailes. 4. el tenis. 5. el futbol y el beisbol.

4. *Change the time reference to the day following. (Example:* Jugamos el lunes. — Jugamos el martes.) 1. Hoy es miércoles. 2. Juegan al beisbol el viernes. 3. No piensan jugar el domingo. 4. Voy a verlos el martes. 5. Vamos al partido del jueves.

C. QUESTIONS. 1. ¿Cuáles son sus diversiones favoritas? 2. ¿Qué programas de radio escucha usted? 3. ¿Le gusta la música clásica? 4. ¿Le gusta más la música de baile? 5. ¿Qué le parecen los programas de la orquesta sinfónica? 6. ¿Prefiere usted mirar la televisión? 7. ¿A qué hora empieza su programa favorito? 8. ¿Le interesan los programas de la mañana? 9. ¿Le parecen mejores los programas de la tarde? 10. ¿Qué días de la semana hay programas buenos? 11. ¿Piensan ustedes ir al cine esta noche? 12. ¿Va usted mucho al cine? 13. ¿Hay muchas películas buenas ahora? 14. Usted juega al tenis, ¿verdad? 15. ¿Pueden ustedes jugar el martes que viene? 16. ¿Cuál es el deporte favorito de los norteamericanos? 17. ¿Qué deportes le gustan más a usted? 18. ¿Va usted al partido del sábado que viene? 19. ¿Quién va a ganar? 20. ¿Cuántos partidos puede ganar nuestro equipo este año?

D. TRANSLATION. 1. My favorite entertainments are radio and television. 2. I also like sports. 3. I go to almost all the football and baseball games. 4. Do you go to the movies a lot? 5. There is a good picture tonight. 6. I prefer to watch the television programs. 7. My favorite program begins at eight thirty. 8. The morning and afternoon programs don't interest me. 9. Do you listen to the programs of the symphony orchestra?   10. I like classical music, but I like dance music better.   11. Can you play tennis with me on Friday?   12. Tennis is one of my favorite sports.   13. Do you like football better than baseball?   14. Our football team is always very good.   15. They say that baseball is the favorite sport of Americans.   16. Do you intend to go to the game on Saturday?   17. Which of the teams seems better to you?   18. Can we win many games this year?   19. I think so.   20. Our team plays very well.

E. CONVERSATION AND COMPOSITION. Topic: Your favorite entertainments.

PRESENT INDICATIVE

(List of Irregularities for Lessons 1–9)

RADICAL CHANGES (-ar, -er, and -ir verbs)	ORTHOGRAPHIC CHANGES (-er and -ir verbs)
stressed $\begin{cases} \text{o} > \text{ue} \\ \text{e} > \text{ie} \\ \text{e} > \text{i} \end{cases}$	$\left. \begin{array}{l} \text{qu} > \text{c} \\ \text{gu} > \text{g} \\ \text{c} > \text{z} \\ \text{g} > \text{j} \end{array} \right\}$ *before* o

acostarse (ue) jugar (ue) preferir (ie)
coger (j) llover (ue) sentir (ie)
dormir (ue) nevar (ie) volver (ue)
empezar (ie) pensar (ie)
entender (ie) poder (ue)

IRREGULAR IN THE FIRST PERSON SINGULAR

conocer: conozco parecer: parezco salir: salgo
hacer: hago saber: sé ver: veo

OTHER IRREGULAR VERBS

Decir		Estar		Ir	
digo	decimos	estoy	estamos	voy	vamos
dices	decís	estás	estáis	vas	vais
dice	dicen	está	están	va	van

Ser		Tener		Venir	
soy	somos	tengo	tenemos	vengo	venimos
eres	sois	tienes	tenéis	vienes	venís
es	son	tiene	tienen	viene	vienen

10 Ayer

Ayer me levanté a las ocho menos cuarto. Me desayuné a las ocho y diez. Tomé el autobús y llegué a la universidad un poco antes de las nueve. Tuve clases toda la mañana. Almorcé a la una. Por la tarde fuí al centro a hacer unas compras. No volví a casa hasta las siete. Por la noche hice una visita a unos amigos. Charlamos un rato, y luego salimos a tomar café. Volví a casa y me acosté a las once. ⁵

(Elena y Pablo.)

ELENA. Buenos días, Pablo. ¿Qué hizo usted ayer? No ¹⁰ le vimos en la clase.

PABLO. Me quedé en casa para curarme de este resfriado. ¡Con el bonito tiempo que hace!

ELENA. ¿Usted tiene un resfriado? Lo siento mucho.

PABLO. Muchas gracias. ¹⁵

ELENA. Claro que estudió usted todo el día.

PABLO. No, pero pensé en ustedes.

ELENA. Es usted muy galante. ¿Cómo pasó el día?

PABLO. Escuché la radio. Los programas fueron malos. Miré la televisión . . . ²⁰

ELENA. Y los programas fueron peores.

PABLO. ¡Claro! Luego dormí un rato, y soñé con el examen. ¿Qué tal fué el examen de ayer?

ELENA. No fué difícil. Lo terminamos todos en unos treinta minutos. ²⁵

VOCABULARY

acosté: me acosté I went to bed
almorzar (ue) to eat lunch; **almorcé** I ate lunch
antes de *prep.* before
el **autobús** bus
ayer yesterday
el **centro** business district; **fuí al centro** I went downtown, I went to the city
¡claro! sure!, of course!
claro que . . . of course . . .
la **compra** purchase
curar to cure, to treat
charlamos we chatted
desayuné: me desayuné I ate breakfast
dormí I slept
escuché I listened (to)
estudió (you) studied
el **examen** examination, exam
fué (it) was
fueron (they) were
fuí I went
galante gallant
hice I made
hizo (you) did; **¿qué hizo usted?** what did you do?

levanté: me levanté I got up
llegué I arrived
miré I watched
para to, in order to
pasar to pass, to spend *(time);* **¿cómo pasó el día?** how did you spend the day?
pensé en I thought about
peor worse *or* worst
quedarse to stay, to remain; **me quedé en casa** I stayed (at) home
¿qué tal fué. . .? how was...?
el **rato** short time; **un rato** a (little) while
salimos we went out
soñar (ue) to dream; **soñé con** I dreamed about
terminar to end, to finish; **terminamos** we finished
tomé I took
tuve I had
vimos we saw, did see
la **visita** visit, call; **hice una visita** I made a call, I visited
volví I returned

GRAMMATICAL EXPLANATIONS

1. Idiomatic Forms.

(a) **Pensar en,** *to think of* or *about.* The preposition **en** (rather than **de**) is used except where an opinion is involved.

Pensé en la clase.   *I thought about the class.*
¿Qué piensa usted de la clase?   *What do you think of the class?*

(b) **Soñar con,** *to dream of* or *about.*

Soñé con el examen.   *I dreamed about the exam.*

2. Use of *para* and *a* to Express Purpose. An infinitive used to express purpose is usually introduced by **para,** *in order to.* After verbs of motion (**ir,** *to go,* **venir,** *to come,* etc.) **a,** *to,* is used instead of **para** unless the idea of purpose is stressed.

Me quedé en casa **para curarme** de este resfriado.	*I stayed home to treat this cold.*
Fuimos al centro **a hacer** unas compras.	*We went downtown to make some purchases.*

3. Verbs.

(*a*) **Regular:** curar, pasar, quedarse, terminar.

(*b*) **Radical-Changing:** almorzar (ue), soñar (ue).

4. Preterite Indicative of Regular Verbs. The preterite indicative (narrative past tense) can usually be formed as follows: remove the ending of the infinitive (**-ar, -er,** or **-ir**); add the endings of the preterite.

-ar VERBS		**-er** OR **-ir** VERBS	
tom-ar, *to take*		**com-er,** *to eat*	
I took (did take),		*I ate (did eat),*	
you took, etc.		*you ate,* etc.	
tomé	tomamos	comí	comimos
tomaste	tomasteis	comiste	comisteis
tomó	tomaron	comió	comieron

5. Preterite Indicative of Irregular Verbs.

(*a*) **Radical Changes.** All **-ir** radical-changing verbs have stem-vowel changes in the preterite. These changes occur in the third-person singular and plural (**o > u, e > i**). Examples:

Dormir (o > u)		**Sentir (e > i)**	
dormí	dormimos	sentí	sentimos
dormiste	dormisteis	sentiste	sentisteis
durmió	durmieron	sintió	sintieron

Another verb of this type: **preferir (e > i).**

(*b*) **Orthographic Changes.** For **-ar** verbs spelling changes occur in the final consonant of the stem of certain verbs when before **-e** (**c > qu, g > gu, z > c, gu > gü**). Examples:

Empezar (z > c)		Llegar (g > gu)	
empecé	empezamos	llegué	llegamos
empezaste	empezastcis	llegaste	llegasteis
empezó	empezaron	llegó	llegaron

Other verbs of this type: **almorzar (z > c), jugar (g > gu)**.

For **-er** or **-ir** verbs spelling changes occur in the initial **i** of the endings when the stem ends in a vowel (stressed **i > í** after **a, e,** or **o;** unstressed **i > y** between vowels). Examples:

Creer (í, y)		Leer (í, y)	
creí	creímos	leí	leímos
creíste	creísteis	leíste	leísteis
creyó	creyeron	leyó	leyeron

(c) **Verbs with an Irregular Stem + a Special Set of Endings.** Most of the irregular preterites have an irregular stem and a special set of endings. Example:

Tener	
tuve	tuvimos
tuviste	tuvisteis
tuvo	tuvieron

The other verbs of this type which have been used so far are listed here. This list is an almost complete one for the language.

decir: **dije** (3rd plur.: **dijeron**)	poder: **pude**
estar: **estuve**	saber: **supe**
hacer: **hice** (3rd sing.: **hizo**)	venir: **vine**

The preterite of **hay** (from **haber**) is also of this type: **hubo,** *there was, there were.* Note that in the form **dijeron** the i of the ending **-ieron** has been lost, and in the form **hizo** there is a spelling change (c > z).

(d) **Other Irregular Verbs.** Note that the preterites of **ir** and **ser** are identical.

Ir		Ser	
fuí	fuimos	fuí	fuimos
fuiste	fuisteis	fuiste	fuisteis
fué	fueron	fué	fueron

EXERCISES

A. STRUCTURE PRACTICE.

1. Me levanté ⎫   ⎧ ocho.
Fuí al centro ⎬ a las   ⎨ nueve.
Volví a casa ⎭   ⎩ diez.

Answer. 1. ¿A qué hora se levantó usted ayer?   2. ¿Cuándo fué usted al centro?   3. ¿A qué hora volvió usted a casa?

Translate. 1. I got up at eight.   2. I went downtown at nine.   3. I returned home at ten.

2. Me quedé ⎫   ⎧ leer.
Nos quedamos ⎬ en casa para ⎨ estudiar.
Se quedó ⎭   ⎩ dormir.

Answer. 1. ¿Por qué se quedó usted en casa?   2. ¿Por qué se quedaron ustedes en casa?   3. ¿Por qué se quedó Pablo en casa?

Translate. 1. We stayed home to read.   2. He stayed home to study.   3. I stayed home to sleep.

3. Fuí ⎫   ⎧ almorzar.
Fuimos ⎬ al centro a ⎨ ver a unos amigos.
Fué ⎭   ⎩ hacer unas compras.

Answer. 1. ¿Fué usted al centro a almorzar?   2. ¿A dónde fueron ustedes?   3. ¿Dónde está Elena?

Translate. 1. I went downtown to see some friends. 2. She went downtown to have lunch.   3. We went downtown to make some purchases.

B. DRILL EXERCISES.

1. *Change from the first to the third person singular.* (*Example:* tomé — tomó.) 1. miré.   2. soñé.   3. pasé. 4. pensé.   5. terminé.

2. *Change from the first to the third person plural.* *(Example:* tomamos — tomaron.) 1. cenamos. 2. hablamos. 3. charlamos. 4. ganamos. 5. estudiamos.

3. *Change from the first to the third person singular.* *(Example:* comí — comió.) 1. viví. 2. cogí. 3. salí. 4. volví. 5. entendí.

4. *Change from the third person singular to the third person plural. (Example:* comió — comieron.) 1. vivió. 2. cogió. 3. durmió. 4. sintió. 5. prefirió.

5. *Change from the first to the third person singular. (Example:* tuve — tuvo.) 1. estuve. 2. pude. 3. supe. 4. dije. 5. vine.

C. QUESTIONS. 1. ¿A qué hora se levantó usted ayer? 2. ¿A qué hora se desayunó? 3. ¿Cuántas clases tuvo usted por la mañana? 4. ¿A dónde fueron ustedes por la tarde? 5. ¿Fueron en su coche o tomaron el autobús? 6. ¿Qué hicieron ustedes en el centro? 7. ¿Qué hizo usted cuando volvió a casa? 8. ¿Cuántas horas estudió? 9. ¿Durmió usted un rato? 10. ¿Qué programas de radio escuchó? 11. ¿Qué programas de televisión vieron ustedes? 12. ¿Fueron buenos o malos? 13. ¿Cuándo jugaron ustedes al tenis? 14. ¿Quién ganó? 15. ¿A qué hora cenó usted? 16. ¿Quiénes le hicieron una visita por la noche? 17. ¿De qué charlaron ustedes? 18. ¿Con qué soñó Pablo ayer? 19. ¿En quiénes pensó? 20. ¿Por qué se quedó en casa?

D. TRANSLATION. 1. Yesterday I got up quite early. 2. I had breakfast at eight thirty. 3. I had classes all morning. 4. What did you do in the afternoon? 5. I went downtown to make some purchases. 6. I returned home at three. 7. I slept a while. 8. At four I went to see a friend. 9. We played tennis until six. 10. We ate supper

at six thirty.   11. Did you go out in the evening?   12. I
stayed home to study.   13. How many hours did you study
for the exam?   14. Some friends came to visit me.   15. We
chatted a while.   16. They left at nine.   17. I watched a
television program.   18. I listened to a program of dance
music.   19. I didn't think about the Spanish exam until
ten thirty.   20. I went to bed at eleven.

**E. CONVERSATION AND COMPOSITION. Topic: What
you did yesterday.**

PRETERITE INDICATIVE

(List of Irregularities for Lessons 1–10)

RADICAL CHANGES	ORTHOGRAPHIC CHANGES	
(-ir verbs)	**(-ar** verbs) *consonant of stem*	**(-er** and **-ir** verbs) *i of endings after* **a, e, o**
3rd sing. $\begin{cases} \text{o} > \text{u} \\ \text{e} > \text{i} \end{cases}$ *and pl.*	$\left. \begin{array}{l} \text{c} > \text{qu} \\ \text{g} > \text{gu} \\ \text{z} > \text{c} \\ \text{gu} > \text{gü} \end{array} \right\}$ *before* e	*stressed* i > í *unstressed* i > y

almorzar (c)   empezar (c)   llegar (gu)
creer (í, y)   jugar (gu)   preferir (i)
dormir (u)   leer (í, y)   sentir (i)

IRREGULAR STEM + SPECIAL ENDINGS

decir: dije *(3rd pl.* dijeron)   saber: supe
estar: estuve   tener: tuve
hacer: hice *(3rd sing.* hizo)   venir: vine
poder: pude

OTHER IRREGULAR VERBS

Ir

fuí	fuimos
fuiste	fuisteis
fué	fueron

Ser

fuí	fuimos
fuiste	fuisteis
fué	fueron

GRAMMATICAL NOTES

(Use the following grammatical notes as a guide for reviewing forms and usage. Then test your knowledge of them by using the corresponding Test Exercises on the opposite page.)

1. Idiomatic Forms. *List for Lessons 6-10.*

casa *(after prep.)* home (7)
creer que sí to think so; **creer que no** to think not (9)
ir a (+ *inf.*) to be going to (9)
jugar a (+ *game*) to play (9)
pensar (+ *inf.*) to intend (9)
pensar en to think of *or* about (10)
saber(lo) to know (8)
salir (de) to leave (7)

sentir(lo) to regret (it), to be sorry (8)
ser (+ *numeral*): **somos cinco** there are five of us (6)
soñar con to dream of *or* about (10)
tener . . . años, *etc.* to be . . . (years) old, *etc.* (6)
tener (mucho) calor to be (very) warm *or* hot; **tener (mucho) frío** to be (very) cold (8)

2. Definite Article.

Usage: definite article used with proper nouns when modified, except in exclamations or in direct address (8:2); with names of entertainments, except in adjectival phrases (9:2); with names of the days of the week, except after **ser** (9:3); with hours of the day (7:2).

3. Indefinite Article.

Usage: indirect article omitted before noun objects that refer to types rather than individuals (6:2).

(Continued on page 80)

1. Idiomatic Forms.

1. *(at home)* Creo que están _____ ahora.
2. *(we're going to)* Me parece que _____ ganar.
3. *(They intend)* _____ ir a todos los partidos.
4. *(did you think about)* ¿Por qué _____ el examen?
5. *(I left)* Ayer _____ la universidad a las dos.
6. *(she's very sorry)* Isabel dice que _____.
7. *(there are six of us)* En mi familia _____.
8. *(he dreams about)* A veces _____ sus clases.
9. *(How old is)* ¿_____ su hermano mayor?
10. *(I'm very cold)* Esta mañana _____.

2. Definite Article.

1. *(Poor Helen)* _____ no puede ir con nosotros.
2. *(baseball)* ¿Juegan ustedes _____?
3. *(television)* Me gusta mirar _____.
4. *(Wednesday)* Hoy es _____, ¿verdad?
5. *(on Thursday)* Hay un buen programa _____ a las tres.

3. Indefinite Article.

1. *(a car)* Los señores Castro no tienen _____.
2. *(any brothers and sisters)* ¿Tiene _____ María?

(Continued on page 81)

[79]

GRAMMATICAL NOTES, CONTINUED

4. Personal Pronouns.

Forms: special reflexive forms (**se, sí,** and **consigo**) for the third person (6:4).

Usage: object pronouns attached to the infinitive (9:4).

5. Adjectives.

Usage: **pobre** (after noun), *poor, needy,* (before noun) *poor, unfortunate* (8:3).

6. Numerals, Time, Weather.

Lists of related expressions: cardinal numerals 1-100 (6:3); time of day (7:2); days of the week (9:3); months of the year (8:4); weather (8:5).

7. Verbs.

Infinitive: **para** (or after verbs of motion, **a**) used before infinitive to express purpose (10:2).

Present indicative: formed by adding endings to stem (7:3); irregularities often according to patterns for Radical Changes (7:4) or Orthographic Changes (8:6). List on p. 69.

Preterite indicative: formed by adding endings to stem (10:4); irregularities often according to patterns for Radical Changes, Orthographic Changes, or an irregular stem + a special set of endings (10:5). List on p. 77.

Reflexive verbs: often with special meanings (6:5).

Verbs used mainly in the third person: certain verbs (like **gustar, interesar, parecer**) often used with a thing as subject and a person as indirect object (9:5).

TEST EXERCISES, CONTINUED

4. Personal Pronouns.

1. *(himself)* José ____ conoce bien.
2. *(with him)* Felipe no lo tiene ____.
3. *(see her)* Luisa va a ____ esta noche.

5. Adjectives.

1. *(poor girl)* La ____ tiene un resfriado.
2. *(poor boys)* Pablo y Eduardo son ____.

6. Numerals, Time, Weather.

1. *(at a quarter to twelve)* Volví al centro ____.
2. *(in April)* Llueve mucho ____.
3. *(The weather is fine)* ____ en la primavera.

7. Verbs.

1. *(to study)* Se quedaron en casa ____.
2. *(to make)* Fuimos al centro ____ unas compras.
3. *(live)* Mis padres ____ en esta ciudad.
4. *(goes to bed)* José ____ antes de las diez.
5. *(I catch)* Cuando hace frío, ____ un resfriado.
6. *(we studied)* Claro que ____ todo el día.
7. *(Did you sleep)* ¿____ un rato por la tarde?
8. *(I arrived)* ____ a casa a eso de las dos.
9. *(I made)* Por la noche ____ una visita a un amigo.
10. *(is named)* Nuestro tío ____ Jorge González.
11. *(Did you like)* ¿____ los programas del lunes?
12. *(interest me)* Los programas deportivos ____ más.
13. *(seemed to us)* El partido ____ muy bueno.

11 El pasado

A veces recuerdo lo que hacía el año pasado. Mis clases eran más fáciles y tenía más tiempo para mis diversiones. Me paseaba o jugaba al tenis casi todas las tardes. Por la noche miraba la televisión o escuchaba mis discos favoritos en el fonógrafo. Muchas veces salía con mis 5 amigos al cine, a bailar, o a tomar un refresco. Este año tengo que trabajar más. Mi vida es menos divertida.

(Pablo, Elena y Felipe.)

PABLO. Conque ¿estudiaron ustedes anoche para su 10 examen de historia?

ELENA. No, fuimos al cine. Estábamos cansados de tanto estudiar.

FELIPE. Además ya sabíamos bastante historia.

ELENA. Había una película nueva, con buenos actores. 15

FELIPE. Por lo menos las actrices eran buenas.

PABLO. ¿De modo que les gustó la película?

ELENA. Nos gustó mucho. También nos gustaron los dibujos animados.

PABLO. Trabajábamos menos el año pasado, ¿verdad? 20

FELIPE. Ya lo creo. Mucho menos.

ELENA. Entonces nos divertíamos más. Escuchábamos el fonógrafo, mirábamos la televisión . . .

PABLO. Salíamos todas las noches . . .

FELIPE. Y nos quejábamos más que ahora. 25

VOCABULARY

el **actor** actor
la **actriz** actress
   además moreover, besides
   anoche last night
   bailar to dance
   bastante *adj.* enough
   conque (and) so
el **dibujo animado** animated
   cartoon
el **disco** record *(phonograph)*
   divertido, -a amusing, entertaining
   divertirse (ie, i) to enjoy
   oneself, to have a good
   time; **nos divertíamos más**
   we had more fun
   entonces then
   eran (they) were
   escuchaba I listened (to);
   escuchábamos we listened
   (to)
   estábamos we were
el **fonógrafo** phonograph
   había there was, there were
   hacía I did, I used to do
   jugaba I played
   lo que that which, what
   miraba I watched; **mirába-**
   mos we watched

el **modo** way, manner; **de mo-**
   do que so (that), and so
   muchas veces often
   nuevo, -a new
el **pasado** past
   pasado, -a past, last
   pasear *or* **pasearse** to stroll,
   to take a walk; **me pasea-**
   ba I took a walk
   por lo menos at least
   quejarse to complain; **nos**
   quejábamos we com-
   plained
   recordar (ue) to recall, to
   remember
el **refresco** cold drink, refresh-
   ment(s)
   sabíamos we knew
   salía I went out; **salíamos**
   we went out
   tanto, -a as much, so much;
   pl. as many, so many; **tan-**
   to estudiar so much studying
   tener que (+ *inf.*) to have to
   tenía I had (= used to have)
el **tiempo** time
   trabajar to work; **trabajá-**
   bamos we used to work

GRAMMATICAL EXPLANATIONS

1. Idiomatic Form. Tener que (+ infinitive), *to have to*
(do something). The word **que** must come immediately before
the infinitive that it serves to introduce.

Teníamos que trabajar menos.	*We had to work less.*
¿**Tienen** ustedes **que** salir?	*Do you have to leave?*
Tenemos mucho **que** hacer.	*We have a lot to do.*

2. Infinitive as a Noun. The infinitive is the only Spanish verb form used as a noun (subject, object, object of a preposition, etc.). Its function as an abstract verbal noun is often made clearer by the use of the definite article (masculine singular). Note that in many of these cases, English uses the gerund.

El bailar era una de mis diversiones favoritas.	*Dancing was one of my favorite entertainments.*
No quiero estudiar esta noche.	*I don't want to study tonight.*
Estoy cansado de estudiar.	*I'm tired of studying.*

3. Preterite (Narrative Past Tense) and Imperfect (Descriptive Past Tense). In Spanish there are two simple past tenses: the preterite and the imperfect. The preterite is a *narrative* tense; it tells what happened. The imperfect is a *descriptive* tense; it tells what the situation was (what "was happening" or "used to happen," or how or what the person or thing "was").

Ayer cuando llegué a casa de Pablo, hablaban de lo que hacíamos el año pasado.	*Yesterday when I arrived* (pret.) *at Paul's house, they were talking* (imperf.) *about what we used to do* (imperf.) *last year.*
El año pasado bailábamos, íbamos al cine o mirábamos la televisión casi todas las noches.	*Last year we used to dance, go to the movies, or watch television almost every night.* (Imperf.: tells what the situation used to be.)
Anoche yo estaba cansado de estudiar. Ya sabía bastante historia, y además había una buena película.	*Last night I was tired of studying. I already knew enough history, and besides there was a good movie.* (Imperf.: tells what the situation was last night.)
No estudié más. Fuí al cine y vi una película nueva. Me gustó mucho.	*I didn't study any more. I went to the movies and saw a new picture. I liked it a lot.* (Pret.: tells what happened.)

When a past state, normally a situation (imperfect), is viewed as an event (preterite), the meaning of the verb may be altered. Compare: **conocía,** *I knew* (= *was acquainted with*), **conocí,** *I met* (= *became acquainted with*); **prefería,** *I pre-ferred,* **preferí,** *I decided* or *chose;* **sabía,** *I knew,* **supe,** *I found out, I learned.*

4. Verbs.

(a) **Regular:** bailar, pasearse, quejarse, trabajar.

(b) **Radical-Changing:** divertirse (ie, i), recordar (ue).

5. Imperfect Indicative of Regular Verbs. The imperfect indicative can usually be formed as follows: remove the ending of the infinitive (**-ar, -er,** or **-ir**); add the endings of the imperfect.

-ar VERBS		**-er** OR **-ir** VERBS	
tom-ar, *to take*		**com-er,** *to eat*	
I was taking (used to take, took, did take), you were taking, etc.		*I was eating (used to eat, ate, did eat), you were eating,* etc.	
tomaba	tomábamos	comía	comíamos
tomabas	tomabais	comías	comíais
tomaba	tomaban	comía	comían

6. Imperfect Indicative of Irregular Verbs. Only three verbs are irregular in the imperfect indicative: **ir,** *to go;* **ser,** *to be;* and **ver,** *to see.*

Ir		Ser		Ver	
iba	íbamos	era	éramos	veía	veíamos
ibas	ibais	eras	erais	veías	veíais
iba	iban	era	eran	veía	veían

EXERCISES

A. STRUCTURE PRACTICE.

1. Estábamos cansados }
    Estaba cansada } de { estudiar.
    Estaba cansado }   { leer.
                        { trabajar.

Answer. 1. ¿Estaban ustedes cansados ayer por la tarde? 2. ¿Estaba cansada Elena? 3. ¿Estaba cansado Felipe?

Translate. 1. She was tired of studying. 2. He was tired of reading. 3. We were tired of working.

2. No jugué al tenis ⎞   ⎛ hacía mal tiempo.
    No fuí al cine   ⎬ porque ⎨ tenía un resfriado.
    Me quedé en casa   ⎠   ⎝ tenía que estudiar.

Answer. 1. ¿Por qué no jugó usted al tenis? 2. ¿Por qué no fué usted al cine? 3. ¿Por qué se quedó usted en casa?

Translate. 1. I didn't play tennis because I had a cold. 2. I stayed home because the weather was bad. 3. I didn't go to the movies because I had to study.

3. Recuerdo   ⎞   ⎛ nos divertíamos mucho.
    Recordamos ⎬ que ⎨ nos paseábamos mucho.
    Recuerdan   ⎠   ⎝ trabajábamos poco.

Answer. 1. ¿Piensa usted en nuestra vida del año pasado? 2. ¿Recuerdan ustedes lo que hacíamos entonces? 3. ¿Qué recuerdan Pablo y Felipe?

Translate. 1. We remember that we used to have a lot of fun. 2. They remember that we used to take a lot of walks. 3. I remember that we used to work little.

B. Drill Exercises.

1. *Change from the first person singular to the first person plural. (Example:* tomaba — tomábamos.) 1. bailaba. 2. vivía. 3. iba. 4. era. 5. veía.

2. *Change from the third person singular to the third person plural. (Example:* tomaba — tomaban.) 1. trabajaba. 2. sentía. 3. iba. 4. era. 5. veía.

3. *Change to refer to a past situation or habit, using the imperfect. (Example:* Es la una. — Era la una.) 1. Son las dos. 2. Hace buen tiempo. 3. Todos están bien. 4. Les gusta bailar. 5. Tienen que estudiar.

4. *Change to refer to a past occurrence, using the imperfect for the descriptive element, the preterite for the narrative.* (*Example:* Son las dos cuando salgo de casa. — Eran las dos cuando salí de casa.) 1. Hace mal tiempo cuando salgo de casa. 2. Todos están bien cuando los veo. 3. Están cansados cuando voy a su casa. 4. Tiene diez y ocho años cuando viene a la universidad. 5. No habla inglés cuando llega aquí.

C. QUESTIONS. 1. ¿Por qué no estudió usted anoche? 2. ¿Fué usted al cine? 3. ¿A quiénes hizo usted una visita ayer? 4. ¿Qué hacían sus amigos cuando usted llegó? 5. ¿De qué se quejaban? 6. ¿Por qué se quedó José en casa ayer? 7. ¿Tenía un resfriado cuando usted le vió? 8. ¿Para qué examen tenía que estudiar? 9. ¿A dónde pensaban ir ustedes? 10. ¿Por qué no lo hicieron? 11. ¿Tenía usted que trabajar menos el año pasado? 12. ¿Cuántas clases tenía? 13. ¿Cuáles eran sus diversiones favoritas? 14. ¿Qué hacía usted por la tarde? 15. ¿Qué hacía usted por la noche? 16. ¿Qué programas de televisión le gustaban? 17. ¿Qué programas de radio escuchaba? 18. ¿Cuáles eran sus discos favoritos? 19. ¿Son los mismos que le gustan ahora? 20. ¿Le gusta recordar lo que hacía el año pasado?

D. TRANSLATION. 1. Yesterday I visited some friends. 2. When I arrived, they were talking about what we used to do last year. 3. They were remembering that we had to study a lot less. 4. We had a lot more fun then. 5. We went out almost every evening. 6. I used to take a walk or play tennis almost every day. 7. I liked to dance or go to the movies. 8. We always had refreshments before returning home. 9. I often listened to my favorite records. 10. This year my life is less entertaining. 11. Today we

have a history exam.   12. I didn't study last night because
I was tired.   13. Besides there was a good movie, with my
favorite actress.   14. I wasn't interested in history.   15. I
already knew enough.   16. My sister and I went to the
movies.   17. We liked the picture.   18. *She* also liked the
animated cartoons.   19. It was almost eleven o'clock when
we returned home.   20. I don't know why we have so
many exams.

E. CONVERSATION AND COMPOSITION. Topic: Your
memories.

IMPERFECT

(Reference List of Expressions for Lessons 1–11)

IMPERFECT* (Situation or circumstances)	Meaning in imperfect	Meaning if changed to preterite (completed past action or state)
conocer: conocía a Eduardo	knew	(met, recognized)
creer: creía eso	believed	(at first believed)
entender: entendía el inglés	understood	(understood on that occasion)
estar: estaba aquí estaba bien	was	(was = came, became, next was)
hablar: hablaba español	spoke	(spoke on that occasion)
hacer: hacía buen tiempo	made (was)	(became, next was)
llamarse: se llamaba José	was named	(called himself)
ser: era fácil era guapo era mejicano era la una	was	(proved to be, once was, was for a while)
pensar: pensaba estudiar	intended	(at first intended)
poder: podía hacerlo	could	(suceeded in)
preferir: prefería salir	preferred	(chose, decided)
saber: sabía eso	knew	(learned, found out)
tener: tenía amigos tenía un resfriado tenía veinte años	had	(once had, had for a while)
vivir: vivía en esta ciudad	lived, was living	(once lived, lived for a while)

* In addition, verbs normally narrative become descriptive when the meaning is "was happening" or "used to happen."

12 Comidas

Hago tres comidas diarias: el desayuno, el almuerzo
y la comida, o cena. Me gusta tomar un buen desayuno:
jugo de naranja, huevos, tostadas y café con leche. Al
mediodía no tengo mucho apetito y tomo un almuerzo
ligero: un sandwich, ensalada, leche y postre. Por las 5
noches tengo más apetito y casi siempre tomo una comida
abundante: sopa, carne o pescado, legumbres, pan, café
y postres.

(Felipe, María y Luisa. Al mediodía, en un restaurán.)

FELIPE.   Aquí tenemos la lista. ¿Qué prefieren ustedes? 10
MARÍA.   Yo el cubierto de dos dólares.
LUISA.   Yo también lo prefiero, pero no quiero engor-
dar. Voy a tomar sopa, ensalada y café solo.
FELIPE.   Y ¿de postre?
LUISA.   ¡Ay! ¡Los postres! No quiero pensar en ellos... 15
Bueno, sí, puedo tomar melón. ¿Me hace el favor de
pasarme el agua?
FELIPE.   Con mucho gusto. *(Se la sirve.)* Como les de-
cía, tengo billetes para la revista musical. Me los dió
un amigo que no puede ir. 20
MARÍA.   ¿Puede acompañarnos Miguel?
FELIPE.   Sí. Hablé con él esta mañana.
LUISA.   La revista va a ser muy interesante.
MARÍA.   Eso creo, todos dicen lo mismo. Me parece que
vamos a divertirnos mucho. 25

[90]

VOCABULARY

abundante abundant, hearty
acompañar to accompany, to go with
el **agua** *f.* water
el **almuerzo** lunch
el **apetito** appetite
¡**ay**! ow!, oh!, alas!
el **billete** ticket
bueno *adv.* well
la **carne** meat
la **cena** supper
la **comida** food, meal, dinner; **hago tres comidas** I eat three meals
el **cubierto** (special) lunch *or* dinner; **el cubierto de dos dólares** the $2.00 lunch
dar to give; **me los dió** (he) gave them to me
de as, for
el **desayuno** breakfast
diario, -a daily, a day
el **dólar** dollar
engordar to get fat
la **ensalada** salad
el **favor** favor; ¿**me hace el favor de . . .?** will you please . . .?

el **huevo** egg
el **jugo** juice
la **leche** milk; **café con leche** coffee with cream
la **legumbre** vegetable
ligero, -a light
la **lista** list, menu
lo mismo the same (thing)
el **mediodía** noon; **al mediodía** at noon
el **melón** melon, cantaloupe
musical musical
la **naranja** orange
el **pan** bread
el **pescado** fish
el **postre** dessert; **de postre** for dessert
querer (**ie**; *irreg.*) to want, to wish
el **restaurán** restaurant
la **revista** review, revue
el **sandwich** sandwich
servir (**i**) to serve; **se la sirve** he pours it for her
solo, -a alone; **café solo** black coffee
la **sopa** soup
las **tostadas** (pieces of) toast

GRAMMATICAL EXPLANATIONS

1. Idiomatic Forms.

(a) **Tener (mucho) apetito,** *to be (very) hungry.*

No tengo mucho apetito.   *I'm not very hungry.*

(b) **Hacer el favor de** (+ infinitive), *to do the favor of* or *please* (do something).

¿(Me) hace usted el favor de servirme agua?   *Will you serve (or give) me some water, please?*

2. Definite Article with the Names of Meals. The definite article is regularly used with the names of meals, whether the meaning is general (the meal as a type) or specific (the particular meal).

Tomo **el almuerzo** a la una.	*I have lunch at one.*
Antes de **la cena**, voy al centro.	*Before supper I'm going downtown.*

Note, however, that in adverbial phrases the article is often omitted, the noun being non-specific.

De desayuno voy a tomar huevos y café.	*For breakfast I'm going to have eggs and coffee.*

3. Feminine Articles *el* and *un*. Special feminine forms of the definite and indefinite articles, **el** and **un** (normally masculine), are used before feminine nouns beginning with stressed **a-** or **ha-**.

El agua está fría, ¿verdad?	*The water is cold, isn't it?*

4. Neuter Article *lo*. A neuter form of the definite article, **lo,** is used with adjectives, adverbs, or phrases to refer to an idea.

Todos dicen **lo mismo.**	*Everybody says the same (thing).*

5. Use of Two Object Pronouns. If there is both a direct and indirect object pronoun, the indirect precedes the direct, whether before or after the verb.

Me los dió un amigo mío.	*A friend of mine gave them to me.*
El profesor quiso enseñá**rnoslo.**	*The teacher tried to teach it to us.*

A special third person object form, **se,** *(to) you, him, her, it,* or *them,* is used instead of **le** or **les** before a direct object pronoun **(lo, la, los, las).** For clarity or stress, a prepositional form may be added.

¿Quién **se lo** enseña (a usted)?	*Who is teaching it to you?*
Se lo voy a decir (a ellos).	*I'm going to tell them* (lit. *say*
Voy a decír**selo** (a ellos.)	*it to them*).

6. Present Tense for the Future. The use of the present tense for the future is more common in Spanish than in English. Its use conveys a feeling of proximity, certainty, or determination.

¿Me **hace** el favor de decírselo?   *Will you* (lit. *Do you*) *do me the favor of telling him?*

Mañana lo **hacemos.**   *Tomorrow we'll do it (for sure).*

7. Verbs.

(a) **Regular:** acompañar, engordar.

(b) **Radical-Changing: servir (i).** Note that the stem-vowel of **servir** changes to **i** in both the present and the preterite.

(c) **Other verbs.**

Dar, *to give.*

PRESENT	INDICATIVE		PRETERITE	INDICATIVE
doy	damos		**di**	**dimos**
das	**dais**		**diste**	**disteis**
da	**dan**		**dió**	**dieron**

Querer (ie; irreg.), *to want, to wish.*

PRESENT	INDICATIVE		PRETERITE	INDICATIVE
quiero	queremos		**quise**	**quisimos**
quieres	queréis		**quisiste**	**quisisteis**
quiere	quieren		**quiso**	**quisieron**

EXERCISES

A. STRUCTURE PRACTICE.

1. Mi padre ⎫   ⎧ la ⎫
Mi madre ⎬ nos ⎨ las ⎬ sirvió.
Mi hermana ⎭   ⎩ lo ⎭

Answer. 1. ¿Quién les sirvió la carne? 2. ¿Quién les sirvió las legumbres? 3. ¿Quién les sirvió el café?

Translate. 1. My sister served it to us. 2. My mother served them to us. 3. My father served it to us.

2. Me   ⎫   ⎧ Eduardo.
     Nos ⎬   los dió   ⎨ un amigo.
     Se   ⎭   ⎩ su hermano.

Answer. 1. ¿Quién le dió a usted los billetes?   2. ¿Quién se los dió a ustedes?   3. ¿Quién le dió los billetes a Pablo?

Translate. 1. A friend gave them to me.   2. Edward gave them to us.   3. His brother gave them to him.

3. Me   ⎫   ⎧ ayer.
     Nos ⎬   lo dijo   ⎨ anoche.
     Se   ⎭   ⎩ esta mañana.

Answer. 1. ¿Cuándo le dijo Felipe que tenía los billetes? 2. ¿Cuándo les dijo Eduardo que podía ir?   3. ¿Cuándo dijo Pablo a José que no podía acompañarnos?

Translate. 1. He told me last night.   2. He told him yesterday.   3. He told us this morning.

B. Drill Exercises.

1. *Add an appropriate prepositional form to stress or clarify the indirect object. (Example:* Se lo dijo. — Se lo dijo a él *or* a ella, *etc.)* 1. Me lo dijo.   2. Nos lo dijo. 3. Se la dió.   4. Se los dió.   5. Se la sirvió.

2. *Substitute a pronoun for the noun object. (Example:* Le dió el reloj. — Se lo dió.) 1. Me dió el fonógrafo.   2. Me dió los discos.   3. Le sirvió café.   4. Le pasó el agua. 5. Les leyó la lista.

3. *Express with the present tense instead of* ir a + *the infinitive. (Example:* Van a dármelo mañana. — Me lo dan mañana.) 1. Van a decírmelo esta tarde.   2. Van a dármelos esta noche.   3. Van a decírselo mañana.   4. Van a dárselo esta noche.   5. Van a enseñárnoslo esta tarde.

C. Questions.   1. ¿A qué hora se desayuna usted? 2. ¿Qué toma usted de desayuno?   3. ¿Toma usted lo mismo

todos los días?   4. ¿Dónde almuerza usted?   5. ¿Prefiere
usted un almuerzo ligero?   6. ¿Cuándo tiene usted más
apetito, al mediodía o por la noche?   7. ¿Prefiere usted
comer en casa o en un restaurán?   8. ¿Pueden ustedes cenar
conmigo esta noche?   9. ¿Le gusta la comida mejicana?
10. ¿Prefiere usted la comida italiana?   11. ¿Conoce usted
un buen restaurán francés o italiano?   12. ¿Cuál es el mejor
restaurán de la ciudad?   13. ¿Le gustan a usted los postres
más que las legumbres?   14. ¿Por qué no come postres
Luisa?   15. ¿Cómo prefiere usted el café, solo o con leche?
16. ¿Quiénes van a ver la revista musical?   17. ¿Piensa ir
Felipe?   18. ¿Quién le dió los billetes?   19. ¿Quiénes van
con él?   20. ¿Qué hacen ustedes mañana por la noche?

D. Translation.   1. Here is the menu.   2. The three-
dollar lunch is very good.   3. I'm going to have (take) soup,
a sandwich, and milk.   4. I haven't much appetite at noon
because I eat (take) a hearty breakfast.   5. For breakfast I
have orange juice, eggs, toast, and coffee.   6. I also like to
eat a hearty dinner.   7. I like to have salad, soup, meat or
fish, vegetables, bread, coffee, and dessert.   8. Do you like
Mexican food?   9. We know a Mexican restaurant that is
very good.   10. Why don't we eat supper there tonight?
11. Will you pass me the bread, please?   12. I don't know
why they don't serve us some water.   13. Do you take black
coffee or coffee with cream?   14. What are you going to
have for dessert?   15. I don't eat desserts because I don't
want to get fat.   16. You *can* have cantaloupe, can't you?
17. Did you go to see the musical review?   18. A friend
who couldn't go gave us the tickets.   19. It was very interesting.   20. Before going to the review, we had dinner at a
French restaurant.

E. Conversation and Composition.   Topic: Your
meals.

13 Programas

Todos los años tenemos una serie de programas artísticos que me parecen excelentes. El primer programa de este año consistió en un concierto por una orquesta sinfónica muy famosa. El segundo fué un programa de baile, con unos bailarines magníficos, y el tercero, una revista musical, por una compañía muy conocida. En la serie de este año figuran también una ópera, una zarzuela, una comedia, un programa de variedades, etc.

(Elena, Felipe y José.)

ELENA.   Parece que la revista fué un éxito completo. 10

FELIPE.   Sí, lo fué. La compañía es excelente.

JOSÉ.   Cantaban muy bien y no representaban mal.

FELIPE.   La serie de este año me parece mejor que la del año pasado.

ELENA.   ¿Cuál de los programas te gustó más? 15

FELIPE.   El primero fué el mejor de todos.

JOSÉ.   Ya sé por qué te gustó. ¡Porque tocaron la novena sinfonía de Beethoven!

ELENA.   Más divertida fué la revista musical.

JOSÉ.   Y ¿qué me decís del programa de baile? ¡Qué 20 bailarina más guapa!

FELIPE.   ¡Guapísima! Y ¡qué bien bailaba!

ELENA.   Bailaba mejor el primer bailarín, aunque os gustó más la bailarina.

JOSÉ.   Sí, él no bailaba mal. 25

VOCABULARY

artístico, -a artistic, cultural
aunque although, even though, even if
el **bailarín** dancer; la **bailarina** dancer, danseuse, ballerina
cantar to sing
la **comedia** play, comedy
la **compañía** company
completo, -a complete
el **concierto** concert
conocido, -a well-known
consistir en to consist of
etc. (abbrev. of **etcétera**) etc.
excelente excellent
el **éxito** success
famoso, -a famous
figurar to figure, to appear
guapísimo, -a very good-looking, extremely good-looking

lo it, so; **lo fué** it was (so)
magnífico, -a magnificent, wonderful
noveno, -a ninth
la **ópera** opera
primer, primero, -a first
¡**qué**! how!, what a!; ¡**qué bailarina más guapa!** what a good-looking dancer; ¡**qué bien bailaba!** how well she danced!
representar to act, to perform (a play)
segundo, -a second
la **serie** series
la **sinfonía** symphony
tercer, tercero, -a third
tocar (qu) to play (music)
la **variedad** variety; **variedades** variety, vaudeville
la **zarzuela** musical comedy

GRAMMATICAL EXPLANATIONS

1. Use of *lo* as Predicate Complement. The neuter pronoun **lo**, *it, so,* used as a predicate complement, stands for an idea previously expressed by a noun, an adjective, or a phrase.

Parece que la revista fué un éxito completo.—Sí, **lo fué**.

It seems that the revue was a complete success.—Yes, it was.

2. Ordinal Numerals, *First* to *Tenth*. Ordinal numerals usually precede the nouns that they modify, and always agree with them in gender and in number (usually singular).

primero, -a	*first*		**sexto, -a**	*sixth*
segundo, -a	*second*		**séptimo, -a**	*seventh*
tercero, -a	*third*		**octavo, -a**	*eighth*
cuarto, -a	*fourth*		**noveno, -a**	*ninth*
quinto, -a	*fifth*		**décimo, -a**	*tenth*

When the masculine singular forms **primero** and **tercero** precede the nouns that they modify, they are shortened to **primer** and **tercer**.

Me gustó el **primer** concierto.   *I liked the first concert.*
El **tercer** programa no fué malo.   *The third program wasn't bad.*

3. The Ending -ísimo. The ending **-ísimo** (**-ísima**, etc.), attached to an adjective, is an emphatic form meaning *very, quite,* or *extremely.*

La bailarina era **guapísima**.   *The dancer was very good-looking.*

4. Exclamatory Forms. Interrogative words serve also as exclamatory words. The most common one is **¡qué!** (+ a noun, adjective, or adverb), *what (a)!, how!* When an adjective follows a noun after **¡qué!**, it is preceded by **más,** *more,* or **tan,** *so.*

¡**Qué** bien bailaban!   *How well they danced!*
¡**Qué** linda muchacha!
¡**Qué** muchacha **más** linda!   } *What a pretty girl!*
¡**Qué** muchacha **tan** linda!

5. Comparisons of Equality. Comparisons of equality are formed as follows.

> **tan,** *as* + adjective or adverb + **como,** *as*
> **tanto, -a, -os, -as,** *as much* (plur. *as many*) + noun + **como,** *as*
> **tanto como** (after a verb), *as much as*

6. Comparisons of Inequality. Comparisons of inequality are usually formed as follows.

más, *more, most* }   { (adjective }   { **que,** *than* (usual form)
menos, *less, least* } + { or adverb) } + { **de,** *than* (+ a numeral)
                                                { **de,** *of, in* (after a
                                                {   superlative)

Note that the same forms are used for comparative and superlative. The context makes the meaning clear.

El **primer** programa fué **más in-**   *The first program was more in-*
teresante que el segundo.   *teresting than the second.*
Tenemos **más de** diez programas.   *We have more than ten pro-*
                                           grams.
Esta compañía es **la más famosa**   *This company is the most fam-*
de todas.   *ous of all.*

There are very few irregular comparatives or superlatives in Spanish. The words **mayor,** *older, oldest,* and **menor,** *younger, youngest,* are irregular comparative or superlative forms (from **grande,** *large,* and **pequeño,** *small*). The other irregular forms are listed here.

ADJECTIVES					ADVERBS			
bueno	**mejor**	mucho	**más**		bien	**mejor**	mucho	**más**
malo	**peor**	poco	**menos**		mal	**peor**	poco	**menos**

7. Verbs.

(*a*) **Regular:** cantar, consistir, figurar, representar.

(*b*) **Orthographic-Changing:** tocar (qu).

EXERCISES

A. STRUCTURE PRACTICE.

1.

Fué tan { bueno / divertido / interesante } como { el primero. / el segundo. / el tercero. }

Answer. 1. ¿Fué bueno el programa de anoche? 2. ¿Fué divertido? 3. ¿Fué interesante?

Translate. 1. It was as entertaining as the first (one). 2. It was as good as the third. 3. It was as interesting as the second.

2.

Es { mejor / más conocida / más interesante } que { la cuarta. / la quinta. / la sexta. }

Answer. 1. ¿Es la tercera sinfonía tan buena como la cuarta? 2. ¿Es tan conocida como la quinta? 3. ¿Es tan interesante como la sexta?

Translate. 1. It is more interesting than the fourth. 2. It is better than the sixth. 3. It is better-known than the fifth.

3.

Fué $\left\{\begin{array}{l}\text{el mejor}\\\text{el peor}\\\text{el menos interesante}\end{array}\right\}$ de la serie.

Answer. 1. ¿Cómo fué el primer programa? 2. ¿Cómo fué el segundo? 3. ¿Qué tal le pareció el tercer programa?

Translate. 1. It was the best in the series. 2. It was the least interesting in the series. 3. It was the worst in the series.

B. Drill Exercises.

1. *Use in exclamations.* (*Example:* muchacha linda — ¡Qué muchacha tan linda!) 1. muchacho guapo. 2. bailarina guapa. 3. compañía excelente. 4. revista divertida. 5. programa interesante.

2. *Change to comparisons of superiority.* (*Example:* Tocan tan bien como el año pasado. — Tocan mejor que el año pasado.) 1. El primer programa fué tan bueno como el segundo. 2. Fué tan interesante como el tercero. 3. La tercera sinfonía es tan buena como la cuarta. 4. Es tan conocida como la quinta. 5. Me gusta la séptima tanto como la novena.

3. *Change the comparison to the opposite meaning.* (*Example:* Tocan mejor este año. — Tocan peor este año.) 1. El primer programa fué el mejor de todos. 2. Me gustó más que los otros. 3. El tercer programa fué más divertido que el segundo. 4. La serie de este año es mejor que la del año pasado. 5. El cuarto programa fué el más interesante de todos.

C. Questions. 1. ¿Le gusta la serie de programas que tenemos este año? 2. ¿Fué usted a todos los programas el año pasado? 3. ¿Qué tal le pareció la serie? 4. ¿Qué pro-

grama le gustó más? 5. ¿Cuál fué el primer programa de
la serie? 6. ¿Fué el primero mejor que el segundo?
7. ¿Cuál fué el peor? 8. ¿Cuál de los conciertos le gustó
más? 9. ¿Qué tal le pareció el programa de la orquesta
sinfónica? 10. ¿Cuáles de las sinfonías de Beethoven le
gustan a usted? 11. ¿Prefiere usted los programas de baile?
12. ¿Qué programa de baile le pareció mejor? 13. ¿Bailaba
mejor el bailarín o la bailarina? 14. ¿Qué programas tenemos para este año? 15. ¿Qué tal le parece la serie? 16. ¿A
qué programas piensa usted ir? 17. ¿Le interesan las revis-
tas musicales? 18. ¿Le parecen más divertidos los programas de variedades? 19. ¿Qué zarzuela vió usted ayer?
20. ¿Cuál es la ópera más conocida?

D. TRANSLATION. 1. All the programs seem excellent
to me. 2. This year's series is better than last year's.
3. The first program was the best, wasn't it? 4. I liked the
musical comedy better. 5. The company wasn't bad.
6. They didn't act well, but they sang very well. 7. What
do you say about the dance program? 8. How well they
danced! 9. What a pretty ballerina! 10. She was extremely good-looking. 11. The program was a complete
success. 12. The variety program was, too. 13. Which of
the concerts did you like best? 14. We liked the program
of the symphony orchestra. 15. They played Beethoven's
ninth symphony. 16. You prefer the seventh, don't you?
17. We already have tickets for the opera. 18. A friend
gave them to us. 19. Are you going to see the play?
20. We intend to go to all the programs in the series.

E. CONVERSATION AND COMPOSITION. Topic: Programs that you like or don't like.

14 De tiendas

Esta tarde voy de tiendas con mi hermana. Vamos a un gran almacén a hacer varias compras. A mí no me gusta ir de compras; a ella sí. Para ella es un recreo comprarse un sombrero, un vestido o un par de zapatos. Esta tarde va a comprar sólo una blusa blanca. Yo, en cambio, 5 tengo varias compras que hacer: un sombrero, camisas, corbatas y pañuelos.

(*En un almacén. Un dependiente, Felipe y Elena.*)

DEPENDIENTE.   Buenas tardes. ¿En qué puedo servirles?
FELIPE.   Quiero ver los nuevos modelos de sombreros. 10
DEPENDIENTE.   Tenemos un buen surtido, de diferentes precios. Éstos son muy baratos; aquéllos, un poco más caros. (*Felipe y Elena miran varios sombreros.*)
ELENA.   Ese gris claro que tienes en la mano te sienta muy bien. 15
FELIPE.   Creo que me gusta más aquel verde oscuro. Voy a probármelo, a ver. (*Se lo pone.*)
ELENA.   Te sienta perfectamente. Estás muy elegante.
FELIPE. (*Al dependiente.*) ¿Cuánto es?
DEPENDIENTE.   Vale sólo ocho dólares. No es caro. 20
FELIPE.   Pues me quedo con éste. Aquí tiene usted un billete de diez dólares.
DEPENDIENTE.   Tome usted la vuelta. Que ustedes sigan bien.
FELIPE.   Adiós. Buenas tardes. 25

VOCABULARY

el **almacén** department store
aquel, aquella, adj. that
aquéllos, -as pron. those
aquí tiene usted here you have, here is, here are
barato, -a cheap, inexpensive
el **billete** bill, bank note
blanco, -a white
la **blusa** blouse
el **cambio** change, exchange; **en cambio** on the other hand
la **camisa** shirt
caro, -a expensive
claro, -a light (color)
comprar to buy
la **corbata** tie
el **dependiente,** la **dependienta** (store) clerk
diferente different
elegante elegant, stylish, fancy; **estás muy elegante** you look swell
ese, esa adj. that
éste, ésta pron. this (one); **éstos, éstas** these
gran, grande large, big, great
gris gray; **ese gris claro** that light gray one
ir de compras to go shopping

la **mano** hand
el **modelo** model, style
oscuro, -a dark
el **pañuelo** handkerchief
el **par** pair
perfectamente perfectly
poner to put; **ponerse** to put on (clothes)
el **precio** price; **de diferentes precios** at different prices
probar (ue) to prove; to test, to try (on)
pues well (then)
quedarse con to keep, to take
que ustedes sigan bien goodby
el **recreo** recreation
sentar (ie) to suit, to become, to be becoming
el **sombrero** hat
el **surtido** stock, supply
la **tienda** shop; **de tiendas** shopping
tome usted (lit. "take") here is, here are
valer to be worth; to cost
verde green
el **vestido** clothing; dress
la **vuelta** change (money)
el **zapato** shoe

GRAMMATICAL EXPLANATIONS

1. Idiomatic Forms. Aquí tiene usted ("here you have") and **tome usted** ("take") are used when offering something.

Aquí tiene usted un billete de diez dólares.

Here is a ten-dollar bill.

Tome usted la vuelta.

Here is your change.

2. Definite Article with Names of Parts of the Body, etc.
When no ambiguity would result, the definite article usually
replaces the possessive adjectives with names of the parts of the
body, clothing, etc. Note that the number of the subject and
verb usually does not affect the number of the object.

Lo tiene en **la mano.**	*He has it in his hand.*
Se pone **el sombrero.**	*He puts on his hat.*
Se ponen **el sombrero.**	*They put on their hats.*

3. Use of *gran, grande*. The adjective **grande,** *large, big,
great,* when in an unstressed position (before the noun) has a
subjective and often figurative meaning *(important, impres-
sive).* In this position the singular form is shortened to **gran.**

Fuí a un **gran** almacén.	*I went to a big department store.*
Los sombreros **grandes** no me sientan bien.	*Large hats aren't becoming to me.*

4. Use of Adjectives as Nouns. The use of adjectives as
nouns is much more common in Spanish than in English, which
often supplies a noun or the pronoun *one.*

De estos sombreros, **el verde** (= el sombrero verde) me parece el mejor.	*Of these hats, the green one seems best to me.*

5. Demonstrative Adjectives. In Spanish there are three
demonstrative adjectives: **este,** *this* (near me), **ese,** *that* (near
you, or in your thoughts), and **aquel,** *that* (over there, not near
us). The forms of these adjectives are as follows.

SINGULAR		PLURAL		MEANING
MASC.	FEM.	MASC.	FEM.	
este	esta	estos	estas	*this, these*
ese	esa	esos	esas	*that, those*
aquel	aquella	aquellos	aquellas	*that, those*

The demonstrative adjectives normally precede the nouns
that they modify, and agree with them in gender and number.

Le sienta bien **esa** corbata.	*That tie* (that you have on) *is very becoming to you.*
Me gusta **aquel** sombrero gris.	*I like that gray hat* (over there).

6. Demonstrative Pronouns. The demonstrative adjectives may be used as pronouns. When so used, they take written accents.

Me gusta este sombrero más que ése (= ese sombrero).	*I like this hat better than that one.*
Aquéllos son más caros.	*Those are more expensive.*
¿Son **éstas** las camisas que usted compró?	*Are these the shirts that you bought?*

In addition to the masculine and feminine forms, there are corresponding neuter pronouns (without written accents) which do not refer to nouns but to ideas or general concepts.

Eso es lo que dicen.	*That is what they say.*
¿Qué es **esto**?—No sé lo que es.	*What is this? — I don't know what it is.*

7. Verbs.

(a) **Regular:** comprar.

(b) **Radical-Changing:** probar (ue), sentar (ie).

(c) **Other Verbs.**

Poner, *to put,* has an irregular stem in the first person singular present indicative: **pongo.** It also has an irregular stem in the preterite: **puse, pusiste, puso, pusimos, pusisteis, pusieron.**

Valer, *to be worth,* has an irregular stem in the first person singular present indicative: **valgo.**

EXERCISES

A. Structure Practice.

1. Éste / Ése / Aquél } es mejor que { el blanco. / el otro. / el verde.

Answer. 1. ¿Prefiere usted ese pañuelo o el blanco? 2. ¿Prefiere usted este sombrero o el otro? 3. ¿Prefiere usted aquel vestido o el verde?

Translate. 1. That one is better than the white one.
2. This one is better than the green one.   3. That one is
better than the other one.

2.   Sí, ese sombrero $\Big\}$ le sienta muy bien.
Sí, esa corbata   es muy elegante.
Sí, esa camisa $\Big\}$ me gusta mucho.

Answer. 1. ¿Me sienta bien este sombrero?   2. ¿Le parece bien esta corbata?   3. ¿Le gusta esta camisa?

Translate. 1. Yes, that tie is very becoming to you.
2. Yes, that shirt is very stylish.   3. Yes, I like that hat a lot.

3.   Esto $\Big\}$ $\Big\{$ compré.
Eso   es lo que   dijeron.
Aquello $\Big\}$ $\Big\{$ nos gustaba.

Answer. 1. ¿Son éstas sus compras?   2. ¿Le dijeron que
no podían ir de compras?   3. ¿Recuerda usted que nos paseábamos mucho?

Translate. 1. That is what I bought.   2. This is what
we used to like.   3. That is what they said.

B. Drill Exercises.

1. *Use the proper form of **este** with each noun or phrase.
(Example:* tienda — esta tienda.) 1. compras.   2. camisa.
3. par de zapatos.   4. pañuelos blancos.   5. gran almacén.

2. *Give the form of the demonstrative pronoun corresponding to each of the following. (Example:* este pañuelo
— éste.) 1. este vestido.   2. esta corbata.   3. ese modelo.
4. esos zapatos.   5. aquellas tiendas.

3. *Answer in the affirmative, using the demonstrative
pronoun **ése, ésa**, etc. (Example:* ¿Le gusta este sombrero?
— Me gusta ése.) 1. ¿Prefiere usted este modelo?   2. ¿Le
gusta esta blusa?   3. ¿Compra usted esta corbata?   4. ¿Quiere
usted estas camisas?   5. ¿Se queda usted con estos pañuelos?

C. QUESTIONS.   1. ¿Le gusta ir de tiendas?   2. ¿Qué compras tiene que hacer?   3. ¿Cuándo piensa ir de compras?   4. ¿A dónde va?   5. ¿Va usted solo (sola)?   6. ¿Es nuevo ese sombrero?   7. ¿Qué le parecen los nuevos modelos de sombreros?   8. ¿Le parece bien aquel sombrero verde?   9. ¿Qué sombrero prefiere usted?   10. ¿Cuántos pañuelos quiere usted?   11. ¿Le sienta bien a su hermana el vestido nuevo?   12. ¿Le sienta mejor que los viejos?   13. ¿Cuándo se compró la blusa nueva?   14. ¿Cuándo compró usted esos zapatos?   15. ¿Qué compras tiene que hacer su hermano?   16. ¿Fué usted de tiendas la semana pasada?   17. ¿Qué compró?   18. ¿Qué compró su hermana?   19. ¿Tenía el almacén un buen surtido?   20. ¿Por qué no vamos de tiendas esta tarde?

D. TRANSLATION.   1. I want to see some white shirts. 2. We have a good supply, at different prices.   3. These shirts are very inexpensive.   4. Those are a little more expensive.   5. How much do these cost?   6. I'll take this one. 7. Here's a twenty-dollar bill.   8. Here's your change. 9. Don't you want to buy some ties?   10. These are very stylish.   11. Which of these hats do you like best?   12. The new style hats are not becoming to me.   13. I like that dark green one that you have in your hand.   14. The light gray one is very becoming to you.   15. Do you have any other purchases to make?   16. Yesterday I went shopping with my brother.   17. We went to a big department store. 18. He bought some shirts and ties.   19. I bought a hat, some handkerchiefs, and a pair of shoes.   20. You like to go shopping, don't you?

E. CONVERSATION AND COMPOSITION. Topic: Some recent shopping trips.

Excursiones

Me gusta hacer excursiones al campo. Cerca de la ciudad hay muchos lugares hermosos e interesantes. Mañana pensamos hacer una excursión a un sitio hermosísimo, cerca de un río y con muchos árboles. Pasaremos varias horas agradables en el campo. Daremos un ⁵ paseo para tomar el sol, merendaremos después y cantaremos sentados alrededor del fuego . . . Por supuesto que vamos a volver a casa, a eso de las siete u ocho de la noche, cansados, pero contentos.

(Pablo, José y Elena.) ¹⁰

PABLO. Mañana hacemos otra jira campestre. ¿Podrán ustedes ir con nosotros?

JOSÉ. Quizá. ¿Adónde van? ¿A qué hora salen?

PABLO. Vamos al lago Azul. Saldremos de mi casa a eso de las cuatro. ¹⁵

ELENA. Yo pensaba estudiar, pero me gustan tanto las excursiones al campo . . .

JOSÉ. A las cuatro ya estarás cansada de estudiar.

ELENA. ¡Ya lo estoy ahora!

PABLO. Si no tienen coche, iré a su casa a buscarlos a ²⁰ las tres y media.

JOSÉ. No vale la pena. Podemos tomar el tranvía número 10 en la calle 40.

PABLO. Luego nos veremos mañana, en mi casa, a las cuatro, o un poco antes. ²⁵

VOCABULARY

¿adónde? *or* ¿a dónde? where? *(to what place?)*
alrededor de *prep.* around
antes *adv.* before, beforehand
el árbol tree
azul blue
buscar (qu) to look for; ir a buscar to stop by for *(a person)*
la calle street; en la calle 40 at 40th Street
campestre *adj.* country, in the country
el campo field, country
cantaremos we'll sing
contento, -a contented, happy
daremos un paseo we'll take a walk
estarás you'll be
la excursión excursion, outing, (short) trip
el fuego fire
hermoso, -a beautiful
iré I'll go
la jira picnic; hacer una jira to go on a picnic
el lago lake

luego then, so, therefore
el lugar place, spot
merendar (ie) to have a (light) lunch *or* supper; merendaremos we'll have picnic supper
el número number
pasaremos we'll spend
el paseo walk, stroll; dar un paseo to take a walk
la pena pain, trouble
podrán (you) will be able
quizá *or* quizás perhaps, maybe
el río river
saldremos we'll leave
sentado, -a seated
si if
el sitio place, spot
supuesto: por supuesto of course, naturally
tomar el sol to get some sunshine, to get out in the sun
el tranvía trolley, streetcar
veremos we'll see; nos veremos we'll see each other, we'll meet

GRAMMATICAL EXPLANATIONS

1. Idiomatic Forms.

(a) **Dar un paseo** (lit. "to give a walk"), *to take a walk.*

Daremos un paseo en el campo.   *We'll take a walk in the country.*

(b) **Tomar el sol** (lit. "to take the sun"), *to get some sunshine, to get out in the sun.*

Nos gusta tomar el sol.   *We like to get out in the sun.*

(c) **Hacer una jira,** *to go on a picnic.*

Mañana hacen otra jira (campestre).	*Tomorrow they're going on another picnic (in the country).*

(d) **Hacer una excursión,** *to go on an excursion* (or *outing*), *to make* (or *take*) *a trip.*

No podré hacer la excursión con ustedes.	*I won't be able to go on the excursion with you.*

2. Definite Article in References to Public Places. The definite article is regularly used in references to public places (streets, squares, buildings, streetcars, busses, etc.), which are specific in nature and usually involve a noun and a modifier (either expressed or understood).

Nos veremos en **la calle 40** (cuarenta).	*We'll meet at 40th Street.*
Tomaremos **el tranvía** número 10 (diez).	*We'll take trolley number 10.*

3. Verbs.

(a) **Radical-Changing:** merendar (ie).

(b) **Orthographic-Changing:** buscar (qu).

4. Future Indicative of Regular Verbs. The future indicative can usually be formed as follows: to the *full infinitive* add the endings of the future. Note that the endings for the future are the same for all verbs.

-ar, -er, OR **-ir** VERBS
tomar, *to take*

I shall take (will take),
you will take, etc.

tomaré	tomaremos
tomarás	tomaréis
tomará	tomarán

5. Future Indicative of Irregular Verbs. The *endings* of the future are never irregular. There are very few irregular future *stems*. Those given here (for verbs used so far) form an almost complete list for the language.

decir:	**diré**	saber:	**sabré**
hacer:	**haré**	salir:	**saldré**
poder:	**podré**	tener:	**tendré**
poner:	**pondré**	valer:	**valdré**
querer:	**querré**	venir:	**vendré**

The future of **hay** (from **haber**) is irregular: **habrá,** *there will be.*

EXERCISES

A. STRUCTURE PRACTICE.

1. Daré un paseo ⎫ esta tarde.
Iremos al campo ⎬ mañana.
Harán una jira ⎭ el sábado.

Answer. 1. ¿Qué hará usted esta tarde? 2. ¿Cuándo irán ustedes al campo? 3. ¿Cuándo harán una jira sus amigos?

Translate. 1. We'll go to the country on Saturday. 2. I'll take a walk tomorrow. 3. They will go on a picnic this afternoon.

2. Saldré ⎫ ⎧ las cuatro.
Llegaré ⎬ a eso de ⎨ las cinco.
Volveré ⎭ ⎩ las seis.

Answer. 1. ¿Saldrá usted temprano? 2. ¿A qué hora llegará? 3. ¿Cuándo volverá?

Translate. 1. I'll arrive about four o'clock. 2. I'll leave about five. 3. I'll return at about six o'clock.

3. Haré ⎫ ⎧ al campo.
Haremos ⎬ una excursión ⎨ al lago Azul.
Harán ⎭ ⎩ a un lugar hermoso.

Answer. 1. ¿Qué hará usted mañana? 2. ¿Qué excursión harán ustedes? 3. ¿Adónde irán sus amigos?

Translate. 1. We'll take a trip to the country. 2. I'll

go on an excursion to Blue Lake. 3. They'll go on an outing to a beautiful spot.

B. DRILL EXERCISES.

1. *Give the first person singular future indicative of each verb. (Example:* tomar — tomaré.) 1. comer. 2. vivir. 3. buscar. 4. ver. 5. escuchar.

2. *Change from the first to the third person singular. (Example:* Lo haré esta tarde. — Lo hará esta tarde.) 1. Lo sabré esta noche. 2. Se lo diré mañana. 3. Lo tendré en casa. 4. Vendré aquí temprano. 5. Podré ir al campo.

3. *Change from the first to the third person plural. (Example:* Saldremos a las tres. — Saldrán a las tres.) 1. Iremos al campo. 2. Daremos un paseo. 3. Tomaremos el sol. 4. Haremos una jira. 5. Haremos una excursión.

C. QUESTIONS. 1. ¿Le gusta hacer excursiones al campo? 2. ¿Cuándo piensan ustedes hacer otra jira? 3. ¿Podrán ir sus hermanos? 4. No tendrán que estudiar, ¿verdad? 5. ¿Adónde van a ir ustedes? 6. ¿Irán si hace mal tiempo? 7. ¿Quiénes tienen coche? 8. ¿Quién irá a su casa a buscarlos? 9. ¿En qué calle pueden tomar el autobús o el tranvía? 10. ¿Qué autobús tomarán? 11. ¿A qué hora saldrán ustedes de casa? 12. ¿A qué hora llegarán al campo? 13. ¿Darán un paseo antes de tomar la merienda? 14. ¿Jugarán al beisbol? 15. ¿Escucharán la radio? 16. ¿Les gusta charlar sentados alrededor del fuego? 17. ¿A qué hora volverán ustedes a casa? 18. ¿Qué harán por la noche? 19. ¿Le gustó la jira de la semana pasada? 20. ¿Qué lugares cerca de aquí le parecen más hermosos?

D. TRANSLATION. 1. We're going on another picnic tomorrow. 2. Will you be able to go with us? 3. We're going to the lake or to the river.   4. Near the lake there is a very beautiful spot.   5. I like it better than the river. 6. We can take bus number 15 at 30th Street.   7. Paul told me that we can go in his car.   8. He'll stop by for us at three.   9. We'll arrive about three thirty.   10. We'll take a walk to get some sunshine.   11. Maybe we'll play baseball.   12. We'll have picnic supper about six.   13. Then we'll sing or listen to the radio.   14. We like to chat seated around the fire.   15. We'll return home about eight o'clock. 16. I think that we're going to have a lot of fun.   17. Of course we won't go if the weather is bad.   18. I believe that the weather will be very pleasant.   19. Will your brother be able to go with us?   20. He says that at three o'clock he'll be tired of studying.

E. Conversation and Composition. Topic: Plans for a picnic or outing.

GRAMMATICAL NOTES⎯⎯⎯⎯⎯⎯

(Use the following grammatical notes as a guide for reviewing forms and usage. Then test your knowledge of them by using the corresponding Test Exercises on the opposite page.)

1. Idiomatic Forms. *List for Lessons 11-15.*

aquí tiene usted here is, here are (14)

dar un paseo to take a walk (15)

hacer el favor de (+ *inf.*) to do the favor of; please . . . (12)

hacer una excursión to go on an excursion *or* trip (15)

hacer una jira to go on a picnic (15)

tener (mucho) apetito to be (very) hungry (12)

tener que (+ *inf.*) to have to (11)

tomar el sol to get some sunshine (15)

tome usted here is, here are (14)

2. Definite and Indefinite Articles.

Forms: feminine **el, un,** before stressed **a-** or **ha-** (12:3); neuter **lo,** with adjective, adverb, or phrase, to refer to an idea (12:4).

Usage: definite article used with the infinitive, to clarify its function as a noun (11:2); with names of meals—except when non-specific, as after **de,** *for* (12:2); with names of parts of the body or clothing when the reference is clear (14:2); in most references to public places, usually with a modifier (15:2).

3. Personal Pronouns.

Forms: **se** for **le** or **les** before **lo, la, los, las** (12:5).

Usage: indirect object pronoun before direct (12:5); neuter **lo,** *it, so,* as predicate complement, standing for an idea previously expressed by a noun, adjective, or phrase (13:1).

(Continued on page 116)

[114]

(Complete the Spanish sentences with the idea indicated. Check your answers by using the corresponding Grammatical Notes on the opposite page.)

1. Idiomatic Forms.

1. *(I took a walk)* ____ antes de almorzar.
2. *(Will you please)* ¿____ hablar con él?
3. *(did they go on)* ¿Cuándo ____ la excursión?
4. *(we're going on)* Mañana ____ otra jira campestre.
5. *(I'm very hungry)* Por la noche ____.
6. *(we had to)* El año pasado ____ estudiar menos.
7. *(get some sunshine)* Nos paseábamos para ____.
8. *(Here is)* ____ la vuelta.

2. Definite and Indefinite Articles.

1. *(the)* ¿Está fría ____ agua?
2. *(the same)* Eduardo dijo ____.
3. *(the best)* Eso será ____.
4. *(Going)* ____ al cine me gustaba mucho.
5. *(supper)* Antes de ____ iremos al centro.
6. *(breakfast)* De ____ tomo tostadas y café.
7. *(his hat)* Se puso ____.
8. *(street)* Pueden tomar el autobús en ____ Mayor.

3. Personal Pronouns.

1. *(them to him)* José tiene billetes; ____ dió un amigo.
2. *(teach it to us)* El señor Pérez va a ____.
3. *(It to them)* ____ diremos esta noche.
4. *(it is)* Eso no parece difícil, pero ____.

(Continued on page 117)

GRAMMATICAL NOTES, CONTINUED

4. Adjectives.

Forms: shortened forms **primer** and **tercer** before masculine singular noun (13:2); shortened form **gran** before masculine or feminine singular noun (14:3); ending **-ísimo** (**-ísima**) used to mean *very, quite, extremely* (13:3).

Usage: **grande** (after noun), *big, large,* (before noun) *big, great* (14:3); use of adjectives as nouns more common than in English (14:4); comparisons of equality (**tan...como,** *as... as,* etc.) and inequality (**más...que,** *more...than,* etc.) almost always regular (13:5-6).

5. Demonstrative Adjectives and Pronouns.

Forms: masculine and feminine demonstrative adjectives used, with written accents, as pronouns (14:5-6); neuter pronouns (**esto, eso, aquello**), without written accents, used to refer to ideas or general concepts (14:6).

Usage: two demonstrative adjectives for *that* or *those*— "near you," etc., and "over there," etc. (14:5).

6. Exclamatory Forms.

Common forms: ¡**qué!** *what (a)!, how!* (+ noun, adjective, or adverb); **qué** + noun + **tan** or **más** + adjective (13:4).

7. Verbs.

Future indicative: formed by adding endings to infinitive or irregular stem (15:4-5).

Imperfect indicative: formed by adding endings to stem (11:5-6); used as descriptive past tense (11:3).

Infinitive: used as noun, often with the definite article to clarify its function as an abstract verbal noun (11:2).

Present indicative: used for future to indicate proximity, certainty, or determination (12:6).

Preterite indicative: used as narrative past tense (11:3).

TEST EXERCISES, CONTINUED

4. Adjectives.

1. *(first)* El ____ programa no fué malo.
2. *(third)* El ____ fué el mejor de la serie.
3. *(big)* Nos gusta ir a esa ____ ciudad.
4. *(extremely good-looking)* Las bailarinas eran ____.
5. *(large hats)* Ella compró dos ____.
6. *(the green one)* El vestido gris es mejor que ____.
7. *(as good as)* El coche viejo es ____ el nuevo.
8. *(more famous than)* Esa orquesta es ____ la otra.
9. *(better-known than)* Esta sinfonía es ____ la quinta.

5. Demonstrative Adjectives and Pronouns.

1. *(this)* Prefiero ____ blusa blanca.
2. *(Those)* ____ son más caras.
3. *(these)* Me quedo con ____ pañuelos.
4. *(That)* ____ es lo que me dijeron.
5. *(these)* ¿Son ____ las compras que usted hizo?
6. *(That)* ____ corbata le sienta muy bien.

6. Exclamatory Forms.

1. *(How well)* ¡____ bailaban todos!
2. *(good-looking)* ¡Qué muchacho ____!

7. Verbs.

1. *(We'll arrive)* ____ a las cuatro y media.
2. *(will they do)* ¿Qué ____ por la noche?
3. *(knew)* Felipe ya ____ bastante filosofía.
4. *(was)* Nuestra vida ____ más divertida.
5. *(working)* Estábamos cansados de ____.
6. *(Dancing)* ____ era mi diversión favorita.
7. *(we're going)* Esta noche ____ al cine.
8. *(we'll finish)* Mañana lo ____.
9. *(I studied)* Anoche ____ un rato.

16 | Viajes

El viajar mucho sería para mí un gran recreo. Me gustaría hacer viajes largos, en los Estados Unidos y en muchos países extranjeros. Con cuánto gusto iría a Latinoamérica, para conocer Méjico, Colombia, el Perú, la Argentina, etc. Después visitaría España, Francia, 5 Inglaterra y otros países europeos. Me gusta soñar con tales viajes, aunque no sé cuándo podré hacerlos, pues no soy rico y tengo que trabajar. Por ahora mis viajes serán mucho más cortos.

(Felipe, Elena y José.) 10

FELIPE. Ya que no tenemos nada que hacer este fin de semana, ¿por qué no acompañamos al tío Paco en su viaje a la capital?

ELENA. Papá y mamá ya nos dieron permiso.

JOSÉ. Bueno, y ¿qué haríamos en la capital? 15

FELIPE. ¡Hombre!, visitaríamos los monumentos históricos, iríamos al teatro...

ELENA. Iríamos de compras, comeríamos en restauranes elegantes...

FELIPE. Siempre se divierte uno en una gran ciudad. 20

JOSÉ. Y todo eso, costaría mucho, ¿verdad?

FELIPE. Tú tienes bastante dinero. Además el tío Paco paga los billetes y el hotel.

ELENA. No debemos perder la ocasión de ir con él.

JOSÉ. Desde luego...¡Con un programa tan divertido! 25

VOCABULARY

la **Argentina** Argentina
la **capital** capital
Colombia *f.* Colombia
comeríamos we would eat
corto, -a short
costar (ue) to cost; **costaría** (it) would cost
deber to owe; to be obliged (must, ought, should)
desde luego of course
el **dinero** money
los **Estados Unidos** the United States
europeo, -a European
extranjero, -a foreign
el **fin** end; **fin de semana** weekend
Francia *f.* France
gustaría (it) would please; **me gustaría** I would like
haríamos (we) would do
histórico, -a historical
el **hombre** man; la **mujer** woman
el **hotel** hotel
Inglaterra *f.* England
iría I would go
iríamos we would go

largo, -a long
Latinoamérica *f.* Latin America
la **mamá** mamma, mother
Méjico *m.* Mexico
el **monumento** monument
nada nothing, not...anything
la **ocasión** occasion, opportunity
Paco Frank
pagar (gu) to pay (for)
el **país** country *(nation)*
el **papá** dad, papa, father
perder (ie) to lose; to miss
el **permiso** permission
el **Perú** Peru
pues since *(cause)*
rico, -a rich
sería (it) would be
tal such, such a
el **teatro** theatre
uno, -a *indef. pron.* one
viajar to travel
el **viaje** trip
visitar to visit; **visitaría** I would visit; *etc.*
ya que since *(cause)*

GRAMMATICAL EXPLANATIONS

1. Idiomatic Forms.

(a) **Hacer un viaje,** *to take* (or *make*) *a trip.*

Me gustaría hacer un viaje.   *I'd like to take a trip.*

(b) **Pagar,** *to pay (for).* When both the amount paid and the thing paid for are expressed, **por,** *for,* is required.

Mi tío **pagó** el billete.   *My uncle paid for the ticket.*
¿**Pagó** mucho **por** el billete?   *Did he pay much for the ticket?*

2. Definite Article with Place Names. The definite article is used as part of the names of a few countries, cities, etc. Listed below are some of the most common names of this type.

la **Argentina**, Argentina	la **Habana**, Havana
el **Brasil**, Brazil	la **India**, India
el **Canadá**, Canada	el **Paraguay**, Paraguay
el **Ecuador**, Ecuador	el **Perú**, Peru
los **Estados Unidos**, the	el **Salvador**, Salvador
United States	el **Uruguay**, Uruguay

The article is also used with the names of other countries, cities, etc. when the meaning is limited by an adjective or phrase. Compare:

España es un país histórico.	*Spain is a historical country.*
¿Le interesa la **España** histórica o la **España** de hoy?	*Are you interested in historical Spain or in Spain of today?*

3. Double Negative. The use of two or more negatives is normal in Spanish. If, however, one of the longer forms (*nothing, nobody, never,* etc.) precedes the verb, the word **no** is omitted.

No tenemos **nada** que hacer. ⎫	*We haven't anything to do.* Or:
Nada tenemos que hacer. ⎭	*We have nothing to do.*

4. Meanings of the Conditional. The conditional in Spanish usually has the same meanings as in English.

(*a*) It replaces the future in a past sequence. Compare:

Me dice que **estará** aquí.	*He tells me that he will be here.*
Me dijo que **estaría** aquí.	*He told me that he would be here.*

(*b*) It may state the conclusion to an *if*-clause. Note that the if-clause need not necessarily be expressed.

Nos **divertiríamos** mucho en la capital.	*We would have a good time in the capital* (if we should go).

5. Verbs.

(*a*) **Regular:** deber, viajar, visitar.

(*b*) **Radical-Changing:** costar (ue), perder (ie).

(*c*) **Orthographic-Changing:** pagar (gu).

6. Conditional of Regular Verbs. The conditional can usually be formed as follows: to the *full infinitive* add the endings of the conditional. Note that the endings of the conditional are the same for all verbs.

-ar, -er, OR -ir VERBS
tomar, *to take*
I should take (would take),
you would take, etc.

tomaría	tomaríamos
tomarías	tomaríais
tomaría	tomarían

7. Conditional of Irregular Verbs. The *endings* of the conditional are never irregular. The *stem* is always the same as that of the future.

decir:	**diría**	saber:	**sabría**
hacer:	**haría**	salir:	**saldría**
poder:	**podría**	tener:	**tendría**
poner:	**pondría**	valer:	**valdría**
querer:	**querría**	venir:	**vendría**

The conditional of **hay** (from **haber**) is **habría,** *there would be.*

EXERCISES

A. STRUCTURE PRACTICE.

1. No tengo   ⎫   ⎧ mañana.
   No tenemos   ⎬ nada que hacer ⎨ el lunes.
   No tiene   ⎭   ⎩ esta noche.

Answer. 1. ¿Qué tiene usted que hacer mañana?   2. ¿Qué tienen ustedes que hacer el lunes?   3. ¿Qué tiene que hacer Elena esta noche?

Translate. 1. We don't have anything to do tomorrow. 2. I don't have anything to do tonight.   3. She doesn't have anything to do on Monday.

2. Me ⎫
   Nos ⎬ gustaría hacer un viaje a ⎫ Méjico.
   Le ⎭   ⎬ Colombia.
                                     ⎭ la Argentina.

Answer. 1. ¿Le gustaría hacer viajes largos? 2. ¿Qué viaje les gustaría a ustedes? 3. ¿Qué viaje le gustaría a Felipe?

Translate. 1. I would like to take a trip to Colombia. 2. We would like to take a trip to Argentina. 3. He would like to take a trip to Mexico.

3. En España   ⎫ vería muchos monumentos.
   En Inglaterra ⎬ haría muchas excursiones.
   En el Perú   ⎭ visitaría lugares interesantes.

Answer. 1. ¿Qué vería usted en España? 2. ¿Qué haría usted en Inglaterra? 3. ¿Qué haría usted en el Perú?

Translate. 1. In England I would see many monuments. 2. In Peru I would go on many excursions. 3. In Spain I would visit interesting places.

B. Drill Exercises.

1. *Use the prepositions a and de with each place name.* (*Example:* el Perú — al Perú, del Perú.) 1. los Estados Unidos. 2. Méjico. 3. la Habana. 4. el Brasil. 5. el Canadá.

2. *Give the first person singular conditional of each verb.* (*Example:* pagar — pagaría.) 1. costar. 2. viajar. 3. perder. 4. ir. 5. servir.

3. *Use each statement as a dependent clause in the conditional, after **Dijo que**. (Example:* Lo sabrá mañana. — Dijo que lo sabría mañana.) 1. Hará el viaje. 2. Podrá ir con ellos. 3. Se lo dirá esta noche. 4. Saldrá en enero. 5. Tendrá que volver en marzo.

C. QUESTIONS. 1. ¿Qué tiene usted que hacer este fin de semana? 2. ¿Quiénes piensan ir a la capital? 3. ¿Por qué no vamos nosotros también? 4. ¿Cuánto costaría el viaje? 5. ¿Cuándo podríamos salir? 6. ¿Qué haría usted en la capital? 7. ¿Cuándo tendríamos que volver? 8. ¿Prefiere usted ir al teatro o visitar monumentos históricos? 9. ¿Cuáles son los monumentos más conocidos de esta ciudad? 10. ¿Cuáles son los mejores restauranes? 11. ¿Le gustan los viajes largos? 12. ¿Por qué no hacen ustedes un viaje este verano? 13. ¿Preferiría usted viajar en los Estados Unidos o en un país extranjero? 14. ¿Qué países extranjeros le gustaría conocer? 15. ¿Qué países europeos le gustaría visitar? 16. ¿Qué haría usted en Francia? 17. ¿Preferiría usted ir a España o a Latinoamérica? 18. ¿Le gustaría ir a la India? 19. ¿Qué viajes hizo usted el verano pasado? 20. ¿Adónde le gustaría ir el verano que viene?

D. TRANSLATION. 1. Some friends of mine made a trip to Mexico last summer. 2. They spent several weeks in the capital. 3. They intend to go to Peru next summer. 4. I would like to travel in many foreign countries. 5. I dream of such trips, but I don't know when I'll be able to make them. 6. Your friends are going to the capital this weekend, aren't they? 7. Their uncle said that he would pay for the tickets. 8. They don't want to miss the opportunity to go with him. 9. Do you have to work this weekend? 10. I don't have anything to do. 11. Would you like to take a trip to the capital? 12. It would cost a lot, wouldn't it? 13. I'm not interested in historical places. 14. I'd prefer to go to the theatre to see a musical revue. 15. My sister says that she would like to go shopping. 16. She would also like to eat in a fancy restaurant. 17. We

could leave Friday afternoon.   18. It would be better to
leave Saturday morning.   19. Would we have to get up
before eight?   20. We would have a very good time.

   E. CONVERSATION AND COMPOSITION. Topic: Trips
that you would like to take.

FULL NAME OF REGISTRANT (PLEASE PRINT)		FILL IN COMPLETELY

FULL NAME OF REGISTRANT (PLEASE PRINT)   FILL IN COMPLETELY

MR. ☒   LAST NAME   FIRST
MRS. ☐   ERICKSON   WILL
MISS ☐

LOCAL ADDRESS — STREET — OR BOX NO.   CITY
806 64TH Ave E.   TACOM

WILL YOU RECEIVE VETERANS BENEFITS WHILE ENROLLED? ☐ YES ☒ NO
DID YOU SERVE IN SOUTHEAST ASIA SINCE JULY 1965 ☐ YES ☒ NO
ARE YOU A MILITAR FEDERAL EMPLOYE OR A DEPENDENT O SAME?

PROGRAM CODE   AGENCY CODE   LAST FALL CODE   IF YOU ARE W
I 00   II 1   III   ☐ FRESHMA

ITEM NUMBER	DEPARTMENT	COURSE NO.	SECTION	CRED *
777	SPANISH 2	52	A	2

CURRENT DATE
1 / 17 / 72

TOTAL NUMBER OF CREDIT HOURS →

P

REGISTRAR   STUD

FORT STEILACOOM   COM

REGISTRATION

		RETURNING TO F.S.C.C. ☑

INITIAL J | **SOCIAL SECURITY NO.** 538 – 20 – 6532 | **NEW TO F.S.C.C.** ☐

STATE	ZIP	
WA	98424	NEW ADDRESS SINCE LAST REGISTRATION? ☐ YES ☑ NO

	HAVE YOU LIVED IN WASHINGTON STATE THE PREVIOUS 12 MONTHS? ☑ YES ☐ NO	IF NOT A U.S. CITIZEN WHAT TYPE OF VISA? STU-DENT ☐ VIS-ITOR ☐ IMMI-GRANT ☐ OTHER ☐	LEAVE BLANK RES. / E.O.C.

...OWARD A COLLEGE DEGREE, COMPLETE

	FOR OFFICE USE ONLY		
THAN 45 M. CR. ☐ SOPHOMORE (MORE THAN 45 ACCUM. CR. HRS.)	TUITION & FEES	14	00

TIME OF DAY ROM	TO	DAYS	ROOM	✓			
5-	8:20	M	207		LABORATORY		
					LATE REGISTRATION		
					INSURANCE		
					COMMUNITY SERVICE		
					TOTAL FEES	14	00
					NOTE		
					CASH	14	00

TO AUDIT CLASS | (✓) INDICATES REPEAT COURSE ↑ | REC. NO. | *014.00*

014.00

...COPY

BW

...NITY ● COLLEGE

PLACE NAMES
(Reference List for Lesson 16)

la Argentina

el Brasil

el Canadá

Colombia

el Ecuador

España

los Estados Unidos

Francia

la Habana

la India

Inglaterra

Latinoamérica

Méjico

el Paraguay

el Perú

el Salvador

el Uruguay

17 Preparativos

Para un viaje tan corto, los preparativos fueron largos. Mi hermana se compró una maleta nueva (sólo tenía tres), y fué a despedirse de varias amigas, a ver si querían algo en Villagrande. Hubo mucho ajetreo al hacer las maletas. Nadie encontraba lo que buscaba. Por fin estamos listos. Saldremos para la estación un poco antes de las diez. 5

(En la estación. El tío Paco, el taquillero, el revisor.)

Tío Paco. Cuatro, de ida y vuelta, primera clase, para Villagrande. 10

Taquillero. Aquí los tiene usted. Son treinta y un dólares con veinte centavos.

Tío Paco. ¿Hay que cambiar de tren?

Taquillero. No, señor, el tren de las diez es directo. Aquí tiene usted un horario. 15

Tío Paco. Gracias. ¿Dónde se factura el equipaje?

Taquillero. La sala de equipajes la encontrará usted ahí a la izquierda, al lado de la sala de espera.

Tío Paco. Muchas gracias.

Taquillero. Servidor. 20

Tío Paco. *(Después de facturar el equipaje.)* ¿Dónde estarán los muchachos? ¡Ah!, aquí vienen. ¡Hola, muchachos! Falta poco para las diez. Hay que subir al tren. Creo que está para salir.

Revisor. ¡Señores viajeros, al tren! 25

VOCABULARY

¡ah! ah!, oh!

ahí there, over there

el ajetreo bustle, activity

al (+ *inf.*) on *(doing some-thing)*

algo something

cambiar to change; **cambiar de tren** to change trains

el centavo cent; **son treinta y un dólares con veinte centavos** that will be $31.20

despedirse (i) to take leave, to say good-by; **despedirse de** to say good-by to

después de *prep.* after

directo, -a direct; **es directo** (it) is a through train

encontrar (ue) to find

el equipaje baggage, luggage

la espera wait, waiting

la estación station

estarán (they) probably are; **¿dónde estarán?** where do you suppose (they) are?

estar para (+ *inf.*) to be about to

facturar to check *(baggage);* **¿dónde se factura?** where is (it) checked?

faltar to be lacking; **falta poco para las diez** it's al-most ten

hay que (+ *inf.*) it is neces-sary to *or* one must

el horario timetable

la ida going; **de ida** one-way; **de ida y vuelta** round-trip

izquierdo, -a left; **a la iz-quierda** to the left

el lado side; **al lado de** beside

la maleta suitcase; **hacer la ma-leta** to pack the suitcase

nadie nobody, no one, not . . . anyone

por fin finally, at last

los preparativos preparations

el revisor conductor *(on a train)*

la sala (large) room; **sala de equipajes** baggage room

servidor (de usted) your ser-vant, at your service

subir to go *or* come up; **su-bir al tren** to get on the train

el taquillero ticket agent

el tren train

el viajero traveler; **¡señores viajeros, al tren!** all aboard!

la vuelta return; *see* **ida**

GRAMMATICAL EXPLANATIONS

1. Idiomatic Forms.

(a) **Con,** *with,* used for **y,** *and,* in certain number combi-nations.

Treinta y un dólares **con** *(or* **y)** cuarenta y cinco centavos.

Thirty-one dollars and forty-five cents.

(b) **Ser**, *to be,* used in quoting prices.

Son veinticinco dólares.	*That makes twenty-five dollars.*

(c) **Despedirse (de)**, *to take leave (of), to say good-by (to).*

Se despidieron de sus amigos.	*They said good-by to their friends.*

(d) **Estar para** (+ infinitive), *to be about to* (do something).

El tren estaba para salir.	*The train was about to leave.*

(e) **Hay que** (+ infinitive), *it is necessary to* or *one must* (do something).

Hay que cambiar de tren.	*It is necessary to change trains.*

(f) **Al** (+ infinitive), *on* (doing something). This form is frequently used instead of an adverbial clause of time. Note that the subject of the infinitive need not be the same as the subject of the main verb.

Los vi **al salir** de casa.	*I saw them on leaving home.*
Al hacer (nosotros) las maletas, hubo mucho ajetreo.	*When we were packing our suitcases, there was much activity.*
Al vernos el tío Paco, dijo que debíamos subir al tren.	*When Uncle Frank saw us, he said that we ought to get on the train.*

2. Object Pronoun Used to Repeat a Preceding Noun Object. When a noun object precedes the verb (for emphasis), it is usually repeated as an object pronoun.

La sala de equipajes la encontrará usted ahí al lado.	*You will find the baggage room over there (to the side).*

3. Future and Conditional of Conjecture. In Spanish the future and the conditional are frequently used, with a shift of time reference, to express conjectures or feelings of uncertainty. The same ideas are expressed in English in a variety of ways. For example, a question like **¿Dónde estarán?**, besides its literal meaning *(Where will they be?),* may express a feeling of uncertainty with regard to the present *(Where can they be?, Where do you suppose they are?,* or simply *I wonder where* *they are).* Similarly, a statement like **Serán las diez** *(It will be ten o'clock)* may express present uncertainty *(It's probably ten o'clock, It must be ten o'clock,* or *I suppose it's about ten o'clock).* In such cases in Spanish, the *future* is used for the present, and the *conditional* for the past.

Ya estarán en casa.	*They're probably at home already.*
Serían las tres cuando llegaron.	*It must have been about three o'clock when they arrived.*

4. Substitutes for the Passive Voice. The passive voice is used much less frequently in Spanish than in English. Several other constructions serve to express the same idea.

(a) **Indefinite Third Person Plural.** The use of an indefinite third person plural subject ("they") is more common than in English.

Me dicen que la ciudad es hermosa.	*I am told* (or *They tell me) that the city is beautiful.*

(b) **Reflexive forms.** When the subject is a thing or an idea (not a living being), the verb can be used reflexively to express a passive idea.

Se dice que son interesantes.	*It is said* (lit. *It says itself) that they are interesting.*
¿Dónde **se compran** los billetes?	*Where are the tickets bought?* Or: *Where does one buy the tickets?*

The pronoun **se** can serve as subject when a living being is the object or when the verb is intransitive.

No **se veía** al revisor.	*You couldn't see the conductor.* Or: *The conductor wasn't seen.*
Se sube al tren aquí.	*You get* (or *One gets) on the train here.*

5. Verbs.

(a) **Regular:** cambiar, facturar, faltar, subir.

(b) **Radical-Changing:** despedirse (i), encontrar (ue).

EXERCISES

A. STRUCTURE PRACTICE.

1.

Creo			se compran aquí.
Dicen	}	que {	es muy hermosa.
Se dice			es muy interesante.

Answer. 1. ¿Dónde se compran los billetes? 2. ¿Es hermosa la capital?   3. ¿Es interesante el viaje?

Translate. 1. I believe that it is very interesting. 2. It is said that it is very beautiful. 3. They say that they are bought here.

2.

Creo			faltará poco para las diez.
Parece	}	que {	costará unos setenta dólares.
Dice			estará para salir ahora.

Answer. 1. ¿Sabe usted la hora? 2. ¿Saben ustedes cuánto cuesta el viaje? 3. ¿Cree su tío que el tren está para salir?

Translate. 1. He says that it must be almost ten o'clock. 2. It seems that it's probably about to leave. 3. I think that it must cost about seventy dollars.

3.

	yo,		compraba los billetes.
Al llegar	nosotros,	}	facturaba el equipaje.
	mi hermano,		subimos al tren.

Answer. 1. ¿Qué hacía su tío cuando usted llegó? 2. ¿Qué hacía al llegar ustedes? 3. ¿Qué hicieron ustedes al llegar su hermano?

Translate. 1. When we arrived, he was checking the baggage. 2. When I arrived, he was buying the tickets. 3. When my brother arrived, we got on the train.

B. DRILL EXERCISES.

1. *Change to conjectures, by shifting from the present to the future or from the past to the conditional. (Example:* ¿Dónde están? — ¿Dónde estarán?) 1. Están en la sala de espera. 2. ¿Qué hora es? 3. Falta poco para las diez. 4. Estaban entonces en la estación. 5. Estaban contentos de hacer el viaje.

2. *Express with al + the infinitive instead of the adverbial clause. (Example:* Se lo dije cuando salí de casa. — Se lo dije al salir de casa.) 1. Cuando hicimos las maletas, hubo mucho ajetreo. 2. Los vi cuando llegué a la estación. 3. Cuando llegué yo, compraban los billetes. 4. Cuando llegó mi hermano, estábamos en la sala de espera. 5. Cuando nos vió el tío Paco, dijo que debíamos subir al tren.

3. *Express with an indefinite third person plural subject instead of the reflexive form. (Example:* Se dice que el viaje es interesante. — Dicen que el viaje es interesante.) 1. ¿Por qué se cree eso? 2. Se hace la excursión mañana. 3. Se hacen los preparativos hoy. 4. Se sube al tren aquí. 5. ¿Dónde se factura el equipaje?

C. QUESTIONS. 1. ¿Qué hora será? 2. ¿A qué hora sale el tren para Villagrande? 3. ¿A qué hora llega? 4. ¿Hay que cambiar de tren? 5. ¿Cuánto cuesta un billete de primera clase? 6. ¿Compró usted billetes de ida y vuelta? 7. ¿Dónde se factura el equipaje? 8. ¿Cuándo debemos facturarlo? 9. ¿Quién le dió el horario? 10. ¿Estará el tren para salir? 11. ¿Quiénes querían hacer el viaje? 12. ¿Por qué no quería hacerlo José? 13. ¿Cuándo se despidió usted de sus amigos? 14. ¿Por qué compró su hermana una maleta nueva? 15. ¿Por qué hubo mucho ajetreo

al hacer las maletas?   16. ¿Qué tal fué su viaje a la capital?
17. ¿Le parece tan hermosa como dicen?   18. ¿Quién pagó
los billetes?   19. ¿A qué hora llegó el tren?   20. ¿Qué dijo
el revisor antes de salir el tren?

D. TRANSLATION.   1. Two round-trip first-class tickets
to Villagrande.   2. At what time does the train leave?
3. Is it necessary to change trains?   4. The ten o'clock train
is a through train.   5. Here is a timetable.   6. That makes
$61.40.   7. I'm going to check the baggage.   8. Where is
the baggage room?   9. You will find it over there to the
left.   10. How much did the tickets cost?   11. Our friends
must be in the waiting room.   12. They want to say good-
by to us.   13. When did you buy that new suitcase?
14. There was much activity when we were packing the
suitcases.   15. Nobody could find what he wanted.
16. What time do you suppose it is?   17. It must be almost
ten o'clock.   18. Do you suppose the train is about to
leave?   19. All aboard!   20. I believe that the trip will be
interesting.

E. CONVERSATION AND COMPOSITION.   Topic: What
you did before setting out on a recent trip.

REFLEXIVE FORMS

(Reference List of Examples for Lessons 1–17)

REFLEXIVE VERBS

acostarse	divertirse	pasearse
desayunarse	levantarse	quedarse
despedirse	llamarse	quejarse

RECIPROCAL PLURAL

Nos veremos en mi casa.

Todos se conocen.

Se entendían perfectamente.

Nos visitamos todos los días.

PASSIVE MEANING

comprar: ¿Dónde se compran los billetes?

creer: Se cree que es así.

curar: ¿Cómo se cura un resfriado?

dar: Se darán varios ejemplos.

decir: ¿Cómo se dice eso en español?

enseñar: ¿Qué ciencias se enseñan en la Universidad?

estudiar: ¿Qué lenguas se estudian más?

facturar: ¿Dónde se factura el equipaje?

ganar: Así se ganan muchos partidos.

jugar: Se juega el partido esta tarde.

hablar: Aquí se habla español.

hacer: ¿Cómo se hace eso?

representar: Se representaron las comedias.

saber: No se sabe por qué.

servir: Se sirvió un refresco.

terminar: ¿Cuándo se terminó el monumento?

tomar: ¿A qué hora se toma el almuerzo?

SE AS SUBJECT

bailar: Se bailaba todas las noches.

comer: Se come bien en ese restaurán.

charlar: Se charló un poco de todo.

entender: No se les entendía.

estar: Se está bien aquí.

ir: ¿Por dónde se va a la estación?

salir: Creo que se sale por aquí.

subir: ¿Dónde se sube al tren?

ver: No se veía al revisor.

13 Un fin de semana

Este fin de semana resulta tan divertido como suponíamos. Hemos ido a ver una comedia y una revista musical. Mi hermana ha hecho sus compras y comimos en varios restauranes famosos. Claro que no hemos visto muchos de los monumentos y lugares históricos que pensábamos visitar. Lo hemos dejado para última hora y ya no nos queda mucho tiempo. Acabamos de comprar una guía con plano, y mañana daremos otro paseíto por la ciudad. 5

(Felipe, José y Elena.) 10

FELIPE. ¡Buena la hemos hecho! Ni siquiera hemos visitado el Museo de Arte Moderno.

JOSÉ. Nos interesaba más esa visita a la universidad.

ELENA. Aún queda tiempo.

JOSÉ. ¿Te olvidas de que mañana es domingo? 15

ELENA. No saldremos hasta las tres. Supongo que el museo estará abierto el domingo.

FELIPE. Según la guía el domingo lo abren a las doce.

ELENA. ¿Habrá terminado ya el tío Paco sus negocios? Porque si no, podríamos quedarnos hasta el lunes. 20

FELIPE. Se lo preguntaremos esta noche.

JOSÉ. De todos modos me parece que lo mejor sería tomar un taxi, recorrer la ciudad para ver los edificios ...y leer la guía.

FELIPE. Por lo menos sería una cosa muy cómoda. 25

VOCABULARY

abierto, -a open
abrir to open
acabar to finish; acabar de
  (+ inf.) to have just (done
  something)
el arte m. or f. art
aún still, yet
cómodo, -a comfortable, convenient
dejar to leave; lo hemos dejado we have left it
el edificio building
la guía guide, guidebook
haber (+ past part.) to have
  (done something); ha (she)
  has; hemos we have; ¿habrá will (he) have?, do you
  suppose (he) has?
hecho done, made; ¡buena
  la hemos hecho! we've
  made a fine mess of it!
ido gone
moderno, -a modern
modo: de todos modos any-
  way, at any rate
el museo museum
el negocio business affair, deal;
  pl. business (affairs)

olvidar or olvidarse to forget; ¿te olvidas de que...?
  are you forgetting that...?
el paseíto little walk or tour
el plano (city) map
preguntar to ask (a ques-
  tion); se lo preguntaremos
  we'll ask him about it
quedar to remain; ya no nos
  queda mucho tiempo we
  haven't much time left
recorrer to go through, to
  look over
resultar to result; to turn
  out, to prove to be
según according to
siquiera even, at least; ni
  siquiera not even
suponer to suppose; supongo I suppose
el taxi taxi, taxicab
terminado finished
último, -a last, latest; para
  última hora until the very
  last (minute)
visitado visited
visto seen

GRAMMATICAL EXPLANATIONS

1. Idiomatic Forms.

(a) **Acabar de** (+ infinitive), *to have just* (done something). The present and imperfect of **acabar** may have this
meaning. In other tenses, **acabar** has its literal meaning, *to
finish*.

Acabo de comprar una guía.   *I've just bought a guidebook.*
Acababan de visitar el museo.   *They had just visited the mu-
                                      seum.*

(b) **Olvidar (que)** or **olvidarse (de que),** *to forget (that).* The forms are comparable to *forget* and *forget about* in English.

Olvidé que era domingo.	*I forgot that it was Sunday.*
Me olvidé de que era domingo.	*I forgot about its being Sunday.*

2. Use of the Perfect Tenses. The use of the perfect tenses in Spanish differs in some ways from that in English.

(a) The two parts of the verb form cannot be separated.

¿**Ha visto** usted esas ciudades?	*Have you seen those cities?*
No las **había visto** mi hermana.	*My sister hadn't seen them.*

(b) To emphasize a present perspective or result, the present perfect may be used with an expressed time reference to the past.

Los **he visto** la semana pasada. }
Los **vi** la semana pasada.   }   *I saw them last week.*

(c) The future perfect is used mainly for conjectures.

Ya **habrán llegado.**	*They have probably* (or *They must have*) *arrived already.*

3. Verbs.

(a) **Regular:** abrir, acabar, dejar, olvidar, preguntar, quedar, recorrer, resultar.

(b) **Irregular.**

Haber, *to have* (done something).

PRESENT INDICATIVE		PRETERITE INDICATIVE	
he	hemos	hube	hubimos
has	habéis	hubiste	hubisteis
ha	han	hubo	hubieron

FUTURE INDICATIVE		CONDITIONAL	
habré	habremos	habría	habríamos
habrás	habréis	habrías	habríais
habrá	habrán	habría	habrían

In past perfects the tense of **haber** normally used is the imperfect, which is regular: había, habías, etc.

Suponer, *to suppose,* is conjugated like **poner,** *to put.*

4. Past Participle of Regular Verbs. The past participle can usually be formed as follows: remove the ending of the infinitive (**-ar, -er** or **-ir**); add the ending of the past participle.

-ar VERBS	-er OR -ir VERBS
tom-ar, *to take*	com-er, *to eat*
tomado *taken*	comido *eaten*

5. Past Participle of Irregular Verbs. The irregularities listed here (for verbs used so far) include almost all the common ones. Note that the orthographic changes (**i** > **í**) are like those of the preterite.

abrir:	**abierto**	hacer:	**hecho**	suponer:	**supuesto**
creer:	creído	leer:	leído	ver:	**visto**
decir:	**dicho**	poner:	**puesto**	volver:	**vuelto**

EXERCISES

A. STRUCTURE PRACTICE.

1. Acabo ⎱
Acabamos ⎰ de visitar ⎰ el museo.
Acaban ⎰ el monumento.
la universidad.

Answer. 1. ¿Qué ha visitado usted?   2. ¿Qué han hecho ustedes?   3. ¿Dónde han estado los muchachos?

Translate. 1. We have just visited the museum.   2. I have just visited the university.   3. They have just visited the monument.

2. Lo ⎱ he ⎱
La ⎰ hemos ⎰ visto muchas veces.
Los ⎰ ha ⎰

Answer. 1. ¿Ha visto usted el Museo de Arte Moderno?   2. ¿Han visto ustedes la universidad?   3. ¿Ha visto José esos famosos monumentos?

Translate. 1. I have seen it many times.   2. We have seen them many times.   3. He has seen it many times.

3.
$$No \begin{Bmatrix} lo \\ la \\ los \end{Bmatrix} \begin{Bmatrix} había \\ habíamos \\ habían \end{Bmatrix} visitado.$$

Answer. 1. ¿Había visitado usted el museo? 2. ¿Conocían ustedes la capital? 3. ¿Cuándo habían visitado los muchachos esos monumentos históricos?

Translate. 1. We hadn't visited it. 2. I hadn't visited them. 3. They hadn't visited it.

B. Drill Exercises.

1. *Give the past participle of each verb. (Example:* tomar — tomado.*)* 1. dejar. 2. olvidar. 3. preguntar. 4. quedar. 5. facturar.

2. *Give the past participle of each verb. (Example:* comer — comido.*)* 1. perder. 2. querer. 3. recorrer. 4. vivir. 5. servir.

3. *Change to the corresponding past perfect form. (Example:* he visto — había visto.*)* 1. he dicho. 2. hemos puesto. 3. has abierto. 4. ha hecho. 5. han vuelto.

4. *Change to refer to the past, by using the imperfect of* **acabar.** *(Example:* Acabo de llegar. — Acababa de llegar.*)* 1. Acabo de comprar la guía. 2. Acabamos de llegar a la capital. 3. Acaban de visitar el museo. 4. Acabo de dar un paseo. 5. Acaban de volver al hotel.

C. Questions. 1. ¿Cuántos años ha vivido usted en esta ciudad? 2. ¿Cuáles son los monumentos más conocidos de la ciudad? 3. ¿Los ha visto usted todos? 4. ¿Tiene usted una guía de la ciudad? 5. ¿La ha estudiado? 6. ¿Qué ciudades grandes ha visitado usted? 7. ¿Cuál le ha parecido más interesante? 8. ¿Cuál tiene los mejores

museos?   9. ¿Conoce usted el Museo de Arte Moderno?
10. ¿A qué hora lo abren el domingo?   11. ¿Qué museos
conoce usted?   12. ¿Qué museos ha visitado usted este año?
13. ¿Qué viajes ha hecho usted este año?   14. ¿Cuál de los
viajes le ha gustado más?   15. ¿Cuál es el viaje más largo
que usted ha hecho?   16. ¿Cuántas veces ha ido usted al
teatro este mes?   17. ¿Cuántas veces ha ido al cine?   18. ¿En
qué restauranes ha comido usted esta semana?   19. ¿Qué
programas de televisión le han gustado más?   20. ¿Qué fin
de semana ha resultado más interesante este año?

   D. TRANSLATION.   1. I haven't taken many trips this
year.   2. This is my first visit to this city.   3. This weekend is proving to be very entertaining.   4. Yesterday we
saw several historical places.   5. We have just visited the
famous University.   6. Tomorrow we'll take another little
walk to see the buildings of the city.   7. Maybe the best
would be to take a taxi to go through the city.   8. Philip
said that he had just bought a guidebook.   9. Where do
you suppose he has put it?   10. I haven't seen it.   11. We
haven't much time left.   12. We haven't visited the Museum of Modern Art.   13. Why have you left it until the
very last?   14. We were more interested in the musical
revue.   15. We also wanted to make some purchases.
16. I believe that on Sunday they open the Museum at
twelve.   17. We would like to stay until Monday.   18. We
have had a very good time.   19. Did you ask your uncle
if he had finished his business?   20. I'll ask him about it
this evening.

   E. CONVERSATION AND COMPOSITION.   Topic: Interesting things you have done recently.

19 | Museos

Hay varios museos de la ciudad que son muy conocidos. El Museo de Arte Moderno contiene cuadros y esculturas de los mejores artistas modernos. La Academia de Bellas Artes, además de su biblioteca, tan rica en libros raros, contiene una preciosa colección de pinturas 5 italianas de los siglos XVI (diez y seis) y XVII (diez y siete). De mucho valor, también, es el Museo de Ciencias Naturales, cuyo magnífico edificio se construyó a principios del siglo XX, entre 1910 (mil novecientos diez) y 1912 (mil novecientos doce). 10

(José, Felipe y Elena; después un guardia.)

José. ¡Vaya una colección de pinturas antiguas! Nunca había visto tantas.

Felipe. Es magnífica. Dicen que la colección entera le fué donada al museo, hace pocos años, por un colec- 15 cionista millonario.

Elena. Ya estará abierto el Museo de Arte Moderno.

Felipe. Creo que no está lejos de aquí. Voy a preguntar... Dispense usted, guardia, ¿por dónde se va al Museo de Arte Moderno? 20

Guardia. En la primera bocacalle, hay que doblar a la izquierda y luego todo derecho. En la cuarta bocacalle, a mano derecha, lo encontrará usted.

Felipe. Muchas gracias.

Guardia. No hay de qué. Servidor de usted. 25

VOCABULARY

la **academia** academy
además de besides, in addition to
antiguo, -a ancient, old
el **artista,** la **artista** artist
bello, -a beautiful; **bellas artes** fine arts
la **biblioteca** library
la **bocacalle** (street) intersection
la **colección** collection
el **coleccionista,** la **coleccionista** collector
construir to construct, to build; **se construyó** was built
contener to contain; **contiene** (it) contains
el **cuadro** picture
cuyo, -a whose
derecho, -a right; straight; **a mano derecha** on the right; **todo derecho** straight ahead
dispense usted pardon me
doblar to turn (*a corner*)
donar to donate, to give
entero, -a entire, whole
la **escultura** sculpture
el **guardia** policeman, officer

italiano, -a Italian
lejos far; **lejos de** far from
el **libro** book
mil (one) thousand; **mil novecientos** nineteen hundred
millonario, -a very wealthy
natural natural
no hay de qué you're welcome
novecientos, -as nine hundred
nunca never, not...ever
la **pintura** painting
poco, -a little; *pl.* few; **hace pocos años** a few years ago
¿por dónde? which way?; **¿por dónde se va a...?** which way is...?, how do you get to?
precioso, -a precious, lovely
el **principio** beginning; **a principios de** toward the beginning of
raro, -a rare
el **siglo** century
el **valor** value, worth
¡vaya una colección! what a collection!

GRAMMATICAL EXPLANATIONS

1. Cardinal Numerals, 101-1,000,000.

101 ciento uno. -a
102 ciento dos
200 doscientos, -as
201 doscientos uno,
    doscientas una

202 doscientos dos,
    doscientas dos
300 trescientos, -as
400 cuatrocientos, -as
500 quinientos, -as

600 seiscientos, -as	1999 mil novecientos
700 setecientos, -as	noventa y nueve
800 ochocientos, -as	2000 dos mil
900 novecientos, -as	2001 dos mil uno, -a
1000 mil	2002 dos mil dos
1001 mil uno, -a	100.000 cien mil
1002 mil dos	200.000 doscientos mil,
1100 mil ciento	doscientas mil
1101 mil ciento uno, -a	999.000 novecientos noventa
1102 mil ciento dos	y nueve mil
1200 mil doscientos, -as	1.000.000 un millón

(a) The plural forms **doscientos, -as, trescientos, -as,** etc. agree in gender with the words that they modify.

Había doscientas treinta y una pinturas.	*There were two hundred thirty-one paintings.*

(b) The word **millón,** *million,* is followed by **de,** *of,* when it precedes a noun.

Tienen un millón **de** dólares.	*They have a million dollars.*

(c) The use of commas and periods in numerals in Spanish is the reverse of that in English.

El museo costó $2.000.000.	*The museum cost $2,000,000.*
El billete cuesta $1,25.	*The ticket costs $1.25.*

2. Dates. Note the use of the cardinal numerals after the *first* (day or century) and the use of **mil** from *one thousand* on. The preposition **de** is used to connect the parts of a date (day + month + year).

El 1ro (= **primero**) de mayo.	*May 1st.* Or: *The first of May.*
El 2 (= **dos**) de mayo.	*May 2nd.* Or: *The second of May.*
El siglo **XX** (= **veinte**).	*The twentieth century.*
El 4 de julio de 1776 (**mil setecientos** setenta y seis).	*July 4, 1776.*

The article is normally required with the days of the month (except in dating letters, etc.) No preposition is used for "on."

Llegamos el 30 de abril.	*We arrived (on) April 30th.*

3. Passive Voice. The passive voice is formed by using the appropriate forms of the verb **ser,** *to be* + the past participle. The participle agrees in gender and number with the subject. The agent is usually introduced by **por.**

La colección **fué donada** al museo **por** un millonario.	*The collection was given to the museum by a wealthy man.*

(a) In some cases the passive voice cannot be used in Spanish (for example, to change an *indirect* object into a passive subject), and in other cases its use would seem rather formal or even quite unnatural. As has been noted (Lesson 17, §4), the use of an indefinite subject or a reflexive form is often preferable.

Me han dicho que es una colección preciosa.	*I have been told* (lit. *They have told me) that it is a lovely collection.*
Se cree que es la más rica del país.	*It is believed to be the richest in the country.*

(b) When no action is involved, the past participle is used as a descriptive adjective, referring to a resultant *condition.* In these cases **estar** is used.

¿Cuándo abrirán el museo?—Ya **está abierto.**	*When will they open the museum?—It is already open.*
Este edificio **está** bien **construido.**	*This building is well constructed.*

4. Verbs.

(a) **Regular:** doblar, donar.

(b) **Irregular.**

Construir, *to construct, to build.* Verbs ending in the sound -**uir** have a spelling change (**i** > **y** between vowels) and also add **y** to the stem before endings not beginning with **i.**

PRESENT INDICATIVE		PRETERITE INDICATIVE	
construyo	construimos	construí	construimos
construyes	construís	construiste	construisteis
construye	construyen	construyó	construyeron

Contener, *to contain,* is conjugated like **tener,** *to have.*

EXERCISES

A. Structure Practice.

1.

$$\text{Llegó} \begin{cases} \text{el primero} \\ \text{el dos} \\ \text{el tres} \end{cases} \text{de} \begin{cases} \text{enero.} \\ \text{febrero.} \\ \text{marzo.} \end{cases}$$

Answer. 1. ¿Cuándo llegó su primo? 2. ¿En qué mes llegó su tío? 3. ¿Acaba de llegar su abuelo?

Translate. 1. He arrived the second of January. 2. He arrived the first of March. 3. He arrived the third of February.

2.

$$\begin{aligned}\text{Aquel museo} \\ \text{Ese monumento} \\ \text{Este edificio} \end{aligned} \Big\} \text{fué construido en} \Big\{ \begin{aligned}\text{mil setecientos.} \\ \text{mil ochocientos.} \\ \text{mil novecientos.} \end{aligned}$$

Answer. 1. ¿Cuándo fué construido aquel museo? 2. ¿Se construyó ese monumento en el siglo XIX? 3. ¿Es antiguo este edificio?

Translate. 1. That museum was built in 1900. 2. This building was constructed in 1800. 3. That monument was built in 1700.

3.

$$\begin{aligned}\text{La colección} \\ \text{La biblioteca} \\ \text{Esa escultura} \end{aligned} \Big\} \text{fué donada por} \Big\{ \begin{aligned}\text{un millonario.} \\ \text{un coleccionista.} \\ \text{una mujer rica.} \end{aligned}$$

Answer. 1. ¿Cuándo se compró la colección de pinturas? 2. ¿Por quién fué donada la biblioteca? 3. ¿Quién donó esa escultura?

Translate. 1. The collection was donated by a rich woman. 2. That sculpture was given by a collector. 3. The library was given by a very wealthy man.

B. DRILL EXERCISES.

1. *Read in Spanish.* 1. 200. 2. 301. 3. 570. 4. 787.
5. 1900. 6. 2.500. 7. 100.000. 8. 421 pinturas.
9. $650,25. 10. $1.000.000.

2. *Change each date to a day later. (Example:* el 1ʳᵒ de
enero — el 2 de enero.) 1. el 1ʳᵒ de febrero. 2. el 31 de
marzo. 3. el 4 de julio. 4. el 14 de agosto. 5. el 25 de
diciembre.

3. *Change the subject and verb to the plural. (Example:*
El monumento fué construido en 1920. — Los monumentos
fueron construidos en 1920.) 1. La biblioteca fué cons-
truida en 1930. 2. El edificio fué empezado en 1940.
3. Fué terminado en 1950. 4. La colección fué donada al
museo por un millonario. 5. La comedia fué representada
por una compañía excelente.

C. QUESTIONS. 1. ¿Cuáles son los edificios más conocidos de la ciudad? 2. ¿Qué colecciones contiene el Museo
de Arte Moderno? 3. ¿Cuántas esculturas contiene?
4. ¿Por dónde se va al Museo? 5. ¿Cuándo fué construido
el edificio? 6. ¿Cómo es la biblioteca de la Academia de
Bellas Artes? 7. ¿Qué famosa colección de pinturas contiene la Academia? 8. ¿Por quién fué donada la colección?
9. ¿Cuándo le fué donada? 10. ¿Cuántas pinturas contiene? 11. ¿Cuándo se construyó el Museo de Ciencias
Naturales? 12. ¿Cuánto costó el edificio? 13. ¿Estará
abierto ahora? 14. ¿Qué días de la semana está abierto?
15. ¿Cuántas veces lo ha visitado usted? 16. ¿Cuál de los
museos le gusta más? 17. ¿Cuál es el más antiguo?
18. ¿Cuándo llegaron sus amigos a la ciudad? 19. ¿Qué
museos han visitado ustedes? 20. ¿Qué excursiones les han
gustado más?

D. TRANSLATION. 1. What a collection of modern paintings! 2. We had never seen so many. 3. That museum also has many sculptures by the best modern artists. 4. At the Academy of Fine Arts we saw a collection of Italian paintings. 5. The entire collection was given to it by a wealthy collector. 6. The Academy also has some Spanish paintings of the 17th century. 7. The library of the Academy contains many rare books. 8. I have been told that the collection is magnificent. 9. I don't know when they open the library. 10. It is probably open now. 11. I prefer to visit the Museum of Natural Sciences. 12. It is not far from here, is it? 13. How do you get to the Museum? 14. At the first intersection you have to turn right. 15. You'll find it at the fourth intersection, on the left. 16. Was that building constructed in the 19th century? 17. The guidebook says that it was built between 1912 and 1914. 18. Your friends arrived on the first of January, didn't they? 19. They arrived the second of January. 20. We have visited all the museums of the city.

E. CONVERSATION AND COMPOSITION. Topic: Some museums that you have seen or would like to see.

DIRECTIONS
(Reference List; cf. Lessons 17, 19)

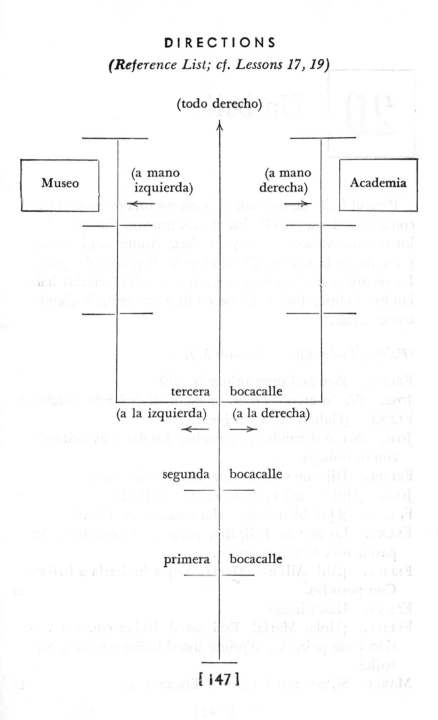

20 Un baile

Para el baile de esta noche tenemos una orquesta muy conocida. Toca no sólo los ritmos nuevos, sino también los mejores valses, tangos y rumbas. Ahora son las ocho y media de la noche. El salón se va llenando de gente. La orquesta está tocando y ya hay muchas parejas bai- 5 lando. Felipe, José y Elena están a un lado, haciendo comentarios.

(Felipe, José y Elena; después María.)

FELIPE.   Esto está muy animado, ¿eh?

JOSÉ.   ¡Ya lo creo! Todos se están divirtiendo mucho. 10

ELENA.   ¿Habéis visto a Miguel?

JOSÉ.   No sé si vendrá esta noche. Estaba muy ocupado con su trabajo.

FELIPE.   Dijo esta tarde que vendría sin falta.

JOSÉ.   ¿Quién será esa muchacha tan linda?   15

FELIPE.   ¡Qué bien baila! ¿La conoces tú, Elena?

ELENA.   Lo siento, Felipillo, pero no la conozco. Su pareja no está mal tampoco.

FELIPE.   ¡Ah! Allí está María. Voy a invitarla a bailar. Con permiso.   20

ELENA.   Hasta luego.

FELIPE.   ¡Hola, María! Está usted divina con ese vestido y ese peinado. ¿Quiere usted bailar conmigo este baile?

MARÍA.   Sí, con mucho gusto. Encantada.   25

VOCABULARY

allí there

animado, -a animated, lively, gay

bailando dancing

el comentario comment, remark

divino, -a divine, lovely; está usted divina you look lovely

divirtiendo: se están divirtiendo mucho (they) are having a very good time

encantado, -a delighted

la falta fault, failure; sin falta without fail

Felipillo (dim. of Felipe) Phil

la gente people

haciendo making

invitar to invite; invitar a (+ inf.) to invite to

llenar to fill; se va llenando de gente (it) is (gradually) filling up with people

ocupado, -a busy

la pareja couple; dancing partner

el peinado hairdo, coiffure

permiso: con permiso excuse me

el ritmo rhythm

la rumba rumba

el salón salon, large room, hall

sino but (but instead); no sólo . . . sino (también) not only...but also

tampoco neither, not...either

el tango tango

tocando playing

el trabajo work

el vals waltz

GRAMMATICAL EXPLANATIONS

1. **Use of *sino*.** After a negative statement, **sino,** *but (= but instead, but rather),* is used to introduce a contrasting positive element. It is also used in the combination **no sólo . . . sino (también),** *not only . . . but also.*

No toca un vals, **sino** un tango.   *It isn't playing a waltz, but (= but instead) a tango.*

Toca **no sólo** valses **sino (también)** tangos y rumbas.   *It plays not only waltzes but also tangos and rumbas.*

2. **Object Pronouns with the Present Participle.** Object pronouns follow the present participle, and are attached to it. If the participle is part of a verb phrase, the pronoun may precede the whole phrase.

Están divirtiéndose mucho.   ⎱   *They are having a very good*
Se están divirtiendo mucho.   ⎰   *time.*

3. Progressive Forms. To stress or clarify the idea of action in progress, the appropriate tense of **estar,** *to be,* is used with the present participle (invariable in form).

La orquesta está **tocando** ahora.	*The orchestra is playing now.*
Hace un rato todos **estaban bailando.**	*A little while ago everybody was dancing.*

In Spanish the progressive tenses are rarely used with verbs of motion (**ir,** *to go,* **venir,** *to come,* etc.). Other verbs may replace **estar,** giving a new shade of meaning. For example, when **ir,** *to go,* is so used, it indicates that the action is not only "in progress" but also "moving forward" (in a literal or a figurative sense).

El salón se **va llenando** de gente.	*The room is (gradually) filling up with people.*
Vamos conociendo a mucha gente.	*We're getting to know a lot of people.*

4. Verbs. Regular: invitar, llenar.

5. Present Participle of Regular Verbs. The present participle can usually be formed as follows: remove the ending of the infinitive (**-ar, -er,** or **-ir**); add the ending of the present participle.

-ar VERBS	-er OR -ir VERBS
tom-ar, *to take*	com-er, *to eat*
taking	*eating*
tomando	comiendo

6. Present Participle of Irregular Verbs. Most of the irregularities of the present participles are radical changes (**o > u, e > i**) or orthographic changes (**i > y**) like those of the third person preterite.

construir: construyendo	leer: leyendo
creer: creyendo	poder: pudiendo
decir: diciendo	preferir: prefiriendo
despedirse: despidiéndose	seguir: siguiendo
divertirse: divirtiéndose	sentir: sintiendo
dormir: durmiendo	servir: sirviendo
ir: yendo	venir: viniendo

EXERCISES

A. Structure Practice.

1.

$$No \begin{cases} queremos \\ toca \\ escuchan \end{cases} un\ vals,\ sino \begin{cases} un\ tango. \\ una\ rumba. \\ un\ ritmo\ nuevo. \end{cases}$$

Answer. 1. ¿Quieren ustedes un vals? 2. ¿Toca la orquesta un vals? 3. ¿Escuchan un vals los muchachos?

Translate. 1. It's not playing a waltz but a tango. 2. We don't want a waltz but a new rhythm. 3. They aren't listening to a waltz but a rumba.

2.

$$Ahora \begin{cases} está \\ están \\ están\ todos \end{cases} \begin{matrix} bailando. \\ charlando\ con\ unos\ amigos. \\ escuchando\ la\ música. \end{matrix}$$

Answer. 1. ¿Dónde está Elena? 2. ¿Qué hacen Pablo y María? 3. ¿Por qué no baila nadie ahora?

Translate. 1. She is now chatting with some friends. 2. Now they are listening to the music. 3. Now everybody is dancing.

3.

$$Hace\ un\ rato \begin{cases} estaba \\ estaban \\ todos\ estaban \end{cases} \begin{matrix} bailando. \\ aquí\ charlando. \\ divirtiéndose\ más. \end{matrix}$$

Answer. 1. ¿Ha visto usted a Isabel? 2. ¿Dónde están Miguel y Luisa? 3. ¿Va siendo menos divertido el baile?

Translate. 1. A little while ago everybody was dancing. 2. A little while ago she was here chatting. 3. A little while ago they were having more fun.

B. Drill Exercises.

1. *Give the present participle of each verb. (Example:* tomar — tomando.) 1. bailar. 2. mirar. 3. llenar. 4. visitar. 5. preguntar.

2. *Give the present participle of each verb. (Example:* comer — comiendo.) 1. hacer. 2. poner. 3. llover. 4. abrir. 5. vivir.

3. *Change to the past, by using the imperfect of estar. (Example:* Está tocando. — Estaba tocando.) 1. Estoy leyendo. 2. Está cantando. 3. Estamos paseándonos. 4. Están despidiéndose. 5. Se están divirtiendo.

4. *Use ahora and reverse the order of the contrasting elements. (Example:* No toca un vals, sino un tango. — Ahora no toca un tango, sino un vals.) 1. No hablan del viaje, sino del baile. 2. No está con Isabel, sino con Elena. 3. No está bailando con Luisa, sino con María. 4. No quieren bailar, sino cantar. 5. No están bailando, sino charlando.

C. QUESTIONS 1. ¿Qué tal le parece el baile de esta noche? 2. ¿Le gusta la orquesta? 3. ¿Qué ritmos toca mejor? 4. ¿Qué ritmos prefiere usted? 5. ¿Qué hora será? 6. ¿Hay mucha gente en el salón? 7. ¿Cuántas parejas están bailando ahora? 8. ¿Con quién baila Luisa? 9. ¿Ha visto usted a Pablo? 10. ¿Qué hacía cuando le vieron ustedes? 11. ¿Por qué no está aquí Juanito? 12. ¿Vendrán al baile los señores Pérez? 13. ¿Con quiénes ha bailado usted? 14. ¿Baila bien Eduardo? 15. ¿Dónde estará Miguel? 16. ¿Quién es esa muchacha tan bonita? 17. ¿Qué le parece el peinado de María? 18. ¿Le gusta el nuevo vestido de Elena? 19. ¿Se están divirtiendo ustedes? 20. ¿A qué hora termina el baile?

D. TRANSLATION. 1. The room is gradually filling up with people. 2. Everybody is having a very good time. 3. The orchestra seems excellent to me. 4. I like the tango that they are playing now. 5. It's not a tango but a rumba.

6. May I have (Will you dance with me) this dance?
7. With pleasure. Delighted.   8. Louise says that Philip
dances very well.   9. His sister doesn't dance badly either.
10. Who is that pretty girl who is dancing with Joseph?
11. Mary's new dress is lovely, isn't it?   12. I also like her
new hairdo.   13. Have you seen Paul?   14. He said that
he would come for sure (without fail).   15. When I saw
him this afternoon, he was very busy with his work.   16. I
saw Mr. and Mrs. Pérez a little while ago.   17. They were
talking with Mr. and Mrs. Martin.   18. I haven't seen
Edward.   19. He is dancing with Elizabeth.   20. The
dance ends at twelve.

E. CONVERSATION AND COMPOSITION. Topic: A dance
in progress.

GRAMMATICAL NOTES

(Use the following grammatical notes as a guide for reviewing forms and usage. Then test your knowledge of them by using the corresponding Test Exercises on the opposite page.)

1. Idiomatic Forms. *List for Lessons 16-20.*

acabar de (+ *inf.*) to have just *(done something)* (18)

al (+ *inf.*) on *(doing something)* (17)

con (for y): 31 dólares con 45 centavos $31.45 (17)

despedirse de to say good-by to (17)

estar para (+ *inf.*) to be about to (17)

hacer un viaje to make *or* take a trip (16)

hay que (+ *inf.*) it is necessary to *or* one must (17)

olvidar que *or* **olvidarse de que** to forget that (18)

pagar to pay for (16)

ser *(in quoting prices)*: **son $25** that makes $25 (17)

2. Definite Article.

Usage: definite article regularly used with the names of a few countries, cities, etc., and with other place names when the meaning is limited by an adjective or phrase (16:2); with days of the month, except in dating letters, etc. (19:2).

3. Personal Pronouns.

Usage: Object pronoun used to repeat noun object preceding the verb (17:2); object pronouns attached to the present participle, or before whole verb phrase (20:2).

4. Negative Constructions.

Usage: use of two or more negatives normal, but **no** omitted if longer form precedes the verb (16:3); after negative statements, **sino,** *but* (= *but instead, but rather*), used to introduce

(Continued on page 156)

(Complete the Spanish sentences with the idea indicated. Check your answers by using the corresponding Grammatical Notes on the opposite page.)

1. Idiomatic Forms.

1. *(They have just returned)* _____ al hotel.
2. *(on arriving)* Los vi _____ a la estación.
3. *(I said good-by to)* _____ mis amigos.
4. *(is about to)* Dice que el tren _____ salir.
5. *(to take)* Me gustaría _____ un viaje largo.
6. *(It will be necessary to)* _____ cambiar de tren.
7. *(I forgot)* _____ que tendríamos que volver el domingo.
8. *(paid for)* Mis tíos _____ los billetes.

2. Definite Article.

1. *(the United States)* Hemos viajado por _____.
2. *(Canada)* ¿Conocen ustedes _____?
3. *(modern Spain)* Parece que no les interesa _____.
4. *(April 1st)* Vendrán a vernos _____.

3. Personal Pronouns.

1. *(gave it)* El dinero me _____ mis padres.
2. *(are having fun)* Creo que todos _____.
3. *(he isn't reading it)* José tiene la guía, pero _____.

4. Negative Constructions.

1. *(anything)* No tienen _____ que hacer esta tarde.
2. *(Nobody)* _____ quería hacer la excursión.
3. *(but)* No quieren cantar, _____ bailar.

(Continued on page 157)

[155]

GRAMMATICAL NOTES, CONTINUED

a contrasting positive element; **sino** also used in the combination **no sólo...sino (también),** *not only...but also* (20:1).

5. Numerals, Dates.

Forms: cardinal numerals 101-1,000,000 (19:1); cardinal numerals used in dates after *first;* **de** used to connect day + month + year (19:2).

6. Verbs.

Conditional: formed by adding endings to infinitive or future stem (16:6-7); used as in English (16:4), and also to express conjectures or feelings of uncertainty with reference to the past (17:3).

Future indicative: used to express conjectures or feelings of uncertainty with reference to the present (17:3).

Passive voice: formed by using **ser,** *to be,* with the past participle, which agrees in gender and number with the subject (19:3); often replaced by an indefinite subject or a reflexive form (17:4, 19:3).

Perfect tenses: formed by using **haber,** *to have,* with the past participle, invariable in form (18:3-5); present perfect sometimes used with an expressed time reference to the past (18:2); future perfect used mainly for conjectures (18:2).

Progressive forms: **estar,** *to be* (sometimes other verbs, like **ir,** *to go*) used with the present participle, to stress or clarify the idea of action in progress (20:3, 20:5-6).

TEST EXERCISES, CONTINUED

4. *(but)* No hablaba con Pablo, ____ con Eduardo.
5. *(but also)* Fueron no sólo a Méjico ____ a Colombia.

5. Numerals, Dates.

1. *(a hundred thousand)* El edificio costó ____ dólares.
2. *(the 25th)* Los veremos ____ de diciembre.
3. *(1950)* Se terminó el 30 de junio ____.

6. Verbs.

1. *(he would go)* Dijo que ____ con nosotros.
2. *(would you do)* ¿Qué ____ en la capital?
3. *(They probably were)* ____ contentos de hacer el viaje.
4. *(It must have been)* ____ la una cuando salieron.
5. *(He is probably)* ____ en casa ahora.
6. *(do you suppose they are)* ¿Quiénes ____?
7. *(was constructed)* Aquel museo ____ en 1940.
8. *(were donated)* Las pinturas ____ por un coleccionista.
9. *(I am told)* ____ que la familia es muy rica.
10. *(are bought)* ¿Dónde ____ los billetes?
11. *(They had left)* ____ cuando llegamos.
12. *(Have you seen)* ¿____ el Museo de Ciencias Naturales?
13. *(I visited it)* ____ hace pocos días.
14. *(do you suppose he has put)* ¿Dónde ____ el horario?
15. *(are talking)* Los muchachos ____ de su viaje.
16. *(is dancing)* ¿Con quién ____ Miguel?
17. *(They're getting to know)* ____ a mucha gente.

21 Noticias

Acabo de hojear el periódico. Me he enterado de que los precios han subido. El tiempo sigue malo; es posible que haya tormenta esta noche. No encuentran una solución para el conflicto entre los obreros y la dirección de la fábrica; es probable que haya otra huelga. Parece 5 dudoso que los partidos políticos lleguen a un acuerdo. No mejora la situación internacional... Las demás noticias son las de siempre: accidentes, crímenes, muertes, nacimientos y bodas.

(Elena y Felipe.) 10

ELENA. ¿Qué noticias hay en el diario de hoy?

FELIPE. Lo de siempre. Hubo un choque de automóviles bastante serio: murieron dos pasajeros.

ELENA. Supongo que fué por exceso de velocidad.

FELIPE. Se sospecha que fué por exceso de bebidas... 15 Una mujer mató anoche a su marido. Parece que el motivo fué exceso de amor.

ELENA. O de celos.

FELIPE. ¿No es lo mismo?... Se casa mi actriz favorita...por tercera vez. 20

ELENA. No digo nada...tratándose de una rubia.

FELIPE. También me gustan las morenas.

ELENA. Y las pelirrojas.

FELIPE. Más noticias: Han subido los precios.

ELENA. Es muy posible que sigan subiendo. 25

VOCABULARY

el **accidente** accident
el **acuerdo** agreement
el **amor** love
el **automóvil** automobile, car
la **bebida** drink
la **boda** wedding
    casarse to get married
los **celos** jealousy
el **conflicto** conflict, disagreement
el **crimen** crime
el **choque** collision; **choque de automóviles** car wreck
    demás remaining, other
el **diario** newspaper
la **dirección** direction; management
    dudoso doubtful
    enterarse de que to find out that
    entre between
el **exceso** excess; **exceso de velocidad** speeding
la **fábrica** factory
    haya there may *or* will be
    hojear to leaf through, to glance at
la **huelga** strike
    internacional international
    lleguen (they) may *or* will arrive

el **marido** husband
    matar to kill
    mejorar to improve
    morir (ue, u; *irreg.***)** to die
el **motivo** motive
la **muerte** death
el **nacimiento** birth
la **noticia** news (item); *pl.* news
el **obrero,** la **obrera** worker
el **partido** party *(political)*
el **pasajero** passenger
    pelirrojo, -a redheaded
    político, -a political
    por because of, for; **por tercera vez** for the third time
    posible possible
    probable probable, likely
    seguir (i; g) to continue, to still be; **que sigan subiendo** that they'll keep on going up
    serio, -a serious
la **situación** situation
la **solución** solution
    sospechar to suspect
la **tormenta** storm
    tratar to treat; **tratarse de** to concern; **tratándose de** since it concerns
la **velocidad** speed

GRAMMATICAL EXPLANATIONS

1. Indicative and Subjunctive Moods. In Spanish the indicative is used to make a statement or ask a question; the statement or question is visualized as *real*. The subjunctive is used to reflect an attitude (usually uncertainty or emotion); any idea thus subordinated is visualized as *unreal*.

2. Uses of the Subjunctive: Uncertainty, Doubt, or Denial.
Listed below are some common expressions which usually
imply *uncertainty, doubt,* or *denial,* and are normally followed
by the subjunctive.

PERSONAL	IMPERSONAL
no creer que, *not to believe that*	**no parecer que,** *not to seem that*
dudar que, *to doubt that*	**ser** (or **parecer**) **dudoso** (**posible,**
no estar seguro de que, *not to*	**imposible, probable**) **que,** *to*
be sure that	*be* (or *to seem*) *doubtful* (*pos-*
negar que, *to deny that*	*sible, impossible, probable*)
	that

If no doubt is felt by the speaker, the indicative is used
after **no creer, no dudar,** or **no estar seguro.** Compare:

No creo que **estén** aquí.	*I don't believe (= It seems doubtful) that they are here.*
No creen que **estamos** aquí.	*They don't believe (= They are unaware) that we are here.*

3. Present Subjunctive for the Future. A verb in the
present subjunctive may refer to either present or future time,
depending on the context.

Es posible que **haya** tormenta esta noche.	*It is possible that there will be a storm tonight.*

4. Verbs.

(a) **Regular:** casarse, dudar, enterarse, hojear, matar, mejorar, sospechar, tratar.

(b) **Radical-Changing:** morir (ue, u; *irreg.*). In addition
to its radical changes, **morir** has an irregular past participle:
muerto.

(c) **Radical- and Orthographic-Changing:** negar (ie; gu),
seguir (i; g).

5. Present Subjunctive of Regular Verbs. The present
subjunctive can usually be formed as follows: remove the ending of the infinitive (**-ar, -er, -ir**); add the endings of the present
subjunctive.

-ar VERBS		**-er** OR **-ir** VERBS	
tom-ar		**com-er**	
tome	tomemos	coma	comamos
tomes	toméis	comas	comáis
tome	tomen	coma	coman

6. Present Subjunctive of Irregular Verbs.

(a) **Radical Changes.** Stem-vowel changes like those of the present indicative occur when the stem is stressed. For **-ir** radical-changing verbs there is an additional change (**o** > **u**, **e** > **i**) in the first and second persons plural. Examples:

-ar OR **-er** VERBS				**-ir** VERBS	
volver (ue)		**dormir (ue, u)**		**sentir (ie, i)**	
vuelva	volvamos	duerma	durmamos	sienta	sintamos
vuelvas	volváis	duermas	durmáis	sientas	sintáis
vuelva	vuelvan	duerma	duerman	sienta	sientan

(b) **Orthographic Changes.** Any verb whose stem requires a spelling change (cf. the present and preterite indicative) has this change throughout the present subjunctive. Examples:

-ar VERBS		**-er** OR **-ir** VERBS	
llegar (gu)		**coger (j)**	
llegue	lleguemos	coja	cojamos
llegues	lleguéis	cojas	cojáis
llegue	lleguen	coja	cojan

(c) **Irregular Stems.** The irregular stems can almost always be derived from the first person singular present indicative. Example: **tener (tengo), tenga, tengas,** etc. The irregular stems cannot be derived in this way for the six verbs that do not end in **-o** in the first person singular present indicative.

Dar		**Estar**		**Haber**	
dé	demos	esté	estemos	haya	hayamos
des	deis	estés	estéis	hayas	hayáis
dé	den	esté	estén	haya	hayan

Ir		**Saber**		**Ser**	
vaya	vayamos	sepa	sepamos	sea	seamos
vayas	vayáis	sepas	sepáis	seas	seáis
vaya	vayan	sepa	sepan	sea	sean

EXERCISES

A. STRUCTURE PRACTICE.

1.   No creo ⎫   ⎧ estén aquí.
        Dudo   ⎬ que ⎨ vuelvan esta tarde.
        No estoy seguro de ⎭ ⎩ puedan acompañarnos.

Answer. 1. ¿Están aquí Pablo y Miguel?   2. ¿Cree usted que volverán esta tarde?   3. ¿Podrán acompañarnos mañana?

Translate. 1. I doubt that they are here.   2. I don't believe that they will be able to go with us.   3. I'm not sure that they will return this afternoon.

2.   No parece ⎫   ⎧ vaya a llover.
        Parece posible ⎬ que ⎨ haya tormenta esta noche.
        Parece probable ⎭   ⎩ haga mal tiempo mañana.

Answer. 1. ¿Cree usted que lloverá esta tarde?   2. ¿Dice el periódico que habrá tormenta?   3. ¿Creen que hará mal tiempo mañana?

Translate. 1. It seems likely (probable) that it's going to rain.   2. It seems possible that the weather will be bad tomorrow.   3. It doesn't seem that there will be a storm tonight.

3.   Es dudoso ⎫   ⎧ lleguen a un acuerdo.
        Es posible ⎬ que ⎨ mejore la situación.
        Es probable ⎭   ⎩ haya otra huelga.

Answer. 1. ¿Llegarán a un acuerdo?   2. ¿Le parece que va a mejorar la situación?   3. ¿Habrá otra huelga?

Translate. 1. It's possible that they will reach an agreement.   2. It's probable that the situation will get better. 3. It's doubtful that there will be another strike.

B. Drill Exercises.

1. *Give the first person singular present subjunctive of each verb. (Example:* tomar — tome.) 1. dejar. 2. tratar. 3. matar. 4. quedar. 5. mejorar.

2. *Give the first person singular present subjunctive of each verb. (Example:* comer — coma.) 1. leer. 2. deber. 3. vivir. 4. abrir. 5. subir.

3. *Change to the corresponding form of the present subjunctive. (Example:* tengo — tenga.) 1. sigo. 2. vuelvo. 3. me despido. 4. salgo. 5. conozco.

4. *Express doubt concerning each idea, by using* **No creo que** *followed by the subjunctive. (Example:* Vienen aquí. — No creo que vengan aquí.) 1. Salen temprano. 2. Tienen que trabajar. 3. Vuelven esta tarde. 4. Deben hacerlo. 5. Pueden acompañarnos.

5. *Express uncertainty concerning each idea, by using* **Es posible que** *followed by the subjunctive. (Example:* Suben los precios. — Es posible que suban los precios.) 1. Mejora la situación. 2. Llegan a un acuerdo. 3. Encuentran una solución. 4. Llueve esta noche. 5. Tenemos mejores noticias.

C. Questions. 1. ¿Ha leído usted el diario de hoy? 2. ¿Hay noticias interesantes? 3. ¿Cuándo hará mejor tiempo? 4. ¿Es posible que haya tormenta esta noche? 5. ¿Le parece probable que llueva mañana? 6. ¿Qué dicen del conflicto entre los obreros y la dirección de la fábrica? 7. ¿Creen que habrá otra huelga? 8. ¿Es posible que mejore la situación? 9. ¿Cuándo cree usted que encontrarán una solución? 10. ¿Le parece dudoso que lleguen a un acuerdo esta semana? 11. ¿Ha mejorado la situación internacional? 12. ¿Cuándo llegarán a un acuerdo los partidos

políticos?   13. ¿Cuántos choques de automóviles hubo ayer?
14. ¿Cuántos pasajeros murieron?   15. ¿Hubo ayer más
nacimentos que muertes?   16. ¿Qué crímenes hubo anoche?
17. ¿Por qué mató una mujer a su marido?   18. ¿Quiénes
van a casarse?   19. ¿Qué otras noticias hay en el periódico
de hoy?   20. ¿Qué noticias le interesan a usted?

D. TRANSLATION.   1. I have just glanced at today's
newspaper.   2. I'm not interested in the crimes or (nor)
the accidents.   3. I'm more interested in the political news.
4. It seems that the international situation hasn't improved.
5. It is doubtful that they will find a solution this week.
6. The political parties still haven't reached an agreement.
7. It's quite likely that prices will continue to go up.   8. It
is possible that there will be another strike next week.
9. The factory management denies that there is a new disagreement.   10. To me it seems doubtful that they will
reach an agreement tomorrow.   11. Last night there was a
rather serious car wreck.   12. Two passengers died this
morning.   13. They suspect that the accident was because
of speeding.   14. It is possible that it will rain tomorrow.
15. I doubt that there will be a storm tonight.   16. My
favorite actor is getting married next week.   17. Is he
marrying a blonde or a brunette?   18. This time he is marrying a redhead.   19. I like to read the paper every day.
20. Of course the news is always the same.

E. CONVERSATION AND COMPOSITION.   Topic: The
news.

PRESENT SUBJUNCTIVE

(List of Irregularities for Lessons 1–21)

RADICAL CHANGES		ORTHOGRAPHIC CHANGES	
-ar and -er verbs	-ir verbs	-ar verbs	-er and -ir verbs
stressed $\begin{cases} o > ue \\ e > ie \end{cases}$	*stressed* $\begin{cases} o > ue \\ e > ie \\ e > i \end{cases}$ *unstressed* $\begin{cases} o > u \\ e > i \end{cases}$	$c > qu$ $g > gu$ $z > c$ $gu > gü$	$qu > c$ $gu > g$ $c > z$ $g > j$
OTHER IRREGULARITIES (Same stem throughout the present subjunctive.)			

acostarse (ue)
almorzar (ue; c)
buscar (qu)
coger (j)
conocer: **conozca**
construir: **construya**
contener: **contenga**
costar (ue)
dar: **dé**
decir: **diga**
despedirse (i)
divertirse (ie, i)
dormir (ue, u)
empezar (ie; c)
encontrar (ue)
entender (ie)
cstar: **esté**
haber: **haya**

hacer: **haga**
ir: **vaya**
jugar (ue; gu)
llegar (gu)
llover (ue)
merendar (ie)
morir (ue, u)
negar (ie; gu)
nevar (ie)
pagar (gu)
parecer: **parezca**
pensar (ie)
perder (ie)
poder (ue)
poner: **ponga**
preferir (ie, i)
probar (ue)
querer (ie)

recordar (ue)
saber: **sepa**
salir: **salga**
seguir (i; g)
sentar (ie)
sentir (ie, i)
ser: **sea**
servir (i)
soñar (ue)
suponer: **suponga**
tener: **tenga**
tocar (qu)
valer: **valga**
venir: **venga**
ver: **vea**
volver (ue)

22 Una carta

15 de mayo

Querido Felipe:

Con gusto recibí su última carta. Sólo siento que
José haya tenido ese resfriado, y me alegro de que esté
mejor ahora. Es una lástima que eso les haya impedido 5
venir a pasar el fin de semana con nosotros. Mi señora
y yo esperamos que lo podrán hacer la semana que
viene. Tendremos mucho gusto en verlos.

De aquí hay poco nuevo que contarle. El lunes
próximo es preciso que vaya a entrevistarme con el 10
gerente a propósito de esa colocación de que ya le escribí
a usted. Parece que todo va bien.

Cariñosos recuerdos míos y de mi señora a toda la
familia, y un saludo muy cordial de su afmo. amigo,

Ramón Villanueva 15

(Elena y Felipe.)

ELENA. ¿Qué noticias trae la carta de don Ramón?
FELIPE. Muy pocas. Tan sólo unas líneas para repetir
su invitación. ¿Quieres leerla?
ELENA. Sí, ¡cómo no! Quiero ver lo que dice... ¡Ah! 20
Me alegro de que vaya progresando lo del nuevo empleo. ¡Ojalá lo consiga!... ¿Qué vas a contestarle a
propósito del viaje?
FELIPE. Temo que tampoco podamos hacerlo este fin
de semana. No hay tiempo para nada. 25

VOCABULARY

afmo. *(abbrev. of* **afectísimo**), **-a** affectionate, devoted; **su afmo. amigo** sincerely yours

alegrarse de que to be glad that

cariñoso, -a affectionate

la **carta** letter

la **colocación** position, job

¡cómo no! sure!, of course!

conseguir (i; g) to get, to secure, to obtain

contar (ue) to tell, to relate

contestar to answer

cordial cordial

de about

el **empleo** job, position

entrevistarse to have an interview

escribir to write

esperar to hope

el **gerente** manager

impedir (i) to prevent; **que eso les haya impedido venir** that that has prevented your coming

la **invitación** invitation

la **lástima** pity; **es (una) lástima que** it's a pity that

la **línea** line

¡ojalá! I hope (so)!; **¡ojalá lo consiga!** I hope he gets it!

preciso, -a necessary; **es preciso que vaya** it is necessary that I go, it is necessary for me to go

progresar to progress

el **propósito** purpose; **a propósito de** apropos of

próximo, -a next

querido, -a dear

Ramón Raymond

recibir to receive; **con gusto recibí** I was delighted to receive

repetir (i) to repeat

tan sólo only, just, merely

temer to fear

traer to bring; **¿qué noticias trae...?** what's the news in...?

GRAMMATICAL EXPLANATIONS

1. Uses of the Subjunctive: Emotion, Volition, or Necessity. In Spanish the subjunctive is used in clauses which are dependent on expressions of emotion (fear, joy, sorrow, etc.), volition (wish, request, preference, etc.), or necessity.

Siento que **haya tenido** un resfriado.
I'm sorry that he has had a cold.

Me alegro de que **esté** mejor.
I'm glad that he is better.

Quieren que **leamos** la carta.
They want us to read the letter.

Será preciso que **hagamos** el viaje.
It will be necessary for us to make the trip.

Listed below are some common expressions which usually imply emotion, volition, or necessity. They are normally followed by the subjunctive.

EMOTION

alegrarse de que, *to be glad that*
esperar que, *to hope that*
sentir que, *to regret that, to be sorry that*
ser (una) lástima que, *to be a pity that*
temer que, *to fear that, to be afraid that*

VOLITION

decir que, *to tell (= to request that)*
pedir que, *to ask* (or *request*) *that*
permitir que, *to permit (that)*
preferir que, *to prefer that*
querer que, *to want (= to wish that)*

NECESSITY
ser preciso que, *to be necessary that*

The word **esperar,** *to hope,* may be followed by either the indicative or the subjunctive, depending on whether the idea of "belief" or the idea of "wish" is stressed.

2. Subjunctive and Infinitive Constructions. As a rule, the infinitive is used in Spanish after verbs of emotion or volition when the subject of the dependent verb is the same as that of the main verb; the subjunctive is used when the subject is different.

Quiero **leer** la carta.
I want to read the letter.

Siento **haberlo dicho.**
I am sorry to have said it. Or: *I am sorry that I said it.*

Prefiero **que usted lo haga.**
I prefer that you do it. Or: *I prefer you to do it.*

Me pide **que vaya con él.**
He requests that I go with him. Or: *He asks me to go with him.*

Les digo **que nos escriban.**
I'm telling them to write to us.

(*a*) An infinitive construction may be used with certain verbs of volition (permission, causation, or command) when they have a pronoun as indirect object.

Me permiten **ir** con ellos. `}`
Permiten **que vaya con ellos.** `}`
They permit me to go with them.

(b) The infinitive construction is used with impersonal expressions when the dependent verb has no subject or when the subject is indicated by the use of an object pronoun.

Es preciso **hacerlo.**	*It is necessary to do it.*
Me es preciso **hacerlo.**	*It is necessary for me to do it.*
Es preciso **que lo haga.**	Or: *It is necessary that I do it.*

(c) Either construction is possible with verbs expressing doubt or disbelief when the subject of both verbs is the same.

No creo **conocerlos.**	*I don't believe that I know them.*
No creo **que los conozca.**	

3. Verbs.

(a) **Regular:** alegrarse, contestar, entrevistarse, esperar, permitir, progresar, recibir, temer.

(b) **Radical-Changing:** contar (ue), impedir (i), pedir (i), repetir (i).

(c) **Radical- and Orthographic-Changing:** conseguir (i; g).

(d) **Other Verbs.**

Escribir, *to write,* has an irregular past participle: **escrito.**

Traer, *to bring,* has an irregular stem in the first person singular present indicative **(traigo)** and throughout the present subjunctive **(traiga, traigas,** etc.). The preterite also has an irregular stem **(traje, trajiste, trajo, trajimos, trajisteis, trajeron).** The participles have orthographic changes **(trayendo, traído).**

EXERCISES

A. STRUCTURE PRACTICE.

1.   Espero   }   { me conteste esta semana.
         Prefiero   } que   { sea la semana que viene.
         Me alegraré de }   { se quede una semana.

Answer. 1. ¿Le contestó don Ramón? 2. ¿Cuándo vendrá a vernos? 3. ¿Piensa quedarse aquí una semana?

Translate. 1. I prefer that he answer me this week.   2. I hope that he will stay a week.   3. I'll be glad that it's next week.

2.   Siento   ⎞   ⎛   no haya llegado.
        Es una lástima   ⎬   que   ⎨   lo haya tenido.
        Temo   ⎠   ⎩   no pueda hacerlo.

Answer. 1. ¿No ha llegado Eduardo?   2. Ha tenido otro resfriado, ¿verdad?   3. ¿Cree usted que podrá acompañarnos mañana?

Translate. 1. I'm afraid that he hasn't arrived.   2. I'm sorry that he has had it.   3. It's a pity that he can't do it.

3.   Nos pide   ⎞   ⎛   le escribamos.
        Es preciso   ⎬   que   ⎨   lo hagamos.
        Nos dice   ⎠   ⎩   vayamos mañana.

Answer. 1. ¿Qué dice la carta de su padre?   2. ¿Harán ustedes el viaje?   3. ¿Cuándo saldrán?

Translate. 1. It's necessary that we go tomorrow.   2. He asks us to do it.   3. He tells us to write to him.

B. Drill Exercises.

1. *Express a feeling of regret concerning each idea, by using **Siento que** followed by the subjunctive. (Example:* No nos han escrito. — Siento que no nos hayan escrito.) 1. No han hecho el viaje.   2. Ha perdido la carta.   3. No ha conseguido la colocación.   4. Ha tenido un resfriado. 5. Eso les ha impedido venir a vernos.

2. *Express a feeling of necessity concerning each dependent idea, by using **Es preciso que** with it. (Example:* Pide que vayamos con él. — Es preciso que vayamos con él.) 1. Prefiere que salgamos el sábado.   2. Quiere que nos divirtamos más.   3. Nos dice que estudiemos menos.   4. Espero que volvamos el lunes.   5. Me alegro de que hagamos el viaje.

3. *Change the dependent verb to refer to the first person plural. (Example:* Quiero hacer el trabajo. — Quiero que hagamos el trabajo.) 1. Siento haber llegado tarde.   2. Me alegro de estar aquí.   3. Será preciso volver esta tarde. 4. Temo no poder hacerlo.   5. Será imposible hacer el viaje.

   C. Questions.   1. ¿Qué noticias trae la carta de sus amigos?   2. ¿Qué les ha impedido hacer el viaje?   3. ¿Cuándo será posible que lo hagan?   4. ¿Cuánto tiempo quiere usted que se queden aquí?   5. ¿Cuándo se escribió la carta? 6. ¿Qué dice la carta de sus padres?   7. ¿Por qué piden que les escriba más?   8. ¿Cuántas veces les ha escrito usted este mes?   9. ¿Quién ha tenido un resfriado?   10. ¿Cuándo quieren que vaya usted a casa?   11. ¿Qué noticias trae la carta de don Ramón?   12. ¿Cuándo quieren que vayamos a verlos?   13. ¿Será posible que hagamos el viaje este fin de semana?   14. ¿Va progresando lo del nuevo empleo? 15. ¿Cree usted que lo conseguirá?   16. ¿Con quién será preciso que se entreviste?   17. ¿Cuándo prefiere usted que hagamos el viaje?   18. ¿Cuándo será preciso que volvamos? 19. ¿Por qué no hay tiempo para nada?   20. ¿Qué piensa usted contestarles a propósito del viaje?

   D. Translation.   1. We were delighted to receive your last letter.   2. My wife and I hope that you can come to see us next week.   3. We're sorry that you have had a cold.   4. We hope that you are better now.   5. From here there's little new to tell you.   6. It will be necessary that I go have an interview with the manager.   7. Affectionate greetings from your good friend Raymond.   8. What's the news in your friend's letter?   9. He writes us only a few lines to repeat his invitation.   10. I'm afraid that we can't make the trip this weekend.   11. I have just received a letter from my uncle.   12. He's glad that they bought (have bought) the new car.   13. He hopes that they can come to see us this weekend.   14. They want us to go to the capital with them.   15. I'm not sure that we can do it. 16. It will be necessary that they go on Friday.   17. I'm afraid that we can't leave before Saturday.   18. It will be necessary for us to return Sunday afternoon.   19. It seems that there isn't time for anything.   20. I have to write five letters tonight.

E. CONVERSATION AND COMPOSITION. Topic: Your most recent correspondence.

SUBJUNCTIVE

(Reference List for Lessons 21–22)

IMPERSONAL EXPRESSIONS

(With noun clause as subject)

ojalá *(exclamatory wish)*

no parecer

parecer dudoso (imposible, posible, probable)

ser dudoso (imposible, posible, probable)

ser (una) lástima

ser preciso

PERSONAL EXPRESSIONS

(With noun clause as object)

*alegrarse de

decir *(request)*

dudar

*esperar

impedir

negar

no creer

no estar seguro de

pedir

permitir

*preferir

*querer

*sentir

*temer

* With infinitive, rather than a clause, when the dependent verb has the same subject as the main verb.

23 | Una visita

(Al teléfono. Felipe y Miguel.)

FELIPE. ¡Diga!

MIGUEL. ¡Oiga! Deseo hablar con Felipe Lamar.

FELIPE. Al aparato.

MIGUEL. Aquí, Miguel Gómez. 5

FELIPE. ¡Hola! ¿Qué hay, Miguel? ¿Qué me cuentas?

MIGUEL. Dime, ¿estás ocupado ahora?

FELIPE. Al contrario. Estoy completamente libre.

MIGUEL. Pues mira... Quiero presentarte a mi primo
Luis, que acaba de llegar de Méjico. Si no tienes 10
inconveniente, iremos a tu casa ahora mismo.

FELIPE. Encantado. Tendré mucho gusto en verlos.

MIGUEL. Entonces, hasta pronto.

FELIPE. Adiós. Hasta luego.

(Más tarde. Miguel, Felipe y Luis.) 15

MIGUEL. ¿Se puede?

FELIPE. Adelante. Pasen ustedes.

MIGUEL. Felipe, permíteme que te presente a mi primo
Luis García... Mi buen amigo Felipe Lamar.

FELIPE. Tanto gusto en conocerle a usted. 20

LUIS. El gusto es mío. Me tiene a sus órdenes.

FELIPE. Siéntense, por favor. ¿Qué tal el viaje?

LUIS. Bien. Lo hice en avión. Es cosa de unas horas.
En tren o en automóvil sería otra cosa.

FELIPE. ¡Oh! Ya lo sé. Una vez lo hice en automóvil. 25

VOCABULARY

adelante forward; come in

el aparato (telephone) apparatus; **al aparato** this is... (speaking)

aquí... this is...(calling)

el avión plane, airplane; **en avión** by plane

completamente completely

contrario, -a contrary; **al contrario** on the contrary

cosa: es cosa de it's a matter of; **sería otra cosa** it would be quite different

desear to desire, to wish

¡diga! say!, tell me!; hello! *(answering the telephone)*

dime tell me *(familiar)*

el inconveniente difficulty, objection; **si no tienes inconveniente** if it's all right (with you)

libre free

Luis Louis

mira look *(familiar)*

mismo *adv.* even, right; **ahora mismo** right now

¡oh! oh!

oír to hear, to listen; **¡oiga!** listen!; hello! *(calling on the telephone)*

la orden order, command; **a sus órdenes** at your service

pasar to pass, to come *or* go in; **pasen ustedes** come in

permíteme permit me *(familiar)*

por favor please

presentar to present, to introduce

pronto soon; **hasta pronto** see you soon

¿qué hay (de nuevo)? what's new?

¿qué me cuentas? what do you say?

sentarse (ie) to sit down; **siéntense (ustedes)** sit down, be seated

¿se puede? may we come in?

tarde late; **más tarde** later

el teléfono telephone; **al teléfono** on the telephone

una vez once

GRAMMATICAL EXPLANATIONS

1. Imperative and Related Forms. In Spanish there are second-person "imperative" forms (corresponding to **tú** and **vosotros**) which are used in familiar affirmative commands. For other wishes, requests, or commands (including negative forms for **tú** and **vosotros**), the present subjunctive is used.

Di (tú) lo que piensas.	*Say what you think.* (Familiar)
No digas (tú) lo que piensas.	*Don't say what you think.*
Diga usted lo que piensa.	*Say what you think.* (Polite)
Digamos lo que pensamos.	*Let's say what we think.*

(*a*) The verb **ir,** *to go,* has a special form, **vamos,** *let's go,* which replaces **vayamos** in affirmative wishes.

(*b*) The phrase **vamos a** (+ the infinitive), *let's* (do something), is often used to emphasize immediate action. Compare:

Volvamos a las tres.	*Let's return at three.*
Vamos a ver lo que dicen.	*Let's see what they say.*

(*c*) The word **que,** *that,* is used with the forms corresponding to **yo, él, ella, ellos,** or **ellas,** and occasionally, for emphasis, with the other forms (implying a governing verb of volition). After **que** the familiar forms require the subjunctive.

Que lo haga José.	*Let* (or *Have*) *Joseph do it.*
Que lo hagas tú.	*You do it.*

2. Object Pronouns with the Imperative and Related Forms. Object pronouns follow the verb, and are attached to it, in the imperative and related forms, except after **no** or **que.**

Dígamelo (usted).	*Tell me.*
No me lo diga (usted).	*Don't tell me.*
Que me lo digan ellos.	*Let them* (or *May they*) *tell me.*

When the reflexive object pronouns **nos** or **os** are attached to the verb, the final consonant of the verb is lost.

Sentémo**nos.**	(= Sentemos + **nos**)	*Let's sit down.*
Senta**os.**	(= Sentad + **os**)	*Sit down.*

The only exception is **idos,** *leave, go away* (from **irse**).

3. Verbs.

(*a*) **Regular:** desear, pasar, presentar.

(*b*) **Radical-Changing:** sentarse (ie).

(*c*) **Irregular. Oír,** *to hear,* has orthographic changes in the endings of the preterite and the participles (stressed **i** > **í,** unstressed **i** > **y**). The present tenses are irregular.

PRESENT INDICATIVE		PRESENT SUBJUNCTIVE	
oigo	oímos	oiga	oigamos
oyes	oís	oigas	oigáis
oye	oyen	oiga	oigan

4. Familiar Affirmative Imperative of Regular Verbs.
The familiar affirmative imperative (corresponding to **tú** and **vosotros**) can usually be formed as follows: remove the ending of the infinitive (**-ar, -er, -ir**); add the endings of the imperative.

-ar VERBS	-er VERBS	-ir VERBS
tom-ar	com-er	viv-ir
toma tomad	come comed	vive vivid

5. Familiar Affirmative Imperative of Irregular Verbs.
The plural form is never irregular. The singular form has the same irregularities as the third person singular present indicative, with the following exceptions.

decir: **di**	poner: **pon**	tener: **ten**
hacer: **haz**	salir: **sal**	valer: **val**
ir: **ve**	ser: **sé**	venir: **ven**

EXERCISES

A. STRUCTURE PRACTICE.

1. Dile ⎱
   No le digas ⎰ que ⎰ ha llegado mi primo.
   Díganle ⎰   ⎰ estamos ocupados.
                        iremos a su casa.

Answer. 1. ¿Qué quieres que le diga a Felipe? 2. Ustedes están ocupados, ¿verdad? 3. ¿Debemos decirle que venga a vernos?

Translate. 1. Don't tell him that we are busy. 2. Tell him that my cousin has arrived. 3. Tell him that we will go to his house.

2. No se lo digas ⎱
   Díselo ⎰ ahora.
   Díganselo ⎰ esta tarde.
                     mañana.

Answer. 1. ¿Quieres que le diga a Elena lo que pasó?
2. ¿Cuándo debo decírselo? 3. ¿Cuándo se lo decimos a Isabel?

Translate. 1. Tell her now. 2. Don't tell her this afternoon. 3. Tell her tomorrow.

3.
Que $\left\{\begin{array}{l} \text{pasen} \\ \text{suban} \\ \text{me llamen} \end{array}\right\}$ si $\left\{\begin{array}{l} \text{tienen el tiempo.} \\ \text{no tienen inconveniente.} \\ \text{están libres.} \end{array}\right.$

Answer. 1. ¿Quiere usted que pasen a la sala? 2. ¿Les digo que suban? 3. ¿Deben llamarle esta noche?

Translate. 1. Have them come in if they are free. 2. Have them come upstairs if they have the time. 3. Have them call me if it's all right with them.

B. Drill Exercises.

1. *Give the familiar singular imperative form for each verb. (Example:* tomar — toma.) 1. dejar. 2. pagar. 3. buscar. 4. llamar. 5. preguntar.

2. *Give the negative for each imperative form. (Example:* di — no digas.) 1. haz. 2. pon. 3. sal. 4. ten. 5. ven.

3. *Change to the negative. (Example:* Hágalo. — No lo haga.) 1. Léalo. 2. Siéntese. 3. Póngaselo. 4. Llámelos. 5. Dígamelo.

4. *Express with* **Quiero** *as a governing verb of volition. (Example:* Que me llamen. — Quiero que me llamen.) 1. Que lo hagan. 2. Que pasen. 3. Que suban. 4. Que se sienten. 5. Que se diviertan.

5. *Emphasize immediate action, by using* **vamos a** + *the infinitive. (Example:* Salgamos. — Vamos a salir.) 1. Volvamos. 2. Sentémonos. 3. Comamos. 4. Cantemos. 5. Empecemos.

C. Questions. 1. ¿Cómo se llama el primo de Miguel? 2. ¿De dónde acaba de llegar? 3. ¿Es español o mejicano?

4. ¿Qué tal fué el viaje?   5. ¿Cómo sería el viaje en automóvil?   6. ¿Quién acaba de llamarle (llamarla) por teléfono?   7. ¿Qué hacía usted cuando le (la) llamó?   8. ¿A qué hora estará usted en casa esta tarde?   9. ¿Qué piensan ustedes hacer esta noche?   10. ¿A qué hora irán sus amigos a buscarlos?   11. ¿Qué monumentos debemos visitar esta tarde?   12.   ¿Prefiere usted ir en coche o en autobús? 13. ¿Adónde vamos primero?   14. ¿Cuándo quiere usted que llamemos a Miguel?   15. ¿Con quién acaba usted de hablar?   16. ¿Qué viajes largos ha hecho usted en automóvil?   17. ¿Cuántos viajes ha hecho usted en avión? 18. ¿Prefiere usted viajar en coche o en tren?   19. ¿Cómo preferiría usted ir a Méjico?   20. ¿Qué viajes largos le gustaría hacer?

D. TRANSLATION.   1. (At the telephone:) Hello.— Hello.   2. I wish to speak with Joseph.   3. This is he (speaking.)—This is Paul (calling).   4. What's new? What do you say?   5. Tell Edward that we'll be able to go on the excursion.   6. Tell him that we can leave at three. 7. Don't tell him that we are busy.   8. Let him think that we have nothing to do.   9. Call him right now if you can. 10. If it's all right, I'll stop by (go to) your house this afternoon.   11. May I come in?   12. Come in. Please sit down. 13. May I present my friend Luis García?   14. It's a pleasure to know you.   15. The pleasure is mine.   16. We are intending to visit Mexico this summer.   17. The trip by plane is a matter of a few hours.   18. By train or by car it is a long trip.   19. We prefer to go by car.   20. Everybody says it's a very beautiful country.

E. CONVERSATION AND COMPOSITION. Topic: A recent visit.

24 Literatura

Alguien ha dicho que los libros son como buenos amigos. Y yo casi diría que no hay ningún amigo que sea más fiel y constante que un buen libro. Cuando me siento aburrido, me gusta coger alguna novela, o alguna colección de cuentos o de poesías, sentarme en un có- 5 modo sillón, y perderme en ese mundo de ideas e imaginación al que nos invitan los buenos libros. Y aunque no se trate de una obra maestra, como dice el dicho antiguo, no hay libro tan malo que no tenga algo bueno.

(Felipe, José y Elena.) 10

FELIPE. ¿Por qué no vamos a ver esa comedia que ponen la semana que viene?

JOSÉ. Podemos ir a la función de la tarde para que nos cueste menos, ¿verdad?

ELENA. Aunque cueste un poco más, yo prefiero ir por 15 la noche.

FELIPE. Aquí tengo la lista de precios. El jueves por la noche hay localidades baratas.

ELENA. ¿Son butacas?

FELIPE. No, son asientos de galería. Pero desde la ga- 20 lería se ve y se oye bastante bien.

JOSÉ. Casi mejor que desde las butacas.

ELENA. Bueno, como queráis...aunque la galería no es muy elegante, que digamos.

FELIPE. Pero es barata. Sacaré los billetes esta tarde. 25

VOCABULARY

aburrido, -a bored
alguien someone, somebody
el asiento seat; asiento de galería balcony seat, seat in the top balcony
la butaca armchair; orchestra seat (theatre)
constante constant, loyal
el cuento story
desde from
el dicho saying, proverbial expression
digamos: que digamos (after a negative statement) let's say, we might say
el que which; al que to which
fiel faithful, trustworthy
la función show, performance; función de la tarde afternoon performance, matinee
la galería (top) balcony
la idea idea

la imaginación imagination
la literatura literature
la localidad seat, ticket
el mundo world
ningún, ninguno, -a no, none, not...any; no hay ningún amigo que sea there is no friend who is
la novela novel
la obra work; obra maestra masterpiece
para que so that, in order that; para que nos cueste so that it will cost us, in order that it may cost us
la poesía poetry; poem; pl. poems, poetry
poner to put on (a play)
sacar (qu) to take out; to get (tickets)
sentirse (ie, i) to feel (used before adjectives)
el sillón (large) armchair, easy chair

GRAMMATICAL EXPLANATIONS

1. Subjunctive in Adjective Clauses. The subjunctive is used in clauses that have indefinite or negative antecedents.

Quiero billetes que **cuesten** menos.	I want some tickets that will cost less. (Indefinite)
No hay billetes que **cuesten** menos.	There aren't any tickets that cost less. (Negative)

The indicative is used if the antecedent is definite. Compare:

¿Hay otros libros que le **gusten** más?	Are there other books that you like better?
Hay varios que me **gustan** más.	There are several that I like better.

2. Subjunctive in Adverbial Clauses.

(a) **Purpose.** The subjunctive is used in all clauses that express purpose. Note, however, that an infinitive, rather than a clause, is used if there is no change of subject.

Iremos por la tarde para que nos **cueste** menos.	*We'll go in the afternoon so that it will cost us less.*
Tomaremos butacas para **ver** mejor.	*We'll take orchestra seats so that we can see better* (or *in order to see better*).

(b) **Concession.** The subjunctive is used in clauses that express a concession based on a supposition. The indicative is used if the concession refers to a known fact. Compare:

Vamos esta noche aunque **cueste** más.	*We're going tonight even if it costs* (= *may cost*) *more.*
Vamos esta noche aunque **cuesta** más.	*We're going tonight although it costs* (= *does cost*) *more.*

(c) **Future Time Clauses.** The subjunctive is used in time clauses that refer to the future. The indicative is used when the reference is to actual events, in present or past time. Compare:

Iremos a ver la comedia cuando **tengamos** el tiempo.	*We'll go see the play when we have the time.*
Nos gusta ir al teatro cuando **tenemos** el tiempo.	*We like to go to the theatre when we have the time.*

Listed below are some common words and phrases that introduce time clauses.

antes de que (or **antes que**), *before*	**en cuanto,** *as soon as*
cuando, *when*	**hasta que,** *until*
	mientras *while, as long as*

Note that **antes de que,** *before,* because of its meaning, always refers to actions that have not, or had not, taken place at the time referred to, and is always followed by the subjunctive.

3. Verbs.

(a) **Radical-Changing:** sentirse (ie, i).

(b) **Orthographic-Changing:** sacar (qu).

EXERCISES

A. STRUCTURE PRACTICE.

1. No tengo ⎫
    No conozco ⎬ ningún libro que ⎧ me guste más.
    No hay ⎭ ⎨ sea más divertido.
    ⎩ se lea más ahora.

Answer. 1. ¿Le gusta ese libro? 2. ¿No prefiere un libro más divertido? 3. El libro es muy conocido, ¿verdad?

Translate. 1. There isn't any book that I like better. 2. I don't know any book that is being read more now. 3. I don't have any book that is more amusing.

2. Iré ⎫
    Las haré ⎬ cuando ⎧ tenga el tiempo.
    Los sacaré ⎭ ⎨ vaya al centro.
    ⎩ termine esta novela.

Answer. 1. ¿No va usted al cine? 2. ¿Pensaba usted hacer unas compras? 3. ¿Cuándo sacará los billetes?

Translate. 1. I'll go when I finish this novel. 2. I'll get them when I go downtown. 3. I'll make them when I have the time.

3. La veremos ⎫
    Iremos ⎬ aunque ⎧ cueste mucho.
    Lo haremos ⎭ ⎨ haga mal tiempo.
    ⎩ tengamos poco tiempo.

Answer. 1. ¿Verán ustedes la comedia si cuesta mucho? 2. ¿Irán al museo si hace mal tiempo? 3. ¿Tendrán tiempo para hacer el viaje?

Translate. 1. We'll go even if it costs a lot. 2. We'll see it even if we have little time. 3. We'll make it even if the weather is bad.

B. DRILL EXERCISES.

1. *Change the main clause to the negative and the dependent clause to the subjunctive. (Example:* Hay un libro

que me gusta más. — No hay ningún libro que me guste
más.) 1. Tengo un libro que es mejor. 2. Conozco una
obra que es más interesante. 3. Hay unas poesías que me
parecen mejores.

2. *Change the dependent clause to refer to a supposition,
by using the subjunctive.* (*Example:* No irá aunque puede.
— No irá aunque pueda.) 1. No sacará las localidades aunque va al centro. 2. Van por la noche aunque cuesta más.
3. Les gustará la comedia aunque es mala.

3. *Change the dependent verb to refer to the first person
plural.* (*Example:* Tomaré butacas para ver mejor. — Tomaré butacas para que veamos mejor.) 1. Quiero buenos
asientos para ver mejor. 2. Miro el periódico para saber
los precios. 3. Volveré temprano para tener más tiempo.
4. Cenaré a las seis para poder salir a las siete. 5. Prefiero
tomar un taxi para llegar antes de las ocho.

4. *Change the main verb to the future and the dependent verb to the present subjunctive.* (*Example:* Voy al teatro cuando tengo tiempo. — Iré al teatro cuando tenga
tiempo.) 1. Los veo cuando voy a la biblioteca. 2. Leo
buenos libros cuando me siento aburrido. 3. Doy un paseo
en cuanto termino mi trabajo. 4. Hago unas compras
cuando voy al centro. 5. Me quedo en el centro hasta que
llegan mis hermanos.

C. QUESTIONS. 1. ¿Qué comedia ponen le semana que
viene? 2. ¿Por qué no vamos nosotros? 3. ¿Qué día será
mejor? 4. ¿Qué tal le parece el viernes? 5. ¿Será mejor ir
el sábado para que Eduardo pueda acompañarnos? 6. ¿Por
qué quiere José que vayamos por la tarde? 7. ¿Quién prefiere ir por la noche? 8. ¿Cuándo prefiere usted que vayamos? 9. ¿Cuáles son los mejores asientos? 10. ¿Prefiere
usted que tomemos butacas aunque cuesten mucho más?

11. ¿Quién podrá sacar las localidades? 12. ¿Cuándo podrá sacarlas? 13. ¿Se quedarán ustedes en el centro hasta que lleguemos? 14. ¿Qué restaurán hay cerca del teatro donde podamos cenar? 15. ¿Qué haremos cuando termine la función? 16. ¿Qué comedias interesantes ha visto usted este año? 17. ¿Cuál es la mejor novela que usted ha leído? 18. ¿Le gustan los cuentos más que las poesías? 19. ¿Cuál de sus amigos prefiere la poesía? 20. ¿Qué libros le gustaría leer este verano?

D. TRANSLATION. 1. I haven't seen the play that they are putting on this week. 2. I have been told that it is very interesting. 3. We intend to go see it even though we may not have much time. 4. I want to go to the matinee so that it will cost us less. 5. My sister prefers to go to the evening performance. 6. She must not have seen the price list. 7. From the balcony you can see and hear rather well. 8. We will go on Saturday so that Louis can go with us. 9. Louis is the boy who has just arrived from Mexico. 10. He's quite interested in American literature. 11. I'll get the tickets when we go downtown this afternoon. 12. Helen will make several purchases while we are in town. 13. We'll stay downtown until our friends arrive. 14. Near the theatre there is a restaurant where they serve Mexican food. 15. We'll have supper there before going to the theatre. 16. We had read the play that they put on last week. 17. Reading is one of my favorite pastimes. 18. The novel that I have just read is very interesting. 19. I don't know any book that I like better. 20. In our English class we have read several plays, novels, and poems.

E. CONVERSATION AND COMPOSITION. Topic: Literature.

25 | Vacaciones

Apenas puedo esperar a que termine el curso. Los últimos días han sido de mucho ajetreo. Con la perspectiva de los exámenes, ¡vaya si me quemo las cejas! ¡Ojalá termine pronto el suplicio!... Sin embargo, tengo ciertas dudas. El año pasado también deseaba que 5 se terminara cuanto antes. Pensaba que en cuanto quedara libre, sería el más feliz de los mortales. Al principio todo fué bien: visitas, bailes, fiestas, unos días en la playa...pero después, me aburrí soberanamente, y deseaba que comenzara el nuevo curso. 10

(Felipe, José y Elena.)

FELIPE. ¡Qué aburridas son estas tardes de lluvia! Si hiciera mejor tiempo, podríamos dar una vuelta.

JOSÉ. Lo que me gustaría más sería ir otra vez a la playa...si tuviera el dinero. 15

ELENA. Y si papá nos diera permiso.

JOSÉ. Si hay una película buena, podemos ir al cine.

FELIPE. ¡Ah! ¡Se me ocurre una idea! Podríamos ir a la exposición de pinturas modernas.

JOSÉ. ¡Vaya una idea! ¡Como si nosotros quisiéramos 20 ver más pinturas, ni modernas ni antiguas!

FELIPE. Más aburridos estamos aquí en casa.

ELENA. Si hubiera venido Luisa, podríamos jugar al bridge... Y ¿por qué no jugamos al dominó?

FELIPE. ¡Sí! ¡El dominó! Voy a traer las fichas. 25

VOCABULARY

aburrido, -a boring (with ser); bored (with estar)
aburrir to bore; aburrirse to get bored, to be bored
al principio at first
apenas hardly, scarcely
el bridge bridge (game)
la ceja eyebrow
cierto, -a certain, a certain
comenzar (ie; c) to commence, to begin; deseaba que comenzara I wanted (it) to begin
cuanto antes as soon as possible
el curso school year
diera might give; si diera if (he) would give
el dominó dominoes (the game)
esperar a que to wait until
la exposición exhibit
feliz happy
la ficha domino (the piece)
la fiesta festival, party
hiciera: si hiciera mejor tiempo if the weather were better
hubiera: si hubiera venido if (she) had come

la lluvia rain
el mortal mortal
ocurrir to occur; (se) me ocurre una idea an idea occurs to me
otra vez again
la perspectiva prospect
la playa beach
quedara: en cuanto quedara libre as soon as I was (= might be) free
quemar to burn; quemarse las cejas to burn the midnight oil
quisiéramos: como si nosotros quisiéramos as if we wanted
sin embargo nevertheless
soberanamente quite, terribly
el suplicio torture
terminara: deseaba que se terminara I wanted it to end
tuviera: si tuviera if I had
las vacaciones vacation
¡vaya si...! of course...!
la vuelta turn; dar una vuelta to take a little walk

GRAMMATICAL EXPLANATIONS

1. Sequence of Tenses with the Subjunctive. If the main verb is in a *past tense* (preterite, imperfect, past perfect, conditional, or conditional perfect), the dependent verb is also in a *past tense* (past or past perfect).

Deseaba que se **terminara**.   *I wanted it to end.*
Sería imposible que **llegasen** el sábado que viene.   *It would be impossible for them to arrive next Saturday.*

In other respects the time reference of the dependent verb itself determines the tense.

Es posible que **estuviesen** allí.	*It is possible that they were there.*
Le he pedido que **vaya** conmigo.	*I have asked him to go with me.*
No creía que mi hermano lo **hubiese hecho.**	*I didn't believe that my brother had done it.*

2. **Subjunctive in Unreal *If*-clauses.** The past or past perfect subjunctive is used in *if*-clauses that are contrary to fact or contrary to expectations.

Si **hiciera** mejor tiempo, daríamos un paseo.	*If the weather were better, we would take a walk.*
Si **viniera** Luisa, podríamos jugar al bridge.	*If Louise should come, we could play bridge.*
Habrían ido al museo si no **hubiese llovido.**	*They would have gone to the museum if it hadn't rained.*
¡Como si ellos **quisieran** ver más pinturas!	*As if they wanted to see any more paintings!*

(*a*) The indicative is used in simple *if*-clauses (those not contrary to fact or contrary to expectations).

Si María **ha llegado,** dígale que quiero verla.	*If Mary has arrived, tell her that I want to see her.*
Iremos al cine si **hay** una película buena.	*We'll go to the movies if there is a good picture.*
Si **hacía** mal tiempo, ¿por qué fueron ustedes a la playa?	*If the weather was bad, why did you go to the beach?*

(*b*) The indicative is also used after **si** meaning *whether* (which introduces an indirect question).

No sé si **podrán** hacer el viaje con nosotros.	*I don't know whether they can take the trip with us.*
Pregúnteles si **pueden** hacerlo.	*Ask them whether they can do it.*

3. **Verbs.**

(*a*) **Regular:** aburrirse, ocurrir, quemar.

(*b*) **Radical- and Orthographic-Changing:** comenzar (ie; c).

4. Past Subjunctive of Regular Verbs. The past subjunctive can usually be formed as follows: remove the ending of the infinitive (**-ar, -er, -ir**); add either set of past subjunctive endings. As a rule, the **-ra** and the **-se** forms may be used interchangeably.

-ar VERBS		-er OR -ir VERBS	
tom-ar		**com-er**	

(-ra Form)

tomara	tomáramos	comiera	comiéramos
tomaras	tomarais	comieras	comierais
tomara	tomaran	comiera	comieran

(-se Form)

tomase	tomásemos	comiese	comiésemos
tomases	tomaseis	comieses	comieseis
tomase	tomasen	comiese	comiesen

5. Past Subjunctive of Irregular Verbs. The irregularities are always the same as those of the third-person plural preterite. Examples:

INFINITIVE	3RD PLUR. PRET.	PAST SUBJUNCTIVE
dormir	durmieron	durmiera *or* durmiese, *etc.*
haber	hubieron	hubiera *or* hubiese, *etc.*
ir	fueron	fuera *or* fuese, *etc.*
tener	tuvieron	tuviera *or* tuviese, *etc.*

EXERCISES

A. STRUCTURE PRACTICE.

1. Iré al cine ⎫   ⎧ tengo el tiempo.
Lo haré con gusto ⎬ si ⎨ usted puede ir conmigo.
Iré a la exposición ⎭   ⎩ no tengo que estudiar.

Answer. 1. ¿Adónde va usted esta tarde? 2. ¿No quiere usted dar una vuelta? 3. ¿Piensa usted ir a la exposición?

Translate. 1. I'll go to the exhibit if I have the time. 2. I'll gladly do it if I don't have to study. 3. I'll go to the movies if you can go with me.

2.   Iría a la playa   }   {   tuviese el tiempo.
         Lo haría   }   si   {   usted pudiese ir conmigo.
         Lo visitaría   }   {   no tuviese que estudiar.

Answer. 1. ¿Le gustaría ir a la playa?   2. ¿No hace usted el viaje?   3. ¿Por qué no visita usted el museo?

Translate.   1. I would go to the beach if you could go with me.   2. I would do it if I didn't have to study.   3. I would visit it if I had the time.

3.   Deseaba   }   {   se terminara.
         Esperaba a   }   que {   llegaran las vacaciones.
         Me alegraba de   }   {   quedáramos libres.

Answer. 1. ¿Siente usted que haya terminado el curso? 2. ¿Por qué lo deseaba?   3. ¿Se alegraba de no tener que estudiar?

Translate.   1. I was waiting for us to be free.   2. I was glad that it was ending.   3. I wanted the vacation to come.

B. DRILL EXERCISES.

1. *Give the first person singular past subjunctive. (Example:* tomar — tomara *or* tomase.) 1. sacar.   2. pasar. 3. contar.   4. llegar.   5. comenzar.

2. *Give the corresponding form of the past subjunctive. (Example:* oyeron — oyeran *or* oyesen.) 1. creyeron.   2. dijeron.   3. pudieron.   4. supieron.   5. tuvieron.

3. *Express a feeling of doubt concerning each idea, by using* **Es dudoso que** *followed by the subjunctive. (Example:* Leyeron el libro. — Es dudoso que leyeran el libro.) 1. Dieron una vuelta.   2. Fueron a la exposición.   3. Escucharon la radio.   4. Se divirtieron mucho.   5. Volvieron a la playa.

4. *Change both verbs to refer to the past. (Example:* Quieren que vayamos a su casa. — Querían que fuéramos a su casa.) 1. Dudo que puedan ir al baile. 2. Deseo que se termine el curso. 3. Esperamos a que lleguen las vacaciones. 4. Es posible que pasemos unos días en la playa. 5. Es una lástima que no tengamos nada que hacer.

5. *Change to simple* if-*clauses referring to the future. (Example:* Darían un paseo si hiciera buen tiempo. — Darán un paseo si hace buen tiempo.) 1. Jugarían al bridge si viniera Luisa. 2. Mirarían la televisión si los programas fueran buenos. 3. Irían al cine si hubiera una película buena. 4. Visitarían el museo si quisieran ver más pinturas. 5. Volverían a la playa si tuvieran el dinero.

C. QUESTIONS. 1. ¿Por qué desea usted que termine el curso? 2. ¿Deseaba usted lo mismo el año pasado? 3. ¿Se aburrió usted un poco antes de que comenzara el nuevo curso? 4. ¿Qué diversiones le gustaron más el verano pasado? 5. ¿Cuánto tiempo pasó usted en la playa? 6. ¿Por qué han sido de mucho ajetreo estos últimos días? 7. ¿Qué haría usted ahora si no tuviese que estudiar? 8. ¿Qué le gustaría hacer mañana? 9. ¿Qué haría usted la semana próxima si no tuviese exámenes? 10. ¿A qué hora se levantaría si no tuviese nada que hacer? 11. ¿Por qué estaban ustedes tan aburridos el domingo pasado? 12. ¿Qué habrían hecho si hubiera hecho mejor tiempo? 13. ¿Habrían mirado la televisión si hubiera habido un programa bueno? 14. ¿Por qué no fueron al cine? 15. ¿Por qué no pudo María hacerles una visita? 16. ¿Qué piensa usted hacer el verano que viene? 17. ¿Cuántos libros piensa leer? 18. ¿Sentirá usted que terminen las vacaciones? 19. ¿Sería usted feliz si fuese rico (rica)? 20. ¿Qué haría usted si tuviese un millón de dólares?

D. TRANSLATION. 1. I would study if I weren't tired.
2. I would watch television if there were a good program.
3. We would go to the movies if there were a good picture. 4. We could take a walk if the weather were better.
5. We could play bridge if Elizabeth had come. 6. I asked Edward to go with us to the exhibit. 7. It is a pity that he had to work. 8. He wanted us to go to his house tonight.
9. Did Paul make the trip to the beach? 10. I doubt that he made it. 11. It was necessary for his parents to leave on Thursday. 12. He couldn't leave before Friday. 13. Besides, he would have had to return on Saturday. 14. In the letter I have just received, my parents tell me to study more. 15. As if it were possible for me to study more!
16. These last days I have been very busy. 17. Next week we have our exams. 18. Of course I'm burning the midnight oil! 19. I can hardly wait until the school year is over. 20. I hope the torture will soon end!

E. CONVERSATION AND COMPOSITION. Topic: Vacation plans and memories.

PAST SUBJUNCTIVE

(List of Irregularities for Lessons 1–25)

Alternate forms: { **-ra:** creyera, *etc.*
                  -se: creyese, *etc.*

conseguir (i) : consiguiera
construir (y) : construyera
contener: contuviera
creer (y) : creyera
dar: diera
decir: dijera
despedirse (i) : me despidiera
divertirse (i) : me divirtiera
dormir (u) : durmiera
estar: estuviera
haber: hubiera
hacer: hiciera
impedir (i) : impidiera
ir: fuera
leer (y) : leyera
morir (u) : muriera

oír (y) : oyera
poder: pudiera
poner: pusiera
preferir (i) : prefiriera
querer: quisiera
repetir (i): repitiera
saber: supiera
seguir (i) : siguiera
sentir (i) : sintiera
ser: fuera
servir (i) : sirviera
suponer: supusiera
tener: tuviera
traer: trajera
venir: viniera

LESSONS 21-25

5TH

REVIEW

GRAMMATICAL NOTES——————

(Use the following grammatical notes as a guide for reviewing forms and usage. Then test your knowledge of them by using the corresponding Test Exercises on the opposite page.)

1. Personal Pronouns.

Usage: object pronouns attached to imperative and related forms, except after **no** or **que** (23:2).

2. Verbs.

(a) **New Tenses.**

Familiar affirmative imperative: always regular in the plural form, and with irregularities in the singular form almost always like those of the third person singular present indicative (23:4-5).

Present subjunctive: with stem almost always like that of the first person singular present indicative (21:5-6); used for present or future time (21:3). List on p. 165.

Past subjunctive: with irregularities always the same as those of the third person plural preterite indicative (25:4-5); used when main verb or dependent verb is in the past (25:1), and in *if*-clauses that are contrary to fact or contrary to expectations (25:2). List on p. 193.

(b) **Usage.**

Imperative and subjunctive: present subjunctive used for wishes, requests, or commands, except for familiar affirmative commands (23:1).

Indicative and subjunctive: indicative used to state a fact or ask a question; subjunctive used to reflect an attitude, usually uncertainty or emotion (21:1).

(Continued on page 196)

(Complete the Spanish sentences with the idea indicated. Check your answers by using the corresponding Grammatical Notes on the opposite page.)

1. Personal Pronouns.

1. *(Tell me)* _____ lo que hiciste anoche.
2. *(Have them do it)* _____ mañana si es posible.

2. Verbs.

(a) New Tenses.

1. *(Come)* _____ a vernos si podéis.
2. *(Return)* _____ a tu casa cuando quieras.
3. *(Continue)* _____ leyendo tu carta.
4. *(Hear)* _____ lo que te digo.
5. *(has)* Siento que Juan _____ un resfriado.
6. *(we leave)* Será preciso que _____ el sábado.
7. *(they'll return)* Dudo que _____ esta noche.
8. *(they would go)* No era probable que _____ al museo.
9. *(they were)* Es posible que _____ allí.
10. *(they make)* Era preciso que _____ el viaje.
11. *(would end)* Deseábamos que _____ el curso.
12. *(it should rain)* No iríamos si _____.

(b) Usage.

1. *(Call)* _____ usted a Miguel antes de salir.
2. *(tell)* No le _____ que puedes hacerlo.
3. *(Make)* _____ el viaje en coche si tienes el tiempo.
4. *(we can)* Estoy seguro de que _____ ir con ustedes.
5. *(will arrive)* ¿Cuándo _____ los señores Villanueva?
6. *(it's going to)* No parece que _____ llover.

(Continued on page 197)

GRAMMATICAL NOTES, CONTINUED

Infinitive and subjunctive: infinitive (rather than dependent clause) used with expressions of emotion, volition, or purpose when there is no change of subject (22:2, 24:2).

(c) **Types of Clauses with the Subjunctive.**

Noun clauses: dependent clauses which are subject or object of expressions of uncertainty, doubt, or denial (21:2), or expressions of emotion, volition, or necessity (22:1).

Adjective clauses: dependent clauses which modify an indefinite or negative antecedent (24:1).

Adverbial clauses: dependent clauses which indicate purpose, a concession based on a supposition, or an indefinite future time (24:2), or which express unreal conditions in *if*-clauses that are contrary to fact or contrary to expectations (25:2).

TEST EXERCISES, CONTINUED

7. *(to know)* Siento no _____ a sus amigos.
8. *(to write)* Prefiero _____ la carta ahora.
9. *(hear)* Tomaremos butacas para _____ mejor.

(c) Types of Clauses with the Subjunctive.

1. *(they haven't arrived)* Es una lástima que _____.
2. *(he is staying)* Me alegro de que _____ una semana.
3. *(we go)* Nos pide que _____ con él.
4. *(seems)* ¿Tienen otro libro que les _____ mejor?
5. *(cost)* No hay billetes que _____ menos.
6. *(we'll have)* Cenaré a las seis para que _____ más tiempo.
7. *(it may be)* No les gustará aunque _____ bueno.
8. *(I see)* Se lo diré cuando le _____.
9. *(would want)* ¡Como si nosotros _____ ver esos cuadros!

Appendix

 A. REGULAR

(Conjugation of three model verbs:

INFINITIVE	tomar, *to take*	
PRESENT INDICATIVE (Lesson 7, §3)	tomo tomas toma	tomamos tomáis toman
PRESENT SUBJUNCTIVE (21:5)	tome tomes tome	tomemos toméis tomen
IMPERATIVE (23:4)	toma	tomad
FUTURE INDICATIVE (15:4)	tomaré tomarás tomará	tomaremos tomaréis tomarán
CONDITIONAL (16:6)	tomaría tomarías tomaría	tomaríamos tomaríais tomarían
IMPERFECT INDICATIVE (11:5)	tomaba tomabas tomaba	tomábamos tomabais tomaban
PRETERITE INDICATIVE (10:4)	tomé tomaste tomó	tomamos tomasteis tomaron
PAST SUBJUNCTIVE (25:4) — -ra Form	tomara tomaras tomara	tomáramos tomarais tomaran
PAST SUBJUNCTIVE (25:4) — -se Form	tomase tomases tomase	tomásemos tomaseis tomasen
PRESENT PARTICIPLE (20:5)	tomando	
PAST PARTICIPLE (18:4)	tomado	
PERFECT TENSES (18:2-3)	(Appropriate tenses of haber, *to have* + tomado.)	

an -ar, an -er, and an -ir verb.)

comer, *to eat*		vivir, *to live*	
como	comemos	vivo	vivimos
comes	coméis	vives	vivís
come	comen	vive	viven
coma	comamos	viva	vivamos
comas	comáis	vivas	viváis
coma	coman	viva	vivan
come	comed	vive	vivid
comeré	comeremos	viviré	viviremos
comerás	comeréis	vivirás	viviréis
comerá	comerán	vivirá	vivirán
comería	comeríamos	viviría	viviríamos
comcrías	comeríais	vivirías	viviríais
comería	comerían	viviría	vivirían
comía	comíamos	vivía	vivíamos
comías	comíais	vivías	vivíais
comía	comían	vivía	vivían
comí	comimos	viví	vivimos
comiste	comisteis	viviste	vivisteis
comió	comieron	vivió	vivieron
comiera	comiéramos	viviera	viviéramos
comieras	comierais	vivieras	vivierais
comiera	comieran	viviera	vivieran
comiese	comiésemos	viviese	viviésemos
comieses	comieseis	vivieses	vivieseis
comiese	comiesen	viviese	viviesen
comiendo		viviendo	
comido		vivido	
(Appropriate tenses of **haber,** *to have* + comido.)		(Appropriate tenses of **haber,** *to have* + vivido.)	

B. ORTHOGRAPHIC

(Conjugation of three typical

Type of change	Final consonant of stem (-ar verbs) $c > qu$ $g > gu$ $z > c$ $gu > g\ddot{u}$ } before **e**	
Example	**sacar,** *to take out*	
PRESENT INDICATIVE (Lesson 8, §6)		
PRESENT SUBJUNCTIVE (21:6)	saque saques saque	saquemos saquéis saquen
PRETERITE INDICATIVE (10:5)	saqué sacaste sacó	sacamos sacasteis sacaron
PAST SUBJUNCTIVE (25:5) ⎧ -*ra* Form ⎨ ⎩ -*se* Form		
PRESENT PARTICIPLE (20:6)		
PAST PARTICIPLE (18:5)		

ORTHOGRAPHIC-CHANGING VERBS

*almorzar
buscar
coger
*comenzar

*conseguir
creer
*empezar
*jugar

* For radical changes, see pages 204-205.

verbs with spelling changes.)

Final consonant of stem (-er or -ir verbs)	Initial i of endings (-er or -ir verbs)
qu > c gu > g c > z g > j } before o or a	stressed i > í after a, e, or o; unstressed i > y between vowels
coger, *to catch*	**leer,** *to read*
cojo cogemos coges cogéis coge cogen	
coja cojamos cojas cojáis coja cojan	
	leí leímos leíste leísteis leyó leyeron
	leyera leyéramos leyeras leyerais leyera leyeran
	leyese leyésemos leyeses leyeseis leyese leyesen
	leyendo
	leído

USED IN THIS TEXT

leer	sacar
llegar	*seguir
*negar	tocar
pagar	

Type	I (-ar and -er verbs)	
Change	$o > ue$ $e > ie$ } when stem is stressed	
Example	**contar,** *to tell, to relate*	
PRESENT INDICATIVE (Lesson 7, §4)	**cuento** **cuentas** **cuenta**	contamos contáis cuentan
PRESENT SUBJUNCTIVE (21:6)	**cuente** **cuentes** **cuente**	contemos contéis cuenten
IMPERATIVE (23:5)	**cuenta**	contad
PRETERITE INDICATIVE (10:5)		
PAST SUBJUNCTIVE (25:5) { *-ra* Form		
-se Form		
PRESENT PARTICIPLE (20:6)		

RADICAL-CHANGING VERBS

acostarse, I	dormir, II
*almorzar, I	*empezar, I
*comenzar, I	encontrar, I
*conseguir, III	entender, I
contar, I	impedir, III
costar, I	*jugar, I
despedirse, III	llover, I
divertirse, II	†morir, II

* For orthographic changes, see pages 202-203.

verbs with vowel changes.)

II (-ir verbs)		III* (-ir verbs)	
o > ue ⎫ e > ie ⎬ when stem is stressed o > u ⎪ before stressed -a-, e > i ⎭ -ie-, -ió		e > i ⎰ when stem is stressed; ⎱ also before stressed -a-, -ie-, -ió	
sentir, *to feel, to regret*		**pedir**, *to ask, to request*	
siento	sentimos	pido	pedimos
sientes	sentís	pides	pedís
siente	sienten	pide	piden
sienta	sintamos	pida	pidamos
sientas	sintáis	pidas	pidáis
sienta	sientan	pida	pidan
siente	sentid	pide	pedid
sentí	sentimos	pedí	pedimos
sentiste	sentisteis	pediste	pedisteis
sintió	sintieron	pidió	pidieron
sintiera	sintiéramos	pidiera	pidiéramos
sintieras	sintierais	pidieras	pidierais
sintiera	sintieran	pidiera	pidieran
sintiese	sintiésemos	pidiese	pidiésemos
sintieses	sintieseis	pidieses	pidieseis
sintiese	sintiesen	pidiese	pidiesen
sintiendo		pidiendo	

USED IN THIS TEXT

*negar, I	repetir, III
nevar, I	*seguir, III
pedir, III	sentar, I
pensar, I	sentarse, I
perder, I	sentir, II
preferir, II	servir, III
probar, I	soñar, I
recordar, I	†volver. I

† Irregular past participles: **morir—muerto; volver—vuelto.**

INFINITIVE	PRESENT INDICATIVE		PRESENT SUBJUNCTIVE		IMPERATIVE SINGULAR
conocer	conozco	conocemos	conozca	conozcamos	
	conoces	conocéis	conozcas	conozcáis	
	conoce	conocen	conozca	conozcan	
dar	doy	damos	dé	demos	da
	das	dais	des	deis	
	da	dan	dé	den	
decir	digo	decimos	diga	digamos	di
	dices	decís	digas	digáis	
	dice	dicen	diga	digan	
estar	estoy	estamos	esté	estemos	está
	estás	estáis	estés	estéis	
	está	están	esté	estén	
haber	he	hemos	haya	hayamos	
	has	habéis	hayas	hayáis	
	ha	han	haya	hayan	
hacer	hago	hacemos	haga	hagamos	haz
	haces	hacéis	hagas	hagáis	
	hace	hacen	haga	hagan	
ir*	voy	vamos	vaya	vayamos	ve
	vas	vais	vayas	vayáis	
	va	van	vaya	vayan	
oír	oigo	oímos	oiga	oigamos	oye
	oyes	oís	oigas	oigáis	
	oye	oyen	oiga	oigan	
parecer	parezco	parecemos	parezca	parezcamos	
	pareces	parecéis	parezcas	parezcáis	
	parece	parecen	parezca	parezcan	
poder	puedo	podemos	pueda	podamos	
	puedes	podéis	puedas	podáis	
	puede	pueden	pueda	puedan	

*Irregular IMPERFECT of ir:

iba	íbamos
ibas	ibais
iba	iban

FUTURE IND. AND CONDITIONAL	PRETERITE INDICATIVE		PAST SUBJUNCTIVE	PARTICIPLES: PRESENT PAST†
	di	dimos	diera, *etc.*	
	diste	disteis	*or*	
	dió	dieron	diese, *etc.*	
diré, *etc.*	dije	dijimos	dijera, *etc.*	diciendo
diría, *etc.*	dijiste	dijisteis	*or*	dicho
	dijo	dijeron	dijese, *etc.*	
	estuve	estuvimos	estuviera, *etc.*	
	estuviste	estuvisteis	*or*	
	estuvo	estuvieron	estuviese, *etc.*	
habré, *etc.*	hube	hubimos	hubiera, *etc.*	
habría, *etc.*	hubiste	hubisteis	*or*	
	hubo	hubieron	hubiese, *etc.*	
haré, *etc.*	hice	hicimos	hiciera, *etc.*	haciendo
haría, *etc.*	hiciste	hicisteis	*or*	hecho
	hizo	hicieron	hiciese, *etc.*	
	fuí	fuimos	fuera, *etc.*	yendo
	fuiste	fuisteis	*or*	ido
	fué	fueron	fuese, *etc.*	
	oí	oímos	oyera, *etc.*	oyendo
	oíste	oísteis	*or*	oído
	oyó	oyeron	oyese, *etc.*	
podré, *etc.*	pude	pudimos	pudiera, *etc.*	pudiendo
podría, *etc.*	pudiste	pudisteis	*or*	podido
	pudo	pudieron	pudiese, *etc.*	

† Irregular PAST PARTICIPLES not included in the table:

abrir—abierto	morir—muerto
escribir—escrito	volver—vuelto

INFINITIVE	PRESENT INDICATIVE		PRESENT SUBJUNCTIVE		IMPERATIVE SINGULAR
poner†	pongo	ponemos	ponga	pongamos	pon
	pones	ponéis	pongas	pongáis	
	pone	ponen	ponga	pongan	
querer	quiero	queremos	quiera	queramos	quiere
	quieres	queréis	quieras	queráis	
	quiere	quieren	quiera	quieran	
saber	sé	sabemos	sepa	sepamos	
	sabes	sabéis	sepas	sepáis	
	sabe	saben	sepa	sepan	
salir	salgo	salimos	salga	salgamos	sal
	sales	salís	salgas	salgáis	
	sale	salen	salga	salgan	
ser*	soy	somos	sea	seamos	sé
	eres	sois	seas	seáis	
	es	son	sea	sean	
tener†	tengo	tenemos	tenga	tengamos	ten
	tienes	tenéis	tengas	tengáis	
	tiene	tienen	tenga	tengan	
traer	traigo	traemos	traiga	traigamos	
	traes	traéis	traigas	traigáis	
	trae	traen	traiga	traigan	
valer	valgo	valemos	valga	valgamos	val
	vales	valéis	valgas	valgáis	
	vale	valen	valga	valgan	
venir	vengo	venimos	venga	vengamos	ven
	vienes	venís	vengas	vengáis	
	viene	vienen	venga	vengan	
ver*	veo	vemos	vea	veamos	ve
	ves	veis	veas	veáis	
	ve	ven	vea	vean	

*Irregular IMPERFECTS:

	ser		ver	
	era	éramos	veía	veíamos
	eras	erais	veías	veíais
	era	eran	veía	veían

FUTURE IND. AND CONDITIONAL	PRETERITE INDICATIVE		PAST SUBJUNCTIVE	PARTICIPLES: PRESENT PAST
pondré, *etc.* pondría, *etc.*	puse pusiste puso	pusimos pusisteis pusieron	pusiera, *etc.* *or* pusiese, *etc.*	poniendo puesto
querré, *etc.* querría, *etc.*	quise quisiste quiso	quisimos quisisteis quisieron	quisiera, *etc.* *or* quisiese, *etc.*	
sabré, *etc.* sabría, *etc.*	supe supiste supo	supimos supisteis supieron	supiera, *etc.* *or* supiese, *etc.*	
saldré, *etc.* saldría, *etc.*				
	fuí fuiste fué	fuimos fuisteis fueron	fuera, *etc.* *or* fuese, *etc.*	
tendré, *etc.* tendría, *etc.*	tuve tuviste tuvo	tuvimos tuvisteis tuvieron	tuviera, *etc.* *or* tuviese, *etc.*	
	traje trajiste trajo	trajimos trajisteis trajeron	trajera, *etc.* *or* trajese, *etc.*	trayendo traído
valdré, *etc.* valdría, *etc.*				
vendré, *etc.* vendría, *etc.*	vine viniste vino	vinimos vinisteis vinieron	viniera, *etc.* *or* viniese, *etc.*	viniendo venido
				viendo visto

† Compound forms:

    contener, like **tener**
    suponer, like **poner**

E. REFERENCE LIST

NOTE. There follow below, in alphabetical arrangement, all the verbs used in this text which have any type of irregularity. Each verb is conjugated in the tenses in which the irregularities occur. On pages 200-209 are given tables showing the patterns for regular verbs, radical and orthographic changes, and other irregularities according to tenses.

Abrir, *to open*

PAST PARTICIPLE

abierto

Acostarse (ue), *to go to bed*

PRESENT INDICATIVE

me acuesto nos acostamos
te acuestas os acostáis
se acuesta **se acuestan**

PRESENT SUBJUNCTIVE

me acueste nos acostemos
te acuestes os acostéis
se acueste **se acuesten**

IMPERATIVE

acuéstate acostaos

Almorzar (ue; c), *to eat lunch*

PRESENT INDICATIVE

almuerzo almorzamos
almuerzas almorzáis
almuerza almuerzan

PRESENT SUBJUNCTIVE

almuerce **almorcemos**
almuerces **almorcéis**
almuerce **almuercen**

IMPERATIVE

almuerza almorzad

PRETERITE INDICATIVE

almorcé almorzamos
almorzaste almorzasteis
almorzó almorzaron

Buscar (qu), *to look for*

PRESENT SUBJUNCTIVE

busque **busquemos**
busques **busquéis**
busque **busquen**

PRETERITE INDICATIVE

busqué buscamos
buscaste buscasteis
buscó buscaron

Coger (j), *to catch*

PRESENT INDICATIVE		PRESENT SUBJUNCTIVE	
cojo	cogemos	coja	cojamos
coges	cogéis	cojas	cojáis
coge	cogen	coja	cojan

Comenzar (ie; c), *to commence, to begin*

PRESENT INDICATIVE		PRESENT SUBJUNCTIVE	
comienzo	comenzamos	comience	comencemos
comienzas	comenzáis	comiences	comencéis
comienza	comienzan	comience	comiencen

IMPERATIVE

comienza	comenzad

PRETERITE INDICATIVE

comencé	comenzamos
comenzaste	comenzasteis
comenzó	comenzaron

Conocer, *to know, be acquainted with*

PRESENT INDICATIVE		PRESENT SUBJUNCTIVE	
conozco	conocemos	conozca	conozcamos
conoces	conocéis	conozcas	conozcáis
conoce	conocen	conozca	conozcan

Conseguir (i; g), *to get, to secure, to obtain*

PRESENT INDICATIVE		PRESENT SUBJUNCTIVE	
consigo	conseguimos	consiga	consigamos
consigues	conseguís	consigas	consigáis
consigue	consiguen	consiga	consigan

IMPERATIVE

consigue	conseguid

PRETERITE INDICATIVE		PAST SUBJUNCTIVE
conseguí	conseguimos	consiguiera, *etc.*
conseguiste	conseguisteis	*or*
consiguió	consiguieron	consiguiese, *etc.*

PRESENT PARTICIPLE

consiguiendo

Construir (y; *irreg.*), *to construct, to build*

PRESENT INDICATIVE

construyo	construimos
construyes	construís
construye	construyen

PRESENT SUBJUNCTIVE

construya	construyamos
construyas	construyáis
construya	construyan

IMPERATIVE

construye   construid

PRETERITE INDICATIVE

construí	construimos
construiste	construisteis
construyó	construyeron

PAST SUBJUNCTIVE

construyera, *etc.*
or
construyese, *etc.*

PRESENT PARTICIPLE

construyendo

Contar (ue), *to tell, to relate*

PRESENT INDICATIVE

cuento	contamos
cuentas	contáis
cuenta	cuentan

PRESENT SUBJUNCTIVE

cuente	contemos
cuentes	contéis
cuente	cuenten

IMPERATIVE

cuenta   contad

Contener, *to contain*, like **tener**, *to have.*

Costar (ue), *to cost*

PRESENT INDICATIVE

cuesto	costamos
cuestas	costáis
cuesta	cuestan

PRESENT SUBJUNCTIVE

cueste	costemos
cuestes	costéis
cueste	cuesten

IMPERATIVE

cuesta   costad

Creer (í, y), *to believe, to think*

PRETERITE INDICATIVE

creí	creímos
creíste	creísteis
creyó	creyeron

PAST SUBJUNCTIVE

creyera, *etc.*
or
creyese, *etc.*

PRESENT PARTICIPLE

creyendo

PAST PARTICIPLE

creído

Dar, *to give; to take* (a walk)

PRESENT INDICATIVE		PRESENT SUBJUNCTIVE	
doy	damos	dé	demos
das	dais	des	deis
da	dan	dé	den

IMPERATIVE

da   dad

PRETERITE INDICATIVE		PAST SUBJUNCTIVE
di	dimos	diera, *etc.*
diste	disteis	*or*
dió	dieron	diese, *etc.*

Decir, *to say, to tell*

PRESENT INDICATIVE		PRESENT SUBJUNCTIVE	
digo	decimos	diga	digamos
dices	decís	digas	digáis
dice	dicen	diga	digan

IMPERATIVE

di   decid

FUTURE INDICATIVE		CONDITIONAL	
diré	diremos	diría	diríamos
dirás	diréis	dirías	diríais
dirá	dirán	diría	dirían

PRETERITE INDICATIVE		PAST SUBJUNCTIVE
dije	dijimos	dijera, *etc.*
dijiste	dijisteis	*or*
dijo	dijeron	dijese, *etc.*

PRESENT PARTICIPLE	PAST PARTICIPLE
diciendo	dicho

Despedirse (i), *to take leave, to say good-by*

PRESENT INDICATIVE		PRESENT SUBJUNCTIVE	
me despido	nos despedimos	me despida	nos despidamos
te despides	os despedís	te despidas	os despidáis
se despide	se despiden	se despida	se despidan

IMPERATIVE

despídete   despedíos

PRETERITE INDICATIVE		PAST SUBJUNCTIVE
me despedí	nos despedimos	me despidiera, *etc.*
te despediste	os despedisteis	*or*
se despidió	se despidieron	me despidiese, *etc.*

PRESENT PARTICIPLE

despidiéndose

Divertirse (ie, i), *to enjoy oneself, to have a good time, to have fun, to be amused*

PRESENT INDICATIVE		PRESENT SUBJUNCTIVE	
me divierto	nos divertimos	me divierta	nos divirtamos
te diviertes	os divertís	te diviertas	os divirtáis
se divierte	se divierten	se divierta	se diviertan

IMPERATIVE

diviértete   divertíos

PRETERITE INDICATIVE		PAST SUBJUNCTIVE
me divertí	nos divertimos	me divirtiera, *etc.*
te divertiste	os divertisteis	*or*
se divirtió	se divirtieron	me divirtiese, *etc.*

PRESENT PARTICIPLE

divirtiéndose

Dormir (ue, u), *to sleep*

PRESENT INDICATIVE		PRESENT SUBJUNCTIVE	
duermo	dormimos	duerma	durmamos
duermes	dormís	duermas	durmáis
duerme	duermen	duerma	duerman

IMPERATIVE

duerme   dormid

PRETERITE INDICATIVE		PAST SUBJUNCTIVE
dormí	dormimos	durmiera, *etc.*
dormiste	dormisteis	*or*
durmió	durmieron	durmiese, *etc.*

PRESENT PARTICIPLE

durmiendo

Empezar (ie; c), *to begin*

PRESENT INDICATIVE		PRESENT SUBJUNCTIVE	
empiezo	empezamos	empiece	empecemos
empiezas	empezáis	empieces	empecéis
empieza	empiezan	empiece	empiecen

IMPERATIVE
empieza empezad

PRETERITE INDICATIVE

empecé	empezamos
empezaste	empezasteis
empezó	empezaron

Encontrar (ue), *to find*

PRESENT INDICATIVE		PRESENT SUBJUNCTIVE	
encuentro	encontramos	encuentre	encontremos
encuentras	encontráis	encuentres	encontréis
encuentra	encuentran	encuentre	encuentren

IMPERATIVE
encuentra encontrad

Entender (ie), *to understand*

PRESENT INDICATIVE		PRESENT SUBJUNCTIVE	
entiendo	entendemos	entienda	entendamos
entiendes	entendéis	entiendas	entendáis
entiende	entienden	entienda	entiendan

IMPERATIVE
entiende entended

Escribir, *to write*

PAST PARTICIPLE
escrito

Estar, *to be*

PRESENT INDICATIVE		PRESENT SUBJUNCTIVE	
estoy	estamos	esté	estemos
estás	estáis	estés	estéis
está	están	esté	estén

IMPERATIVE
está estad

PRETERITE INDICATIVE		PAST SUBJUNCTIVE
estuve	estuvimos	estuviera, *etc.*
estuviste	estuvisteis	*or*
estuvo	estuvieron	estuviese, *etc.*

Haber, *to have* (in compound tenses)

PRESENT INDICATIVE		PRESENT SUBJUNCTIVE	
he	hemos	haya	hayamos
has	habéis	hayas	hayáis
ha	han	haya	hayan

FUTURE INDICATIVE		CONDITIONAL	
habré	habremos	habría	habríais
habrás	habréis	habrías	habríamos
habrá	habrán	habría	habrían

PRETERITE INDICATIVE		PAST SUBJUNCTIVE
hube	hubimos	hubiera, *etc.*
hubiste	hubisteis	*or*
hubo	hubieron	hubiese, *etc.*

NOTE. The third person singular of **haber** is used impersonally to mean *there is, there are, there was,* etc. In the present indicative, the form thus used is **hay**, rather than **ha**.

Hacer, *to do, to make*

PRESENT INDICATIVE		PRESENT SUBJUNCTIVE	
hago	hacemos	haga	hagamos
haces	hacéis	hagas	hagáis
hace	hacen	haga	hagan

IMPERATIVE

haz   haced

FUTURE INDICATIVE		CONDITIONAL	
haré	haremos	haría	haríamos
harás	haréis	harías	haríais
hará	harán	haría	harían

PRETERITE INDICATIVE		PAST SUBJUNCTIVE
hice	hicimos	hiciera, *etc.*
hiciste	hicisteis	*or*
hizo	hicieron	hiciese, *etc.*

PAST PARTICIPLE

hecho

Impedir (i), *to prevent*

PRESENT INDICATIVE		PRESENT SUBJUNCTIVE	
impido	impedimos	impida	impidamos
impides	impedís	impidas	impidáis
impide	impiden	impida	impidan

IMPERATIVE

impide   impedid

PRETERITE INDICATIVE		PAST SUBJUNCTIVE
impedí	impedimos	impidiera, *etc.*
impediste	impedisteis	*or*
impidió	impidieron	impidiese, *etc.*

PRESENT PARTICIPLE

impidiendo

Ir, *to go*

PRESENT INDICATIVE		PRESENT SUBJUNCTIVE	
voy	vamos	vaya	vayamos
vas	vais	vayas	vayáis
va	van	vaya	vayan

IMPERATIVE

ve   id

IMPERFECT INDICATIVE

iba	íbamos
ibas	ibais
iba	iban

PRETERITE INDICATIVE		PAST SUBJUNCTIVE
fuí	fuimos	fuera, *etc.*
fuiste	fuisteis	*or*
fué	fueron	fuese, *etc.*

PRESENT PARTICIPLE

yendo

Jugar (ue; gu), *to play* (a game)

PRESENT INDICATIVE		PRESENT SUBJUNCTIVE	
juego	jugamos	juegue	juguemos
juegas	jugáis	juegues	juguéis
juega	juegan	juegue	jueguen

IMPERATIVE

juega   jugad

PRETERITE INDICATIVE

jugué	jugamos
jugaste	jugasteis
jugó	jugaron

Leer (í, y), *to read*

PRETERITE INDICATIVE

leí	leímos
leíste	leísteis
leyó	leyeron

PAST SUBJUNCTIVE

leyera, *etc.*
or
leyese, *etc.*

PRESENT PARTICIPLE

leyendo

PAST PARTICIPLE

leído

Llegar (gu), *to arrive*

PRESENT SUBJUNCTIVE

llegue	lleguemos
llegues	lleguéis
llegue	lleguen

PRETERITE INDICATIVE

llegué	llegamos
llegaste	llegasteis
llegó	llegaron

Llover (ue), *to rain*

PRESENT INDICATIVE

llueve

PRESENT SUBJUNCTIVE

llueva

Morir (ue, u; *irreg.*), *to die*

PRESENT INDICATIVE

muero	morimos
mueres	morís
muere	mueren

PRESENT SUBJUNCTIVE

muera	muramos
mueras	muráis
muera	mueran

IMPERATIVE

muere   morid

PRETERITE INDICATIVE

morí	morimos
moriste	moristeis
murió	murieron

PAST SUBJUNCTIVE

muriera, *etc.*
or
muriese, *etc.*

PRESENT PARTICIPLE

muriendo

PAST PARTICIPLE

muerto

Negar (ie; gu), *to deny*

PRESENT INDICATIVE		PRESENT SUBJUNCTIVE	
niego	negamos	niegue	neguemos
niegas	negáis	niegues	neguéis
niega	niegan	niegue	nieguen

IMPERATIVE

niega   negad

PRETERITE INDICATIVE

negué	negamos
negaste	negasteis
negó	negaron

Nevar (ie), *to snow*

PRESENT INDICATIVE	PRESENT SUBJUNCTIVE
nieva	nieve

Oír, *to hear, to listen*

PRESENT INDICATIVE		PRESENT SUBJUNCTIVE	
oigo	oímos	oiga	oigamos
oyes	oís	oigas	oigáis
oye	oyen	oiga	oigan

IMPERATIVE

oye   oíd

PRETERITE INDICATIVE		PAST SUBJUNCTIVE
oí	oímos	oyera, *etc.*
oíste	oísteis	*or*
oyó	oyeron	oyese, *etc.*

PRESENT PARTICIPLE	PAST PARTICIPLE
oyendo	oído

Pagar (gu), *to pay (for)*

PRESENT SUBJUNCTIVE		PRETERITE INDICATIVE	
pague	paguemos	pagué	pagamos
pagues	paguéis	pagaste	pagasteis
pague	paguen	pagó	pagaron

Parecer, *to seem*

PRESENT INDICATIVE		PRESENT SUBJUNCTIVE	
parezco	parecemos	parezca	parezcamos
pareces	parecéis	parezcas	parezcáis
parece	parecen	parezca	parezcan

Pedir (i), *to ask, to request*

PRESENT INDICATIVE		PRESENT SUBJUNCTIVE	
pido	pedimos	pida	pidamos
pides	pedís	pidas	pidáis
pide	piden	pida	pidan

IMPERATIVE
pide   pedid

PRETERITE INDICATIVE		PAST SUBJUNCTIVE
pedí	pedimos	**pidiera,** *etc.*
pediste	pedisteis	*or*
pidió	pidieron	**pidiese,** *etc.*

PRESENT PARTICIPLE
pidiendo

Pensar (ie), *to think; to intend*

PRESENT INDICATIVE		PRESENT SUBJUNCTIVE	
pienso	pensamos	piense	pensemos
piensas	pensáis	pienses	penséis
piensa	piensan	piense	piensen

IMPERATIVE
piensa   pensad

Perder (ie), *to lose; to miss*

PRESENT INDICATIVE		PRESENT SUBJUNCTIVE	
pierdo	perdemos	pierda	perdamos
pierdes	perdéis	pierdas	perdáis
pierde	pierden	pierda	pierdan

IMPERATIVE
pierde   perded

Poder (ue; *irreg.*), *to be able (can, may)*

PRESENT INDICATIVE		PRESENT SUBJUNCTIVE	
puedo	podemos	pueda	podamos
puedes	podéis	puedas	podáis
puede	pueden	pueda	puedan

FUTURE INDICATIVE		CONDITIONAL	
podré	podremos	podría	podríamos
podrás	podréis	podrías	podríais
podrá	podrán	podría	podrían

PRETERITE INDICATIVE		PAST SUBJUNCTIVE	
pude	pudimos		pudiera, *etc.*
pudiste	pudisteis		*or*
pudo	pudieron		pudiese, *etc.*

PRESENT PARTICIPLE

pudiendo

Poner, *to put; to put on* (a play)

PRESENT INDICATIVE		PRESENT SUBJUNCTIVE	
pongo	ponemos	ponga	pongamos
pones	ponéis	pongas	pongáis
pone	ponen	ponga	pongan

IMPERATIVE

pon poned

FUTURE INDICATIVE		CONDITIONAL	
pondré	pondremos	pondría	pondríamos
pondrás	pondréis	pondrías	pondríais
pondrá	pondrán	pondría	pondrían

PRETERITE INDICATIVE		PAST SUBJUNCTIVE	
puse	pusimos		pusiera, *etc.*
pusiste	pusisteis		*or*
puso	pusieron		pusiese, *etc.*

PAST PARTICIPLE

puesto

Preferir (ie, i), *to prefer*

PRESENT INDICATIVE		PRESENT SUBJUNCTIVE	
prefiero	preferimos	prefiera	prefiramos
prefieres	preferís	prefieras	prefiráis
prefiere	prefieren	prefiera	prefieran

IMPERATIVE

prefiere   preferid

PRETERITE INDICATIVE		PAST SUBJUNCTIVE
preferí	preferimos	**prefiriera,** *etc.*
preferiste	preferisteis	*or*
prefirió	prefirieron	**prefiriese,** *etc.*

PRESENT PARTICIPLE

prefiriendo

Probar (ue), *to prove; to test, to try (on)*

PRESENT INDICATIVE		PRESENT SUBJUNCTIVE	
pruebo	probamos	pruebe	probemos
pruebas	probáis	pruebes	probéis
prueba	prueban	pruebe	prueben

Querer (ie; *irreg.*), *to want, to wish*

PRESENT INDICATIVE		PRESENT SUBJUNCTIVE	
quiero	queremos	quiera	queramos
quieres	queréis	quieras	queráis
quiere	quieren	quiera	quieran

IMPERATIVE

quiere   quered

FUTURE INDICATIVE		CONDITIONAL	
querré	querremos	querría	querríamos
querrás	querréis	querrías	querríais
querrá	querrán	querría	querrían

PRETERITE INDICATIVE		PAST SUBJUNCTIVE
quise	quisimos	**quisiera,** *etc.*
quisiste	quisisteis	*or*
quiso	quisieron	**quisiese,** *etc.*

Recordar (ue), *to recall, to remember*

PRESENT INDICATIVE		PRESENT SUBJUNCTIVE	
recuerdo	recordamos	recuerde	recordemos
recuerdas	recordáis	recuerdes	recordéis
recuerda	recuerdan	recuerde	recuerden

IMPERATIVE

recuerda   recordad

Repetir (i), *to repeat*

PRESENT INDICATIVE		PRESENT SUBJUNCTIVE	
repito	repetimos	repita	repitamos
repites	repetís	repitas	repitáis
repite	repiten	repita	repitan

IMPERATIVE

repite   repetid

PRETERITE INDICATIVE		PAST SUBJUNCTIVE
repetí	repetimos	repitiera, *etc.*
repetiste	repetisteis	*or*
repitió	repitieron	repitiese, *etc.*

PRESENT PARTICIPLE

repitiendo

Saber, *to know* (a fact)

PRESENT INDICATIVE		PRESENT SUBJUNCTIVE	
sé	sabemos	sepa	sepamos
sabes	sabéis	sepas	sepáis
sabe	saben	sepa	sepan

FUTURE INDICATIVE		CONDITIONAL	
sabré	sabremos	sabría	sabríamos
sabrás	sabréis	sabrías	sabríais
sabrá	sabrán	sabría	sabrían

PRETERITE INDICATIVE		PAST SUBJUNCTIVE
supe	supimos	supiera, *etc.*
supiste	supisteis	*or*
supo	supieron	supiese, *etc.*

Sacar (qu), *to take out; to get* (tickets)

PRESENT SUBJUNCTIVE		PRETERITE INDICATIVE	
saque	saquemos	saqué	sacamos
saques	saquéis	sacaste	sacasteis
saque	saquen	sacó	sacaron

Salir, *to leave, to go out*

PRESENT INDICATIVE		PRESENT SUBJUNCTIVE	
salgo	salimos	salga	salgamos
sales	salís	salgas	salgáis
sale	salen	salga	salgan

IMPERATIVE

sal   salid

FUTURE INDICATIVE		CONDITIONAL	
saldré	saldremos	saldría	saldríamos
saldrás	saldréis	saldrías	saldríais
saldrá	saldrán	saldría	saldrían

Seguir (i; g), *to continue, to still be, to keep on*

PRESENT INDICATIVE		PRESENT SUBJUNCTIVE	
sigo	seguimos	siga	sigamos
sigues	seguís	sigas	sigáis
sigue	siguen	siga	sigan

IMPERATIVE

sigue   seguid

PRETERITE INDICATIVE		PAST SUBJUNCTIVE
seguí	seguimos	**siguiera,** *etc.*
seguiste	seguisteis	*or*
siguió	siguieron	**siguiese,** *etc.*

PRESENT PARTICIPLE

siguiendo

Sentar (ie), *to suit, to become, to be becoming*

PRESENT INDICATIVE		PRESENT SUBJUNCTIVE	
sienta	sientan	siente	sienten

Sentarse (ie), *to sit down*

PRESENT INDICATIVE		PRESENT SUBJUNCTIVE	
me siento	nos sentamos	me siente	nos sentemos
te sientas	os sentáis	te sientes	os sentéis
se sienta	se sientan	se siente	se sienten

IMPERATIVE

siéntate   sentaos

Sentir (ie, i), *to feel, to regret, to be sorry*

PRESENT INDICATIVE		PRESENT SUBJUNCTIVE	
siento	sentimos	sienta	sintamos
sientes	sentís	sientas	sintáis
siente	sienten	sienta	sientan

IMPERATIVE

siente   sentid

PRETERITE INDICATIVE		PAST SUBJUNCTIVE
sentí	sentimos	sintiera, *etc.*
sentiste	sentisteis	*or*
sintió	sintieron	sintiese, *etc.*

PRESENT PARTICIPLE

sintiendo

Ser, *to be*

PRESENT INDICATIVE		PRESENT SUBJUNCTIVE	
soy	somos	sea	seamos
eres	sois	seas	seáis
es	son	sea	sean

IMPERATIVE

sé   sed

IMPERFECT INDICATIVE

era	éramos
eras	erais
era	eran

PRETERITE INDICATIVE		PAST SUBJUNCTIVE
fuí	fuimos	fuera, *etc.*
fuiste	fuisteis	*or*
fué	fueron	fuese, *etc.*

Servir (i), *to serve*

PRESENT INDICATIVE		PRESENT SUBJUNCTIVE	
sirvo	servimos	sirva	sirvamos
sirves	servís	sirvas	sirváis
sirve	sirven	sirva	sirvan

IMPERATIVE
sirve   servid

PRETERITE INDICATIVE		PAST SUBJUNCTIVE
serví	servimos	sirviera, *etc.*
serviste	servisteis	*or*
sirvió	sirvieron	sirviese, *etc.*

PRESENT PARTICIPLE
sirviendo

Soñar (ue), *to dream*

PRESENT INDICATIVE		PRESENT SUBJUNCTIVE	
sueño	soñamos	sueñe	soñemos
sueñas	soñáis	sueñes	soñéis
sueña	sueñan	sueñe	sueñen

IMPERATIVE
sueña   soñad

Suponer, *to suppose,* like poner, *to put.*

Tener, *to have*

PRESENT INDICATIVE		PRESENT SUBJUNCTIVE	
tengo	tenemos	tenga	tengamos
tienes	tenéis	tengas	tengáis
tiene	tienen	tenga	tengan

IMPERATIVE
ten   tened

FUTURE INDICATIVE		CONDITIONAL	
tendré	tendremos	tendría	tendríamos
tendrás	tendréis	tendrías	tendríais
tendrá	tendrán	tendría	tendrían

PRETERITE INDICATIVE		PAST SUBJUNCTIVE
tuve	tuvimos	tuviera, *etc.*
tuviste	tuvisteis	*or*
tuvo	tuvieron	tuviese, *etc.*

Tocar (qu), *to play* (music)

PRESENT SUBJUNCTIVE		PRETERITE INDICATIVE	
toque	toquemos	toqué	tocamos
toques	toquéis	tocaste	tocasteis
toque	toquen	tocó	tocaron

Traer, *to bring*

PRESENT INDICATIVE		PRESENT SUBJUNCTIVE	
traigo	traemos	traiga	traigamos
traes	traéis	traigas	traigáis
trae	traen	traiga	traigan

PRETERITE INDICATIVE		PAST SUBJUNCTIVE
traje	trajimos	trajera, *etc.*
trajiste	trajisteis	*or*
trajo	trajeron	trajese, *etc.*

PRESENT PARTICIPLE

trayendo

PAST PARTICIPLE

traído

Valer, *to be worth; to cost*

PRESENT INDICATIVE		PRESENT SUBJUNCTIVE	
valgo	valemos	valga	valgamos
vales	valéis	valgas	valgáis
vale	valen	valga	valgan

IMPERATIVE

val   valed

FUTURE INDICATIVE		CONDITIONAL	
valdré	valdremos	valdría	valdríamos
valdrás	valdréis	valdrías	valdríais
valdrá	valdrán	valdría	valdrían

Venir, *to come*

PRESENT INDICATIVE		PRESENT SUBJUNCTIVE	
vengo	venimos	venga	vengamos
vienes	venís	vengas	vengáis
viene	vienen	venga	vengan

IMPERATIVE

ven   venid

FUTURE INDICATIVE		CONDITIONAL	
vendré	vendremos	vendría	vendríamos
vendrás	vendréis	vendrías	vendríais
vendrá	vendrán	vendría	vendrían

PRETERITE INDICATIVE		PAST SUBJUNCTIVE
vine	vinimos	viniera, *etc.*
viniste	vinisteis	*or*
vino	vinieron	viniese, *etc.*

PRESENT PARTICIPLE
viniendo

Ver, *to see*

PRESENT INDICATIVE		PRESENT SUBJUNCTIVE	
veo	vemos	vea	veamos
ves	veis	veas	veáis
ve	ven	vea	vean

IMPERATIVE
ve   ved

IMPERFECT INDICATIVE	
veía	veíamos
veías	veíais
veía	veían

PAST PARTICIPLE
visto

Volver (ue; *irreg.*), *to return, to go back*

PRESENT INDICATIVE		PRESENT SUBJUNCTIVE	
vuelvo	volvemos	vuelva	volvamos
vuelves	volvéis	vuelvas	volváis
vuelve	vuelven	vuelva	vuelvan

IMPERATIVE
vuelve   volved

PAST PARTICIPLE
vuelto

Vocabularies

NOTES ON THE VOCABULARIES

Idiomatic phrases are included under the main words of each phrase. *Italics* are used for explanatory notes. Gender of nouns is indicated by *m.* or *f.* after the noun, except when the article is used. For adjectives the singular forms are given.

In the Spanish-English Vocabulary, each irregular verb stem is represented by one form with a cross reference to the infinitive.

In the English-Spanish Vocabulary, verbs that have any type of irregularity are marked with an asterisk (*). These verbs are given on pp. 210-228. The other verbs follow exactly the patterns given on pp. 200-201. The number of the lesson in which words, phrases, and grammatical forms are first used is shown by a raised numeral. Sample entries:

ENTRY	EXPLANATION
excursion excursión[15] *f.;* **to go on an excursion** hacer* una excursión[15]	The word *excursión,* first used in Lesson 15, is feminine; the verb *hacer,* used with it, is irregular.
husband esposo[6] *m.,* marido[21] *m.*	For "husband" *esposo* is first used in Lesson 6 and *marido* in Lesson 21.
Mr. (el) señor *(abbrev.* Sr.)[3]; **Mr. and Mrs.** (los) señores *(abbrev.* Sres.)[3]	Forms and use of titles are explained in Lesson 3.
third tercer, tercero, -a[13]; *(in dates)* tres[19]	The word *tercero,* used in Lesson 13, has three singular forms; in dates the cardinal numeral is used (Lesson 19).

LIST OF ABBREVIATIONS

abbrev. = abbreviation
adj. = adjective
adv. = adverb
art. = article
conj. = conjunction
def. = definite
dem. = demonstrative
dir. = direct
f. = feminine

fam. = familiar
indef. = indefinite
ind. = indirect
inf. = infinitive
m. = masculine
neut. = neuter
obj. = object
part. = participle
pl. = plural

poss. = possessive
prep. = preposition
pres. = present
pron. = pronoun
reflex. = reflexive
rel. = relative
sing. = singular
subj. = subject
vb. = verb

Spanish-English Vocabulary

A

a to; at; *sign of a personal noun object*
abierto, -a open; *see* **abrir**
abogado *m.* lawyer
abril *m.* April
abrir to open
abuela *f.* grandmother
abuelo *m.* grandfather; *pl.* grandparents
abundante abundant, hearty
aburrido, -a bored; boring
aburrir to bore; **aburrirse** to get bored, to be bored
acabar to finish; **acabar de** (+ *inf.*) to have just *(done something)*
academia *f.* academy
accidente *m.* accident
acento *m.* accent; **sin acento** without an accent
acompañar to accompany, to go with
acostarse to go to bed
actor *m.* actor
actriz *f.* actress
acuerdo *m.* agreement
acuesto *etc. see* **acostarse**
adelante forward; come in
además moreover, besides; **además de** *prep.* besides, in addition to
adiós good-by
¿adónde? where? *(to what place?)*
afmo. *(abbrev. of* afectísimo*)*, **-a** affectionate, devoted; **su afmo. amigo** sincerely yours
agosto *m.* August
agradable agreeable, pleasant
agua *f.* water
¡ah! ah!, oh!
ahí there, over there
ahora now

ajetreo *m.* bustle, activity
al (= **a** + **el**) to the, at the; **al** (+ *inf.*) on *(doing something)*, as *or* when (+ *a conjugated verb*)
alegrarse (de que) to be glad (that)
alemán *m.* German *(language);* **alemán, alemana** *adj.* or *noun* German
algo *pron.* something; *adv.* some, a little
alguien someone, somebody
algún, alguno, -a *adj.* some; **alguno, -a** *pron.* someone; *pl.* some
all- *see below, after* **alt-**
almacén *m.* department store
almorcé *see* **almorzar**
almorzar to eat lunch
almuerce *etc. see* **almorzar**
almuerzo *etc. see* **almorzar; almuerzo** *m.* lunch
alrededor de *prep.* around
alto, -a tall
allí there
amable amiable, kind
amiga *f.* friend
amigo *m.* friend; **su afmo.** (= **afectísimo**) **amigo** sincerely yours
amor *m.* love
animado, -a animated, lively, gay
anoche last night
antes *adv.* before, beforehand; **antes de** *prep.* before; **antes (de) que** *conj.* before
antiguo, -a ancient, old
Antonio Anthony
año *m.* year; **tener . . . años** to be . . . (years) old; **¿cuántos años (tiene)?** how old (is he)?
aparato *m.* (telephone) apparatus; **¡al aparato!** *(at the telephone)* this is . . . (speaking)
apenas hardly, scarcely

iii

apetito *m.* appetite; **tener (mucho) apetito** to be (very) hungry
aquel, aquella, aquellos, aquellas *dem. adj.* that, *pl.* those *(over there);* **aquél, aquélla, aquéllos, aquéllas** *pron.* that (one), those; **aquello** *neut. pron.* that *(idea, fact, etc.)*
aquí here; **aquí . . .** *(at the telephone)* this is **. . .** (calling); **aquí tiene usted** here you have, here is, here are
árbol *m.* tree
Argentina: la Argentina Argentina
arte *m. or f.* art; **bellas artes** *f.* fine arts
artista *m. or f.* artist
artístico, -a artistic, cultural
así so, thus, like that; **así así** fair, so-so
asiento *m.* seat
asignatura *f.* subject, course (of study)
aún still, yet
aunque although, even though, even if
autobús *m.* bus
automóvil *m.* automobile, car
avión *m.* plane, airplane; **en avión** by plane
¡ay! ow!, oh!, alas!
ayer yesterday
azul blue

B

bailar to dance
bailarín *m.* dancer
bailarina *f.* dancer, danseuse, ballerina
baile *m.* dance
bajo, -a short *(of stature)*
barato, -a cheap, inexpensive
bastante *adj.* enough; *adv.* enough, rather, fairly
bebida *f.* drink

beisbol *m.* baseball
bello, -a beautiful; **bellas artes** fine arts
biblioteca *f.* library
bien well, fine, all right
billete *m.* ticket; bill, bank note
blanco, -a white
blusa *f.* blouse
bocacalle *f.* (street) intersection
boda *f.* wedding
bonito, -a pretty
Brasil: el Brasil Brazil
bridge *m.* bridge *(game)*
buen, bueno, -a good; **bueno** *adv.* well; **buenos días** good morning, hello; **buenas tardes** good afternoon, hello; **buenas noches** good evening, hello, good night
buscar to look for; **ir a buscar** to stop by for
busque *etc. see* **buscar**
butaca *f.* armchair; orchestra seat *(theatre)*

C

café *m.* coffee; **café con leche** coffee with cream; **café solo** black coffee
call—*see below, after* **calo—**
calor *m.* warmth, heat; **hacer (mucho) calor** to be (very) warm *or* hot *(weather);* **tener (mucho) calor** to be (very) warm *or* hot *(referring to persons)*
calle *f.* street; **en la calle (40)** at (40th) Street
cambiar to change; **cambiar de tren** to change trains
cambio change, exchange; **en cambio** on the other hand
camisa *f.* shirt
campestre *adj.* (in the) country
campo *m.* field, country
Canadá: el Canadá Canada
cansado, -a tired

cantar to sing
capital f. capital
cariñoso, -a affectionate
carne f. meat
caro, -a expensive
carta f. letter
casa f. house, home; en casa at home; salir de casa to leave home; volver a casa to return home
casado, -a married
casarse to get married
casi almost
ceja f. eyebrow; quemarse las cejas to burn the midnight oil
celos m. pl. jealousy
cena f. supper
cenar to eat supper
centavo m. cent
centro m. business district; al centro to the city, to town, downtown; en el centro in the city, in town, downtown
cerca adv. near, nearby; cerca de prep. near
ch— see below, after cu—
cien, ciento hundred, a hundred, one hundred
ciencia f. science
cierto, -a certain, a certain
cinco five; (in dates) fifth; las cinco five (o'clock)
cincuenta fifty; cincuenta y un, cincuenta y uno, -a fifty-one; cincuenta y dos fifty-two; etc.
cine m. sing. cinema, movies
ciudad f. city
claro, -a light (color); ¡claro! sure!, of course!; claro que . . . of course . . .
clase f. class, course
clásico, -a classical
clima m. climate
coche m. car
coger to catch

cojo etc. see coger
colección f. collection
coleccionista m. or f. collector
colocación f. position, job
Colombia f. Colombia
comedia f. play, comedy
comencé see comenzar
comentario m. comment, remark
comenzar to commence, to begin
comer to eat; to eat dinner
comida f. food, meal; dinner
comience etc. see comenzar
comienza etc. see comenzar
como as; como si as if; tan . . . como as . . . as; tanto como as much as; tanto, -a, -os, -as . . . como as much (pl. as many). . . as
¿cómo? how?; ¡cómo no! sure!, of course!; ¿cómo es? what is (he) like?; ¿cómo se llama usted? what is your name?
cómodo, -a comfortable, convenient
compañía f. company
completamente completely
completo, -a complete
compra f. purchase; ir de compras to go shopping
comprar to buy
con with; (treinta dólares) con (cuarenta centavos) (thirty dollars) and (forty cents)
concierto m. concert
conflicto m. conflict, disagreement
conmigo (= con + mí) with me or with myself
conocer to know, to be acquainted with
conocido, -a well-known
conozco etc. see conocer
conque (and) so
conseguir to get, to secure, to obtain
consigo etc. see conseguir; consigo (= con + sí) with himself, herself, itself, oneself, themselves,

yourself *or* yourselves *(polite);* with him, her, it, one, them, you *(used reflexively)*

consigue *etc. see* **conseguir**

consistir en to consist of

constante constant, loyal

construir to construct, to build

construyo *etc. see* **construir**

contar to tell, to relate; **¿qué me cuenta?** what do you say?

contener to contain

contenga *etc. see* **contener**

contento, -a contented, happy

contestar to answer

contiene *etc. see* **contener**

contigo (= **con** + **ti**) with you *or* with yourself *(familiar)*

contrario, -a contrary; **al contrario** on the contrary

corbata *f.* tie

cordial cordial

corto, -a short

cosa *f.* thing; **es cosa de** it's a matter of; **sería otra cosa** it would be quite different

costar to cost

creer to believe, to think; **creer que no** to believe not, to think not; **creer que sí** to believe so, to think so; **¡ya lo creo!** yes, indeed!, I should say so!

creyó *etc. see* **creer**

crimen *m.* crime

cuadro *m.* picture

¿cuál? which (one)?

cuando when

¿cuándo? when?

cuanto: cuanto antes as soon as possible; **en cuanto** *conj.* as soon as

¿cuánto, -a? how much?, *pl.* how many?; **¿cuántos años (tiene)?** how old (is he)?

¡cuánto, -a! how much!, *pl.* how many!, what a lot of!

cuarenta forty; **cuarenta y un, cuarenta y uno, -a** forty-one; **cuarenta y dos** forty-two; *etc.*

cuarto, -a fourth; **cuarto** *m.* quarter *(of an hour);* **(la una) menos cuarto** a quarter to (one); **(la una) y cuarto** a quarter past (one)

cuatro four; *(in dates)* fourth; **las cuatro** four (o'clock)

cuatrocientos, -as four hundred

cubierto *m.* (special) lunch *or* dinner

cuento *etc. see* **contar**; **cuento** *m.* story

cuesto *etc. see* **costar**

curar to cure, to treat

curso *m.* school year

cuyo, -a whose

CH

charlar to chat, to talk

choque *m.* collision, wreck

D

D., D.ª *abbrev. of* **don, doña**

dar to give; **dar un paseo** to take a walk

de of; from; about; as, for; *(after a comparative)* than; *(after a superlative)* of, in

dé *etc. see* **dar**

deber to owe; to be obliged (must, ought, should)

décimo, -a tenth

decir to say, to tell; **¡diga!** *(answering the telephone)* hello!; **que digamos** *(after negative statement)* let's say, we might say

dejar to leave

del (= **de** + **el**) of the

demás remaining, other

dependienta *f.* (store) clerk

dependiente *m.* (store) clerk

deporte *m.* sport
deportivo, -a *adj.* sports
derecho, -a right; straight; **a la derecha** to the right; **a mano derecha** on the right; **todo derecho** straight ahead
desagradable disagreeable, unpleasant
desayunarse to eat breakfast
desayuno *m.* breakfast
desde from; **desde luego** of course
desear to desire, to wish
despedida *f.* farewell, good-by
despedirse to take leave, to say good-by; **despedirse de** to say good-by to
despido *etc. see* **despedirse**
después *adv.* later, afterwards; **después de** *prep.* after
di *see* **dar** *and* **decir**
día *m.* day; **buenos días** good morning, hello
diario, -a daily, a day; **diario** *m.* newspaper
dibujo animado *m.* animated cartoon
dice *etc. see* **decir**
diciembre *m.* December
dicho *see* **decir**; **dicho** *m.* saying, proverbial expression
diez ten; *(in dates)* tenth; **las diez** ten (o'clock); **diez y seis** sixteen; **diez y siete** seventeen; *etc.*
diferente different
difícil difficult, hard
digo *etc. see* **decir**
dije *etc. see* **decir**
dinero *m.* money
diré *etc. see* **decir**
dirección *f.* direction; management
directo, -a direct; **el tren es directo** it is a through train
diría *etc. see* **decir**
disco *m.* record *(phonograph)*
dispense usted pardon me

diversión *f.* entertainment, pastime
divertido, -a amusing, entertaining
divertir to amuse; **divertirse** to enjoy oneself, to have a good time, to have fun
divierto *etc. see* **divertir**
divino, -a divine
divirtió *etc. see* **divertir**
doblar to turn *(a corner)*
doce twelve; *(in dates)* twelfth; **las doce** twelve (o'clock)
dólar *m.* dollar
domingo *m.* Sunday; **el domingo** (on) Sunday
dominó *m. sing.* dominoes *(the game)*
don *m.,* **doña** *f.,* titles of respect used with first names
donar to donate, to give
¿dónde? where?; **¿a dónde?** where? *(to what place?)*; **¿de dónde (es)?** where (is he) from?; **¿por dónde se va a . . . ?** which way is . . . ?, how do you get to . . . ?
doña *see* **don**
dormir to sleep
dos two; *(in dates)* second; **las dos** two (o'clock); **los dos, las dos** the two *or* both
doscientos, -as two hundred
doy *see* **dar**
duda *f.* doubt; **sin duda** without doubt, no doubt
dudar to doubt
dudoso, -a doubtful
duermo *etc. see* **dormir**
durmió *etc. see* **dormir**

E

e and *(used before* i- *or* hi-*)*
Ecuador: el Ecuador Ecuador
edad *f.* age; **¿qué edad (tiene)?** how old (is he)?, what (is his) age?
edificio *m.* building

Eduardo Edward
¿eh? eh?, eh what?, right?
ejemplo *m.* example; **por ejemplo**
for example
el *def. art., m. sing.* the; *also f.*
sing. before stressed a- *or* ha-; **el**
de that of, the one of; **el que**
pron. which
él *subj. pron.* he; *obj. of prep.* him;
a él *obj. pron.* him, to him; **de**
él *poss. adj.* his, of his
elegante elegant, stylish, fancy;
está muy elegante (he) looks
swell
Elena Helen
ella *subj. pron.* she; *obj. of prep.*
her; **a ella** *obj. pron.* her, to her;
de ella *poss. adj.* her, hers, of
hers
ellos, -as *subj. pron.* they; *obj. of*
prep. them; **a ellos, -as** *obj. pron.*
them, to them; **de ellos, -as** *poss.*
adj. their, theirs, of theirs
embargo: sin embargo nevertheless
empecé *see* **empezar**
empezar to begin
empiece *etc. see* **empezar**
empiezo *etc. see* **empezar**
empleo *m.* job, position
en in; at; **en avión** by plane
encantado, -a delighted
encontrar to find
encuentro *etc. see* **encontrar**
enero *m.* January
engordar to get fat
ensalada *f.* salad
enseñar to teach
entender to understand
enterarse to find out
entero, -a entire
entiendo *etc. see* **entender**
entonces then
entre between
entrevistarse to have an interview
equipaje *m.* baggage, luggage; **sala**
(*f.***) de equipajes** baggage room

equipo *m.* team
era *etc. see* **ser**
eres *see* **ser**
es *see* **ser**
escribir to write
escrito *see* **escribir**
escuchar to listen (to)
escultura *f.* sculpture
ese, esa, esos, esas *dem. adj.* that,
pl. those *(near you);* **ése, ésa,**
ésos, ésas *pron.* that (one), those;
eso *neut. pron.* that *(fact, idea,*
etc.); **a eso de** (at) about *(a cer-*
tain time of day)
España *f.* Spain
español *m.* Spanish *(language);*
español, española *adj. or noun*
Spanish, Spaniard
espera *f.* wait, waiting
esperar to hope; **esperar a que** to
wait until
esposa *f.* wife
esposo *m.* husband
esta, ésta *see* **este**
está *etc. see* **estar**
estación *f.* station
Estados: los Estados Unidos the
United States
estar to be *(condition or location);*
estar para (+ *inf.*) to be about
to *(do something);* **está (muy ele-**
gante) he looks (swell)
esté *etc. see* **estar**
este, esta, estos, estas *dem. adj.* this,
pl. these; **éste, ésta, éstos, éstas**
pron. this (one), these; **esto** *neut.*
pron. this *(fact, idea, etc.)*
estoy *see* **estar**
estudiar to study
estuve *etc. see* **estar**
etc. *(abbrev. of* etcétera*)* etc.
europeo, -a European
examen *m.* examination, exam
excelente excellent
exceso *m.* excess; **exceso de velo-**
cidad speeding

excursión *f.* excursion, outing, (short) trip; **hacer una excursión** to go on an excursion, to take (*or* make) a trip
exigente demanding, strict
éxito *m.* success
exposición *f.* exhibit
extranjero, -a foreign

F

fábrica *f.* factory
fácil easy
facturar to check (*baggage*)
falta *f.* fault, failure; **sin falta** without fail
faltar to be lacking; **falta poco para (las diez)** it's almost (ten o'clock)
familia *f.* family
famoso, -a famous
favor *m.* favor; **hacer el favor de** (+ *inf.*) to do the favor of *or* please (*do something*); **por favor** please
favorito, -a favorite
febrero *m.* February
Felipe Philip; **Felipillo** Phil
feliz happy
ficha *f.* domino (*the piece*)
fiel faithful, trustworthy
fiesta *f.* festival, party
figurar to figure, to appear
filosofía *f.* philosophy
fin *m.* end; **fin de semana** weekend; **por fin** finally, at last
física *f.* physics
fonógrafo *m.* phonograph
francés *m.* French (*language*); **francés, francesa** *adj. or noun* French, Frenchman, *etc.*
Francia *f.* France
frío *m.* cold; **hacer (mucho) frío** to be (very) cold (*weather*); **tener (mucho) frío** to be (very) cold (*referring to persons*)

fué *etc. see* **ir** *and* **ser**
fuego *m.* fire
fui *etc. see* **ir** *and* **ser**
función *f.* show, performance; **función de la tarde** afternoon performance, matinee
futbol *m.* football

G

galante gallant
galería *f.* (top) balcony
ganar to earn, to win
gente *f. sing.* people
gerente *m.* manager
gracias *f. pl.* thanks; thank you
gran, grande large, big, great
gris gray
guapo, -a handsome, good-looking; **guapísimo, -a** very (quite, extremely) good-looking
guardia *m.* policeman, officer
guía *f.* guide, guidebook
gustar to please; **me gusta** (it) pleases me, I like (it)
gusto *m.* pleasure; **con gusto recibí** I was delighted to receive

H

ha *etc. see* **haber**
Habana: la Habana Havana
haber (+ *past participle*) to have (*done something*); **hay, había,** *etc., used impersonally* there is, there are, there was, *etc.*; **hay (mucha) humedad** it is (very) humid (*weather*); **hay sol** it is sunny (*weather*); **hay que** (+ *inf.*) it is necessary to *or* one must (*do something*); **no hay de qué** you're welcome; **¿qué hay (de nuevo)?** what's new?
hablar to speak, to talk
habré *etc. see* **haber**

hacer to do, to make; **hace (pocos años)** (a few years) ago; **hacer (mucho) calor** to be (very) warm or hot *(weather);* **hacer (tres) comidas diarias** to eat (three) meals a day; **hacer una excursión** to go on an excursion, to take *(or* make) a trip; **hacer el favor de** (+ *inf.*) to do the favor of *or* please *(do something);* **hacer (mucho) frío** to be (very) cold *(weather);* **hacer una jira** to go on a picnic; **hacer la maleta** to pack the suitcase; **hacer sol** to be sunny *(weather);* **hacer (buen, mal) tiempo** to be (good, bad) weather; **hacer un viaje** to take *(or* make) a trip; **hacer una visita** to make a call, to visit
hago *etc. see* **hacer**
haré *etc. see* **hacer**
hasta *prep.* until; **hasta que** *conj.* until; **hasta (mañana)** see you (tomorrow)
hay *see* **haber**
haya *etc. see* **haber**
haz *see* **hacer**
he *etc. see* **haber**
hecho *see* **hacer**
hermana *f.* sister
hermano *m.* brother; *pl.* brother(s) and sister(s)
hermoso, -a beautiful
hice *etc. see* **hacer**
hija *f.* daughter
hijo *m.* son; *pl.* children
historia *f.* history
histórico, -a historical
hizo *see* **hacer**
hojear to leaf through, to glance at
¡hola! hey!, hi!, hello!
hombre *m.* man
hora *f.* hour; time *(of day);* **¿a qué hora?** at what time?; **¿qué hora es?** what time is it?; **para última**

hora until *(or* for) the very last (minute)
horario *m.* timetable
hotel *m.* hotel
hoy today
hube *etc. see* **haber**
huelga *f.* strike
huevo *m.* egg
humedad *f.* humidity; **hay (mucha) humedad** it is (very) humid *(weather)*

I

iba *etc. see* **ir**
ida *f.* going; **de ida** one-way; **de ida y vuelta** round-trip
idea *f.* idea
ideal ideal
imaginación *f.* imagination
impedir to prevent
impido *etc. see* **impedir**
imposible impossible
inconveniente *m.* difficulty, objection; **si usted no tiene inconveniente** if it's all right (with you)
India: la India India
Inés Agnes
ingeniería *f.* engineering
Inglaterra *f.* England
inglés *m.* English *(language);* **inglés, inglesa** *adj. or noun* English, Englishman, *etc.*
interesante interesting
interesar to interest; **me interesa** (it) interests me, I am interested in (it)
internacional international
invierno *m.* winter
invitación *f.* invitation
invitar to invite; **invitar a** (+ *inf.*) to invite to *(do something)*
ir to go; **irse** to go away; **ir** (+ *pres. part.*) to be *(doing something);* **ir a** (+ *inf.*) to be going

to *(do something);* **ir a buscar** to stop by for; **ir de compras** *or* **ir de tiendas** to go shopping; **vamos a** (+ *inf.*) we are going to *or* let's *(do something);* ¡**vaya** (una colección)! what (a collection)!; ¡**vaya si...**! of course...!
Isabel Elizabeth
italiano *m.* Italian *(language);* **italiano, -a** *adj. or noun* Italian
izquierdo, -a left; **a la izquierda** to the left; **a mano izquierda** on the left

J

jira *f.* picnic
Jorge George
José Joseph
joven young
Juan John; **Juanito** Johnny
juego *etc. see* **jugar**
juegue *etc. see* **jugar**
jueves *m.* Thursday; **el jueves** (on) Thursday
jugar to play *(a game);* **jugar al** (futbol) to play (football)
jugo *m.* juice
jugué *see* **jugar**
julio *m.* July
junio *m.* June

L

la *def. art., f. sing.* the; *dir. obj. pron., f. sing.* her, it, you *(polite);* **la de** that of, the one of
lado *m.* side; **al lado de** beside
lago *m.* lake
largo, -a long
las *def. art., f. pl.* the; *dir. obj. pron., f. pl.* them, you *(polite);* **las de** those of, the ones of
lástima *f.* pity
Latinoamérica *f.* Latin America
le *dir. obj. pron., m. sing.* him, you

(polite); *ind. obj., m. or f. sing.* (to) him, her, it, you *(polite)*
leche *f.* milk; **café** *(m.)* **con leche** coffee with cream
leer to read
legumbre *f.* vegetable
lejos far; **lejos de** far from
lengua *f.* language
les *ind. obj. pron., m. or f. pl.* (to) them, you *(polite)*
levantarse to get up
leyó *etc. see* **leer**
libre free
libro *m.* book
ligero, -a light
lindo, -a pretty
línea *f.* line
lista *f.* list, menu
listo, -a ready
literatura *f.* literature
ll— *see below, after* **lu—**
lo *neut. def. art.* the; *dir. obj. pron., m. sing.* him, it, you *(polite); neut. obj. or predicate complement* it, so; **lo mismo** the same (thing); **lo que** that which, what
localidad *f.* seat, ticket
los *def. art., m. pl.* the; *dir. obj. pron., m. pl.* them, you *(polite);* **los de** those of, the ones of
luego soon, then; so, therefore; **desde luego** of course; **hasta luego** so long, see you later
lugar *m.* place, spot
Luis Louis
Luisa Louise
lunes *m.* Monday; **el lunes** (on) Monday

LL

llamado, -a named
llamar to call; **llamarse** to be named; **me llamo (Felipe)** my name is (Philip); ¿**cómo se llama usted?** what is your name?

llegar to arrive
llegue *etc. see* **llegar**
llenar to fill; **llenarse de** to fill up
with
llover to rain
llueve *etc. see* **llover**
lluvia *f.* rain

M

madre *f.* mother
maestro: obra maestra masterpiece
magnífico, -a magnificent, wonderful
mal *adv.* badly, poorly; **mal, malo, -a** bad
maleta *f.* suitcase
mamá *f.* mamma, mother
mano *f.* hand; **a mano (derecha)** on the (right)
mañana *f.* morning; *adv.* tomorrow; **hasta mañana** see you tomorrow; **por la mañana** (in the) morning; **(las ocho) de la mañana** (eight o'clock) in the morning, (eight) A.M.
María Mary
marido *m.* husband
martes *m.* Tuesday; **el martes** (on) Tuesday
marzo *m.* March
más more, most; *used to form comparative and superlative;* **¡qué (muchacha) más (linda)!** what a (pretty girl)!
matar to kill
matemáticas *f. pl.* mathematics
mayo *m.* May
mayor older *or* oldest
me *dir. and ind. obj. pron.* me, to me; *reflex.* myself
medio, -a half *or* a half; **(la una) y media** half past (one)
mediodía *m.* noon; **al mediodía** at noon

mejicano, -a *adj. or noun* Mexican
Méjico *m.* Mexico
mejor better *or* best
mejorar to improve
melón *m.* melon, cantaloupe
menor younger *or* youngest
menos less, least; *used to form comparative and superlative;* **(la una) menos (cuarto)** (a quarter) to (one); **por lo menos** at least
merendar to have (picnic) lunch *or* supper
mes *m.* month; **de (seis) meses** (six) months old
mi, mis *poss. adj.* my
mí *obj. of prep.* me *or* myself; **a mí** *obj. pron.* me, to me
mientras while, as long as
miércoles *m.* Wednesday; **el miércoles** (on) Wednesday
Miguel Michael
mil thousand, a (*or* one) thousand
millón *m.* million; **un millón de . . .** a million . . .
millonario, -a very wealthy
minuto *m.* minute
mío, -a, -os, -as *poss. adj.* mine, of mine; **el mío,** *etc., pron.* mine
mirar to look (at), to watch
mismo, -a same; selfsame *(used to intensify);* **mismo** *adv.* right, even; **ahora mismo** right now; **lo mismo** the same (thing)
modelo *m.* model, style
moderno, -a modern
modo *m.* way; **de modo que** so (that), and so; **de todos modos** anyway, at any rate
monumento *m.* monument
moreno, -a dark, brunet, brunette
morir to die
mortal *m.* mortal
motivo *m.* motive
muchacha *f.* girl
muchacho *m.* boy, fellow

mucho, -a much; *pl.* many; **mucho**
adv. much, very much, a lot, a
great deal
muero *etc. see* morir
muerte *f.* death
muerto *see* morir
mujer *f.* woman
mundo *m.* world
murió *etc. see* morir
museo *m.* museum
música *f.* music
musical musical
muy very, quite

N

nacimiento *m.* birth
nacionalidad *f.* nationality
nada nothing, not . . . anything
nadie nobody, no one, not . . . anyone
naranja *f.* orange
natural natural
negar to deny
negocio *m.* business affair, deal; *pl.*
business (affairs)
negué *see* negar
nevar to snow
ni neither, nor; **ni siquiera** not
even
niego *etc. see* negar
niegue *etc. see* negar
nieva *etc. see* nevar
ningún, ninguno, -a no, none, not
. . . any
niña *f.* girl, child; **niñita** little girl
niño *m.* boy, child
no no, not, **creer que no** to believe
not, to think not
noche *f.* evening, night; **buenas
noches** good evening, hello, good
night; **por la noche** in the evening, at night; **(las ocho) de la
noche** (eight o'clock) in the evening, (eight) P.M.

norteamericano, -a *adj. or noun*
American
nos *dir. and ind. obj. pron.* us, to
us; *reflex.* ourselves, one another,
each other
nosotros, -as *subj. pron.* we; *obj. of
prep.* us *or* ourselves; **a nosotros,
-as** *obj. pron.* us, to us
noticia *f.* news (item); *pl.* news
novecientos, -as nine hundred
novela *f.* novel
noveno, -a ninth
noventa ninety; **noventa y un, noventa y uno, -a** ninety-one; **noventa y dos** ninety-two, *etc.*
noviembre *m.* November
nublado, -a cloudy
nuestro, -a, -os, -as *poss. adj.* our,
ours, of ours; **el nuestro,** *etc.,
pron.* ours
nueve nine; *(in dates)* ninth; **las
nueve** nine (o'clock); **diez y
nueve** nineteen
nuevo, -a new; **¿qué hay de nuevo?**
what's new?
número *m.* number
nunca never, not . . . ever

O

o or
obra *f.* work; **obra maestra** masterpiece
obrera *f.* worker
obrero *m.* worker
ocasión *f.* occasion, opportunity
och—*see below, after* ocu—
octavo, -a eighth
octubre *m.* October
ocupado, -a busy
ocurrir to occur; **se me ocurre una
idea** an idea occurs to me
ochenta eighty; **ochenta y un,
ochenta y uno, -a** eighty-one;
ochenta y dos eighty-two; *etc.*

ocho eight; *(in dates)* eighth; las
ocho eight (o'clock); **diez y ocho**
eighteen
ochocientos, -as eight hundred
¡oh! oh!
oigo *etc. see* **oír**
oír to hear, to listen; **¡oiga!** *(calling on the telephone)* hello!
¡ojalá! I hope (so)!; **ojalá ...** I
hope (that) ...
olvidar to forget; **olvidarse de que**
to forget that
once eleven; *(in dates)* eleventh;
las once eleven (o'clock)
ópera *f.* opera
orden *f.* order, command; **a sus órdenes** at your service
orquesta *f.* orchestra; **orquesta sinfónica** symphony orchestra
os *dir. and ind. obj. pron.* you, to
you *(fam. pl.); reflex.* yourselves,
one another, each other
oscuro, -a dark
otoño *m.* fall, autumn
otro, -a other, another
oye *etc. see* **oír**

P

Pablo Paul
Paco Frank
padre *m.* father; *pl.* parents
pagar to pay (for)
pague *etc. see* **pagar**
país *m.* country *(nation)*
pan *m.* bread
pañuelo *m.* handkerchief
papá *m.* dad, papa, father
par *m.* pair
para *prep.* for; to, in order to;
para que *conj.* so that, in order
that
Paraguay: el Paraguay Paraguay
parecer to seem
pareja *f.* couple; dancing partner
parezco *etc. see* **parecer**

parienta *f.* relative
pariente *m.* relative
partido *m.* game; party *(political)*
pasado, -a past, last; **pasado** *m.* past
pasajero *m.* passenger
pasar to pass; to spend *(time);* to
come *or* go in
pasear *or* **pasearse** to stroll, to take
a walk
paseo *m.* walk, stroll; **paseíto** little
walk *or* tour; **dar un paseo** to
take a walk
pedir to ask, to request
Pedro Peter
peinado *m.* hairdo, coiffure
película *f.* film, picture, movie
pelirrojo, -a redheaded
pena *f.* pain, trouble
pensar to think; to intend; **pensar
en** to think about
peor worse *or* worst
pequeño, -a small
perder to lose; to miss
perfectamente perfectly
periódico *m.* newspaper
permiso *m.* permission; **con permiso** excuse me
permitir to permit
pero but
perspectiva *f.* prospect
Perú: el Perú Peru
pescado *m.* fish
pido *etc. see* **pedir**
pienso *etc. see* **pensar**
pierdo *etc. see* **perder**
pintura *f.* painting
plano *m.* (city) map
playa *f.* beach
pobre poor; **el pobre (Juan)** poor
(John); **un muchacho pobre** a
poor *(needy)* boy
poco, -a little; *pl.* few; **poco** *adv.*
little; **un poco** *adv.* a little
poder to be able (can, may); **¿se
puede?** may I *(or* we) come in?
podré *etc. see* **poder**

poesía *f.* poetry; poem; *pl.* poems, poetry
político, -a political
pon *see* **poner**
pondré *etc. see* **poner**
poner to put; to put on *(a play);* **ponerse** to put on *(clothes)*
pongo *etc. see* **poner**
por in, during, through; by; because of, for; **¿por dónde?** which way?; **por fin** finally; **por lo menos** at least; **¿por qué?** why?; **por (tercera) vez** for the (third) time
porque because
portugués *m.* Portuguese *(language)*
posible possible
postre *m.* dessert; **de postre** for dessert
precio *m.* price; **de diferentes precios** at different prices
precioso, -a precious, lovely
preciso, -a necessary
preferir to prefer
prefiero *etc. see* **preferir**
prefirió *etc. see* **preferir**
preguntar to ask *(a question)*
preparativos *m. pl.* preparations
presentar to present, to introduce
primavera *f.* spring *(season)*
primer, primero, -a first
prima *f.* cousin
primo *m.* cousin
principio *m.* beginning; **al principio** at first; **a principios de** toward the beginning of
probable probable, likely
probar to prove; to test, to try (on)
profesor *m.* professor, teacher
profesora *f.* professor, teacher
programa *m.* program
progresar to progress
pronto soon; **hasta pronto** see you soon
propósito *m.* purpose; **a propósito de** apropos of

próximo, -a next
pruebo *etc. see* **probar**
pude *etc. see* **poder**
puedo *etc. see* **poder**
pues since *(cause);* well (then)
puesto *see* **poner**
punto *m.* point, dot; **(la una) en punto** (one o'clock) sharp, (one o'clock) on the dot
puse *etc. see* **poner**

Q

que *conj.* that; *(after a comparative)* than; *rel. pron.* that, who; **el (la, los, las) que** which; **lo que** that which
¿qué? what?, which?; **¿qué tal?** how goes it?; **¿qué tal (fué)?** how was?; **no hay de qué** you're welcome; **¿por qué?** why?
¡qué! how!, what (a)!; **¡qué (linda muchacha)!**, **¡qué (muchacha) tan** *or* **más (linda)!** what a (pretty girl)!
quedar to remain; to be; **quedarse** to stay, to remain; **quedarse con** to keep, to take
quejarse to complain
quemar to burn; **quemarse las cejas** to burn the midnight oil
querer to want, to wish
querido, -a dear
querré *etc. see* **querer**
¿quién?, *pl.* **¿quiénes?** *subj.* who?; *obj. of prep.* whom?; **¿a quién?** *obj. of verb* whom?
quiero *etc. see* **querer**
química *f.* chemistry
quince fifteen; *(in dates)* fifteenth
quinientos, -as five hundred
quinto, -a fifth
quise *etc. see* **querer**
quizá *or* **quizás** perhaps, maybe

R

radio *f*. radio
Ramón Raymond
raro, -a rare
rato *m*. short time; un rato a (little) while
recibir to receive
recordar to recall, to remember
recorrer to go through, to look over
recreo *m*. recreation
recuerdo *etc. see* recordar; recuerdos *m. pl*. regards, greetings; recuerdos a (todos) remember me to (everybody)
refresco *m*. cold drink, refreshment(s)
reloj *m*. watch
repetir to repeat
repito *etc. see* repetir
representar to act, to perform *(a play)*
resfriado *m*. cold *(illness);* coger un resfriado to catch (a) cold
restaurán *m*. restaurant
resultar to result, to turn out, to prove to be
revisor *m*. conductor *(on a train)*
revista *f*. review, revue
rico, -a rich
río *m*. river
ritmo *m*. rhythm
rubio, -a fair, blond, blonde
rumba *f*. rumba
ruso *m*. Russian *(language)*

S

sábado *m*. Saturday; el sábado (on) Saturday
saber to know *(a fact);* no (lo) sé I don't know
sabré *etc. see* saber
sacar to take out; to get *(tickets)*
sal *see* salir

sala *f*. (large) room; sala de equipajes baggage room; sala de espera waiting room
saldré *etc. see* salir
salgo *etc. see* salir
salir to leave, to go out; salir de to leave (from), to go out of
salón *m*. salon, large room, hall
saludo *m*. greeting
Salvador: el Salvador Salvador
sandwich *m*. sandwich
saque *etc. see* sacar
se *ind. obj. pron., used before* lo, la, los, las (to) him, her, it, them, you *(polite); reflex. pron., dir. or ind. obj.* himself, herself, itself, oneself, themselves, yourself *or* yourselves *(polite);* one another, each other; *indef. subj. pron.* one, you, they
sé *see* saber *and* ser
sea *etc. see* ser
seguir to continue, to still be, to keep on; que usted siga bien good-by
según according to
segundo, -a second
seguro, -a sure
seis six; *(in dates)* sixth; las seis six (o'clock); diez y seis sixteen
seiscientos, -as six hundred
semana *f*. week; fin *(m.)* de semana weekend
sentado, -a seated
sentar to suit, to become, to be becoming; sentarse to sit down
sentir to feel, to regret, to be sorry; lo siento (mucho) I am (very) sorry; sentirse (+ *adj.*) to feel
señor *m*. sir, Mr., gentleman; *pl.* lady and gentleman, Mr. and Mrs.
señora *f*. ma'am, lady, Mrs., wife
señorita *f*. Miss, young lady
sepa *etc. see* saber
septiembre *m*. September

séptimo, -a seventh

ser to be *(characteristic); used to form passive voice;* somos (cinco) there are (five) of us; son (veinte dólares) that makes *or* will be (twenty dollars)

serie *f.* series

serio, -a serious

servidor (de usted) your servant, at your service

servir to serve

sesenta sixty; sesenta y un, sesenta y uno, -a sixty-one; sesenta y dos sixty-two; *etc.*

setecientos, -as seven hundred

setenta seventy; setenta y un, setenta y uno, -a seventy-one; setenta y dos seventy-two; *etc.*

sexto, -a sixth

si if, whether

sí yes; *used for emphatic affirmative;* sí, señor yes (sir); creer que sí to believe so, to think so

sí *reflex. pron., obj. of prep.* himself, herself, itself, oneself, themselves, yourself *or* yourselves *(polite);* him, her, it, one, them, you *(used reflexively)*

siempre always

siento *etc. see* sentar *and* sentir

siete seven; *(in dates)* seventh; las siete seven (o'clock); diez y siete seventeen

siglo *m.* century

sigo *etc. see* seguir

sigue *etc. see* seguir

sillón *m.* easy chair, (large) armchair

simpático, -a likable, pleasant, nice

sin without; sin duda without doubt, no doubt; sin embargo nevertheless

sinfonía *f.* symphony

sinfónico: orquesta sinfónica symphony orchestra

sino *(after negative)* but *(but rather);* no sólo . . . sino (también) not only . . . but also

sintió *etc. see* sentir

siquiera even, at least; ni siquiera not even

sirvo *etc. see* servir

sitio *m.* place, spot

situación *f.* situation

soberanamente quite, terribly

sobrina *f.* niece *or* cousin's daughter

sobrino nephew *or* cousin's son; *pl.* niece(s) and nephew(s)

sociología *f.* sociology

sois *see* ser

sol *m.* sun, sunshine; hacer *(or* haber) sol to be sunny *(weather);* tomar el sol to get some sunshine, to get out in the sun

solo, -a alone; café solo black coffee

sólo *adv.* only; no sólo . . . sino (también) not only . . . but also

soltero, -a unmarried, single

solución *f.* solution

sombrero *m.* hat

somos *see* ser

son *see* ser

soñar (con) to dream (of *or* about)

sopa *f.* soup

sospechar to suspect

soy *see* ser

Sr., Sra., Srta., Sres. *abbrev. of* señor, señora, señorita, señores

su, sus *poss. adj.* his, her, its, their, your *(polite)*

subir to go *or* come up; subir al tren to get on the train

sueño *etc. see* soñar

supe *etc. see* saber

suplicio *m.* torture

supondré *etc. see* suponer

suponer to suppose

supongo *etc. see* suponer

supuesto *see* suponer; por supuesto of course, naturally

supuse *etc. see* **suponer**
surtido *m.* stock, supply
suyo, -a, -os, -as *poss. adj.* (of) his, hers, theirs, yours *(polite);* **el suyo**, *etc., pron.* his, hers, theirs, yours

T

tal such, such a
también also, too
tampoco neither, not ... either
tan as, so; **tan ... como** as ... as; **¡qué (muchacha) tan (linda)!** what a (pretty girl)!
tango *m.* tango
tanto, -a as much, so much; *pl.* as many, so many; **tanto** *adv.* as much, so much
taquillero *m.* ticket agent
tarde *f.* afternoon; *adv.* late; **buenas tardes** good afternoon, hello; **más tarde** later; **por la tarde** (in the) afternoon; **(la una) de la tarde** (one o'clock) in the afternoon, (one) P.M.; **función** *(f.)* **de la tarde** afternoon performance, matinee
taxi *m.* taxi, taxicab
te *dir. and ind. obj. pron.* you, to you *(fam. sing.); reflex.* yourself
teatro *m.* theatre
teléfono *m.* telephone; **al teléfono** on the telephone
televisión *f.* television
temer to fear; **temer que** to fear that, to be afraid that
temprano *adv.* early
ten *see* **tener**
tendré *etc. see* **tener**
tener to have; **tener ... años,** *etc.* to be ... (years) old, *etc.;* **tener (mucho) apetito** to be (very) hungry; **tener (mucho) calor** to be (very) warm *or* hot *(referring to persons);* **tener (mucho) frío**

to be very cold *(referring to persons);* **tener que** (+ *inf.*) to have to *(do something);* **aquí tiene usted** here you have, here is, here are
tengo *etc. see* **tener**
tenis *m.* tennis
tercer, tercero, -a third
terminar to end, to finish
ti *obj. of prep.* you *or* yourself *(fam.);* **a ti** *obj. pron.* you, to you
tía *f.* aunt
tiempo *m.* time; weather; **hacer (buen, mal) tiempo** to be (good, bad) weather; **¿qué tiempo hace?** how is the weather?
tienda *f.* shop; **ir de tiendas** to go shopping
tiene *etc. see* **tener**
tío *m.* uncle; *pl.* uncle(s) and aunt(s)
tocar to play *(music)*
todo, -a all; **todos** *pron., m. pl.* all, everybody; **todo derecho** straight ahead; **todos los (días)** every (day); **de todos modos** anyway, at any rate
tomar to take; to have *(food or drink);* **tome usted** here is, here are; **tomar el sol** to get some sunshine, to get out in the sun
toque *etc. see* **tocar**
tormenta *f.* storm
tostada *f.* piece of toast; *pl.* toast
trabajar to work
trabajo *m.* work
traer to bring; **¿qué noticias trae ...?** what's the news in ...?
traigo *etc. see* **traer**
traje *etc. see* **traer**
tranvía *m.* trolley, streetcar
tratar to treat; **tratarse de** to concern
trayendo *see* **traer**
trece thirteen; *(in dates)* thirteenth

treinta thirty; *(in dates)* thirtieth; **treinta y un, treinta y uno, -a** thirty-one; **treinta y dos** thirty-two; *etc.*

tren *m.* train; **cambiar de tren** to change trains

tres three; *(in dates)* third; **las tres** three (o'clock)

trescientos, -as three hundred

tu, tus *poss. adj.* your *(fam., one possessor)*

tú *subj. pron.* you *(fam. sing.)*

tuve *etc. see* **tener**

tuyo, -a, -os, -as *poss. adj.* yours, of yours *(fam., one possessor);* **el tuyo,** *etc. pron.* yours

U

u or *(used before* **o-** *or* **ho-)**

Ud., Uds. *(abbrev. of* **usted, ustedes)** you *(polite)*

último, -a last, latest

un, una *indef. art.* a, an; *pl.* some, a few; **un, uno, -a** one; **la una** one (o'clock)

único, -a sole, only

universidad *f.* university

uno, -a *indef. pron.* one

unos, -as some, a few; about

Uruguay: el Uruguay Uruguay

usted, ustedes *subj. pron., and obj. of prep.* you *(polite);* **a usted, a ustedes** *obj. pron.* you, to you; **de usted, de ustedes** *poss. adj.* your, yours, of yours

V

V. *(abbrev. of* **usted)** you *(polite)*

va *etc. see* **ir**

vacaciones *f. pl.* vacation

val *see* **valer**

valdré *etc. see* **valer**

valer to be worth; to cost

valgo *etc. see* **valer**

valor *m.* value, worth

vals *m.* waltz

variedad *f.* variety; *pl.* variety, vaudeville

varios, -as several

vaya *etc. see* **ir**

Vd., Vds. *(abbrev. of* **usted, ustedes)** you *(polite)*

ve *see* **ir**

veces *see* **vez**

veía *etc. see* **ver**

veinte twenty; *(in dates)* twentieth; **veintiún, veintiuno, -a** twenty-one; **veintidós** twenty-two; *etc.*

velocidad *f.* speed; **exceso** *(m.)* **de velocidad** speeding

ven *see* **venir**

vendré *etc. see* **venir**

vengo *etc. see* **venir**

venir to come; **la (semana) que viene** next (week)

veo *etc. see* **ver**

ver to see; **verse** to see each other, to meet

verano *m.* summer

verdad *f.* truth; **¿verdad?** true?, isn't it so?, don't you?, etc.

verde green

vestido *m.* clothing; dress

vez *f.* time; **a veces** at times, sometimes; **muchas veces** many times, often; **otra vez** another time, again; **una vez** once; **por (tercera) vez** for the (third) time

viajar to travel

viaje *m.* trip; **hacer un viaje** to take (*or* make) a trip

viajero *m.* traveler; **¡señores viajeros, al tren!** all aboard!

vida *f.* life

viejo, -a old

viene *etc. see* **venir**

viento *m.* wind; **hacer (mucho) viento** to be (very) windy *(weather)*

viernes *m.* Friday; **el viernes** (on) Friday

vine *etc. see* **venir**

visita *f.* visit; **hacer una visita** to make a call, to visit

visitar to visit

vista *f.* sight, view, meeting; **hasta la vista** so long, good-by

visto *see* **ver**

vivir to live

volver to return, to go back

vosotros, -as *subj. pron.* you *(fam. pl.); obj. of prep.* you *or* yourselves; **a vosotros, -as** *obj. pron.* you, to you

voy *see* **ir**

vuelta *f.* turn; return; change *(money);* **de ida y vuelta** round-trip; **dar una vuelta** to take a little walk

vuelto *see* **volver**

vuelvo *etc. see* **volver**

vuestro, -a, -os, -as *poss. adj.* your, yours, of yours *(fam., two or more possessors);* **el vuestro,** *etc., pron.* yours

VV. *(abbrev. of* **ustedes***)* you *(polite, pl.)*

Y

y and; **(la una) y (cuarto)** (a quarter) past (one)

ya already; **¡ya lo creo!** yes, indeed!, I should say so!; **ya que** since *(cause)*

yendo *see* **ir**

yo *subj. pron.* I

Z

zapato *m.* shoe

zarzuela *f.* musical comedy

zoología *f.* zoology

English-Spanish Vocabulary

A

a *indef. art.* un, una[3]; un[12] *(f.)*
able: to be able poder*[9]
aboard: all aboard! ¡señores viajeros, al tren![17]
about *(of)* de[22]; *(some)* unos, -as[6]; (at) about *(a certain time of day)* a eso de[7]; to be about to *(do something)* estar* para (+ *inf.*)[17]; to dream about soñar* con[10]; to think about pensar* en[10]
abundant abundante[12]
academy academia[19] *f.*
accent acento[3] *m.;* without an accent sin acento[3]
accident accidente[21] *m.*
accompany acompañar[12]
according to según[18]
acquainted: to be acquainted with conocer*[5]
act *(to perform)* representar[13]
activity *(bustle)* ajetreo[17] *m.*
actor actor[11] *m.*
actress actriz[11] *f.*
addition: in addition to además de[19]
affair: business affair negocio[18] *m.*
affectionate cariñoso, -a[22]; *(devoted)* afectísimo *(abbrev.* afmo.), -a[22]
afraid: to be afraid that temer que[22]
after *prep.* después de[17]; (a quarter) after (one) (la una) y (cuarto)[7]
afternoon tarde[7] *f.;* (in the) afternoon por la tarde[7]; (one o'clock) in the afternoon (la una) de la tarde[7]; afternoon performance función *(f.)* de la tarde[24]; good afternoon buenas tardes[1]
afterwards después[5]

again otra vez[25]
age edad[6]; what (is his) age? ¿qué edad (tiene)? *or* ¿cuántos años (tiene)?[26]
agent: ticket agent taquillero[17] *m.*
Agnes Inés[3]
ago: (a few years) ago hace (pocos años)[19]
agreeable agradable[8]
agreement acuerdo[21] *m.*
ah! ¡ah![17]
ahead: straight ahead todo derecho[19]
airplane avión[23] *m.*
alas! ¡ay![12]
all todo, -a[4]; all aboard! ¡señores viajeros, al tren![17]; all right bien[1]; if it's all right (with you) si usted no tiene inconveniente[23]
almost casi[3]; it's almost (ten o'clock) falta poco para (las diez)[17]
alone solo, -a[12]
already ya[8]
also también[2]
although aunque[13]
always siempre[2]
A.M.: (eight) A.M. (las ocho) de la mañana[7]
American *adj. or noun* norteamericano, -a[3]; (he is) an American (es) norteamericano[3]
amiable amable[5]
amusing divertido, -a[11]
an *indef. art.* un, una[3]; un[12] *(f.)*
ancient antiguo, -a[19]
and y[1]; e[4] *(before* i- *or* hi-*);* and so conque *or* de modo que[11]; (thirty dollars) and (forty cents) (treinta dólares) con *or* y (cuarenta centavos)[17]
animated animado, -a[20]

xxi

another otro, -a[4]; one another nos, os, se[6]

answer *vb.* contestar[22]

Anthony Antonio[3]

any: *usually omitted before noun object*[6]; *(some)* algún, alguno, -a[5]; not . . . any ningún, ninguno, -a[24]; at any rate de todos modos[18]

anyone *(after negative)* nadie[17]

anything algo[17]; not . . . anything nada[16]

anyway *(at any rate)* de todos modos[18]

apparatus aparato[23] *m.*

appear *(to figure)* figurar[13]

appetite apetito[12] *m.*

April abril[8] *m.*

apropos of a propósito de[22]

Argentina la Argentina[16]

armchair butaca[24] *f.; (easy chair)* sillón[24] *m.*

around *prep.* alrededor de[15]

arrive llegar*[7]

art arte[18] *m. or f.;* fine arts bellas artes[19] *f. pl.*

artist artista[19] *m. or f.*

artistic artístico, -a[13]

as *(for)* de[12]; *(when)* al[17] (+ *inf.*); as . . . as tan . . . como[4]; as if como si[25]; as long as *(while)* mientras[24]; as many tantos, -as[11]; as many . . . as tantos (-as) . . . como[13]; as much *adv.* tanto[13]; *adj.* tanto, -a[11]; as much . . . as tanto (-a) . . . como[13]; as soon as *conj.* en cuanto[24]

ask *(to inquire)* preguntar[18]; *(to request)* pedir*[22]

at a[7]; *(a place)* en[2]; at different prices de diferentes precios[14]; at last por fin[17]; at least por lo menos[11]; at night por la noche[7]; at your service servidor (de usted)[17], a sus órdenes[23]

August agosto[8] *m.*

aunt tía[6] *f.;* uncle(s) and aunt(s) tíos[6] *m. pl.*

automobile automóvil[21] *m.*

autumn otoño[8] *m.*

away: to go away irse*[23]

B

back: to go back volver*[7]

bad mal, malo, -a[8]

badly mal[2]

baggage equipaje[17] *m.;* baggage room sala *(f.)* de equipajes[17]

balcony *(top balcony)* galería[24] *f.;* balcony seat *or* seat in the top balcony asiento *(m.)* de galería[24]

ballerina bailarina[13] *f.*

bank note billete[14] *m.*

baseball (el) beisbol[9]

be *(characteristic)* ser*[3]; *(condition or location)* estar*[1]; tener* (+ *noun:* años, edad, meses[6]; apetito[12]; calor, frío[8]); *(weather)* estar* (+ *adj.*), haber*, hacer* (+ *noun*)[8]; *(to remain)* quedar[25]; *(in passive voice)* ser*[19]; *(in progressive forms)* estar*, ir*[20]; be able poder*[9]; be about to *(do something)* estar* para (+ *inf.*)[17]; be acquainted with conocer*[5]; be afraid that temer que[22]; be becoming *(to suit)* sentar*[14]; be glad (that) alegrarse (de que)[22]; be lacking faltar[17]; be named llamarse[6]; be obliged *(must)* deber[16]; be sorry *(to regret)* sentir*[8]; be still *(doing something)* seguir* (+ *pres. part.*)[21]; be worth valer*[14]

beach playa[25] *f.*

beautiful hermoso, -a[15], bello, -a[19]

because porque[4]; because of por[21]

become *or* be becoming *(to suit)* sentar*[14]

bed: to go to bed acostarse*[7]

before *(in time)* *adv.* antes[15]; *prep.* antes de[10]; *conj.* antes (de) que[24]
beforehand antes[15]
begin empezar*[9], comenzar*[25]
beginning principio[19] *m.;* **toward the beginning of** a principios de[19]
believe creer*[9]; **to believe not** creer* que no[9]; **to believe so** creer* que sí[9]
beside *prep.* al lado de[17]
besides *adv.* además[11]; *prep.* además de[19]
better *or* **best** mejor[9]; *(with gustar)* más[9]
between entre[21]
big gran, grande[14]
bill *(bank note)* billete[14] *m.*
birth nacimiento[21] *m.*
black coffee café *(m.)* solo[12]
blond, blonde rubio, -a[5]
blouse blusa[14] *f.*
blue azul[15]
book libro[19] *m.*
bore aburrir[25]
bored aburrido, -a[24]; **to get** *(or* **be)** **bored** aburrirse[25]
boring aburrido, -a[25]
both los dos, las dos[3]
boy muchacho[3] *m.,* niño[6] *m.*
Brazil el Brasil[16]
bread pan[12] *m.*
breakfast (el) desayuno[12]; **to eat breakfast** desayunarse[7]
bridge *(game)* (el) bridge[25]
bring traer*[22]
brother hermano[6] *m.;* **brother(s) and sister(s)** hermanos[6] *m. pl.*
brunet, brunette moreno, -a[5]
build construir*[19]
building edificio[18] *m.*
burn quemar[25]; **to burn the midnight oil** quemarse las cejas[25]
bus autobús[10] *m.*
business *(affair, deal)* negocio[18] *m.,* *(affairs)* negocios[18] *m. pl.;* **business district** centro[10] *m.*
bustle ajetreo[17] *m.*
busy ocupado, -a[20]
but pero[2]; *(but instead)* sino[20]; **not only . . . but also** no sólo . . . sino (también)[20]
buy comprar[14]
by por[7]; **by (plane)** en (avión)[23]; **to stop by for** ir* a buscar[15]

C

call *(visit)* visita[10] *f.; vb.* llamar[6]; **this is . . . calling** *(at the telephone)* aquí . . .[23]
can *(to be able)* poder*[9]
Canada el Canadá[16]
cantaloupe melón[12] *m.*
capital capital[16] *f.*
car coche[5] *m.,* automóvil[21] *m.;* **car wreck** choque *(m.)* de automóviles[21]
cartoon *(animated cartoon)* dibujo animado[11] *m.*
catch coger*[8]
cent centavo[17] *m.*
century siglo[19] *m.*
certain *or* **a certain** cierto, -a[25]
chair: easy chair sillón[24] *m.;* *(armchair)* butaca[24] *f.*
change cambio[14] *m.;* *(money)* vuelta[14] *f.; vb.* cambiar[17]; **to change trains** cambiar de tren[17]; **here is your change** tome usted la vuelta[14]
chat *vb.* charlar[7]
cheap barato, -a[14]
check *(baggage)* facturar[17]
chemistry (la) química[4]
child niño[6] *m.,* niña[6] *f.;* **children** niños[6] *m. pl.;* *(sons and daughters)* hijos[6] *m. pl.*
cinema cine[5] *m.*
city ciudad[6] *f.;* *(business district)* centro[10] *m.;* **city map** plano[18] *m.*

class clase[2] f.

classical clásico, -a[9]

clerk *(in a store)* dependiente[14] m., dependienta[14] f.

climate clima[8] m.

clothing vestido[14] m.

cloudy nublado, -a[8]

coffee café[7] m.; **coffee with cream** café con leche[12]; **black coffee** café solo[12]

coiffure peinado[20] m.

cold frío[8] m.; *(illness)* resfriado[8] m.; **cold drink** refresco[11] m.; **to be (very) cold** *(referring to persons)* tener* (mucho) frío[8]; *(weather)* hacer* (mucho) frío[8]; **to catch (a) cold** coger* un resfriado[8]

collection colección[19] f.

collector coleccionista[19] m. or f.

collision choque[21] m.

Colombia Colombia[16] f.

come venir*[5]; **to come in** pasar[23]; **to come up** subir[17]; **come in!** ¡adelante! or ¡pase usted![23]; **may I** *(or we)* **come in?** ¿se puede?[23]

comedy comedia[13] f.; **musical comedy** zarzuela[13] f.

comfortable comodo, -a[18]

command orden[23] f.

commence comenzar*[25]

comment comentario[20] m.

company compañía[13] f.

complain quejarse[11]

complete completo, -a[13]

completely completamente[23]

concern vb. tratarse de[21]

concert concierto[13] m.

conductor *(on a train)* revisor[17] m.

conflict conflicto[21] m.

consist of consistir en[13]

constant constante[24]

construct construir*[19]

contain contener*[19]

contented contento, -a[15]

continue *(to keep on)* seguir*[21] *(+ pres. part.)*

contrary contrario, -a[23]; **on the contrary** al contrario[23]

convenient cómodo, -a[18]

cordial cordial[22]

cost vb. costar*[16]; *(to be worth)* valer*[14]

country *(field)* campo[15] m.; *(nation)* país[16] m.; adj. campestre[15]

couple pareja[20] f.

course *(class)* clase[2] f.; **course (of study)** asignatura[4] f.; **of course!** ¡claro![10], por supuesto[15], desde luego[16], ¡cómo no![22]; **of course...** claro que . . .[10], por supuesto que . . .[15], ¡vaya si . . .![25]

cousin primo[5] m., prima[5] f.

cream: coffee with cream café *(m.)* con leche[12]

crime crimen[21] m.

cultural *(artistic)* artístico, -a[13]

cure vb. curar[10]

D

dad papá[16] m.

daily diario, -a[12]; **daily routine** vida *(f.)* de todos los días[7]

dance baile[9] m.; vb. bailar[11]

dancer bailarín[13] m., bailarina[13] f.

dancing partner pareja[20] f.

danseuse bailarina[13] f.

dark oscuro, -a[14]; *(brunet)* moreno, -a[5]

daughter hija[6] f.

day día[7] m.; **a day** *(daily)* diario, -a[12]

deal *(business)* negocio[18] m.; **a great deal** adv. mucho[4]

dear querido, -a[22]

death muerte[21] f.

December diciembre[8] m.

delighted encantado, -a[20]; **I was delighted to receive** con gusto recibí[22]

demanding *(strict)* exigente[
deny negar*[21]

department store almacén[14] *m.*
desire *vb.* desear[23]
dessert postre[12] *m.; for dessert de*
postre[12]
devoted *(affectionate)* afectísimo
(abbrev. afmo.*)*, -a[22]
die morir*[21]
different diferente[14]; *it would be
quite different* sería otra cosa[23]
difficult difícil[3]
difficulty *(objection)* inconvenien-
tc[23]
dinner (la) comida[12]; *(special dinner)* cubierto[12] *m.; to eat dinner*
comer[7]
direct directo, -a[17]
direction dirección[21] *f.*
disagreeable desagradable[8]
disagreement *(conflict)* conflicto[21]
m.
district: business district centro[10] *m.*
divine divino, -a[20]
do *(to make, to act, etc.)* hacer*[7];
emphatic affirmative[4]; *negative or
interrogative*[2]
dollar dólar[12] *m.*
domino ficha[25] *f.;* dominoes *(the
game)* (el) dominó[25]
Don don *(abbrev.* D.)[3] *m. title*
Doña doña *(abbrev.* D.ª)[3] *f. title*
donate donar[19]
dot punto[7] *m.;* (one o'clock) on the
dot (la una) en punto[7]
doubt duda[8] *f.; vb.* dudar[21]; **no
doubt** *or* **without doubt** sin duda[8]
doubtful dudoso, -a[21]
down: to sit down sentarse*[23]
downtown *(in the city)* en el centro[10]; *(to the city)* al centro[10]
dream (of *or* about) soñar* (con)[10]
dress vestido[14] *m.*
drink bebida[21] *f.;* cold drink refresco[11] *m.*
during *(in)* por[7]

E

each other nos, os, se[6]
early *adv.* temprano[7]
earn ganar[9]
easy fácil[3]; easier más fácil[4]
easy chair sillón[24] *m.*
eat comer[7], *(to have)* tomar[7]; eat
breakfast desayunarse[7]; eat dinner comer[7]; eat lunch almorzar*[10]; eat supper cenar[7]
Ecuador el Ecuador[16]
Edward Eduardo[3]
egg huevo[12] *m.*
eh (what)? ¿eh?[1]
eight ocho[6]; eight (o'clock) las
ocho[7]; eight hundred ochocientos, -as[19]
eighteen diez y ocho[6]
eighteenth *(in dates)* diez y ocho[19]
eighth octavo, -a[13]; *(in dates)*
ocho[19]
eighty ochenta[6]; eighty-one ochenta
y un, ochenta y uno, -a[6]; eighty-
two ochenta y dos[0]; *etc.*
either *(after negative)* tampoco[20]
elegant elegante[14]
eleven once[6]; eleven (o'clock) las
once[7]
eleventh *(in dates)* once[19]
Elizabeth Isabel[2]
end fin[16] *m.; vb.* terminar[10]
engineering ingeniería[5] *f.*
England Inglaterra[16] *f.*
English *(language)* (el) inglés[2];
English, Englishman, *etc., adj. or
noun* inglés, inglesa[3]; **(he is) an
Englishman** (es) inglés[3]
enjoy oneself divertirse*[11]
enough *adj.* bastante[11]; *adv.* bastante[2]
entertaining divertido, -a[11]
entertainment diversión[9] *f.*
entire entero, -a[19]
etc. etc. *(abbrev. of* etcétera)[13]
European curopeo, -a[16]

even *(right)* mismo[23]; *(at least)* siquiera[18]; **not even** ni siquiera[18]; **even if** *or* **even though** aunque[13]
evening noche[5] *f.;* (in the) evening por la noche[7]; (eight o'clock) in the evening (las ocho) de la noche[7]; **good evening** buenas noches[1]
ever *(after negative)* nunca[19]
every todos los, todas las[7]
everybody todos[1] *m. pl.*
exam *or* **examination** examen[10] *m.*
example ejemplo[8] *m.;* **for example** por ejemplo[8]
excellent excelente[13]
excess exceso[21] *m.*
exchange cambio[14] *m.*
excursion excursión[15] *f.;* **to go on an excursion** hacer* una excursión[15]
excuse me con permiso[20]
exhibit exposición[25] *f.*
expensive caro, -a[14]
expression: proverbial expression dicho[24] *m.*
extremely -ísimo[13]
eyebrow ceja[25] *f.*

F

factory fábrica[21] *f.*
fail: without fail sin falta[20]
failure *(fault)* falta[20] *f.*
fair *(blond)* rubio, -a[5]; *(so-so)* así así[1]
fairly *(rather)* bastante[2]
faithful fiel[24]
fall *(autumn)* otoño[8] *m.*
family familia[1] *f.*
famous famoso, -a[13]
fancy elegante[14]
far lejos[19]; **far from** lejos de[19]
farewell despedida[1] *f.*
fat: to get fat engordar[12]
father padre[6] *m.;* *(dad)* papá[16] *m.*
fault falta[20] *f.*
favor favor[12] *m.*

favorite favorito, -a[9]
fear *vb.* temer[22]
February febrero[8] *m.*
feel sentir*[8]; *(with adj.)* sentirse*[24]
fellow *(boy)* muchacho[3] *m.*
festival fiesta[25] *f.*
few pocos, -as[19]; **a few** unos, -as[3]
field campo[15] *m.*
fifteen quince[6]
fifteenth *(in dates)* quince[19]
fifth quinto, -a[13]; *(in dates)* cinco[19]
fifty cincuenta[6]; **fifty-one** cincuenta y un, cincuenta y uno, -a[6]; **fifty-two** cincuenta y dos[6]; *etc.*
figure *(to appear)* figurar[13]
fill *vb.* llenar[20]; **to fill up with** *(to become full of)* llenarse de[20]
film película[9] *f.*
finally por fin[17]
find encontrar*[17]; **find out (that)** enterarse (de que)[21]
fine *(well)* bien[1]; **fine arts** bellas artes[19] *f. pl.* `
finish *vb.* acabar[18], terminar[10]
fire fuego[15] *m.*
first primer, primero, -a[13]; **at first** al principio[25]
fish pescado[12] *m.*
five cinco[4]; **five (o'clock)** las cinco[7]; **five hundred** quinientos, -as[19]
food comida[12] *f.*
football (el) futbol[9]
for *prep.* para[4]; por[21]; **for (dessert)** de (postre)[12]; **for the (third) time** por (tercera) vez[21]; **to stop by for** ir* a buscar[15]
foreign extranjero, -a[16]
forget (that) olvidar (que) *or* olvidarse (de que)[18]
forty cuarenta[6]; **forty-one** cuarenta y un, cuarenta y uno, -a[6]; **forty-two** cuarenta y dos[6]; *etc.*
forward adelante[23]
four cuatro[6]; **four (o'clock)** las cuatro[7]; **four hundred** cuatrocientos, -as[19]

fourteen catorce[6]
fourteenth *(in dates)* catorce[19]
fourth cuarto, -a[13]; *(in dates)* cuatro[19]
France Francia[16] *f.*
Frank Paco[16]
free libre[23]
French *(language)* (el) francés[2] *m.;*
French, Frenchman, *etc., adj. or noun* francés, francesa[3]; (he is) a Frenchman (es) francés[3]
Friday viernes[9] *m.;* (on) Friday *adv.* el viernes[9], *adj.* del viernes[9]
friend amigo[5] *m.,* amiga[5] *f.*
from de[3]; desde[24]; far from lejos de[19]; to be from *(a place)* ser* de[3]; to leave from salir* de[7]
fun: to have fun divertirse*[11]

G

gallant galante[10]
game partido[9] *m.*
gay *(animated)* animado, -a[20]
gentleman señor[3] *m.;* lady and gentleman señores[3] *m. pl.*
George Jorge[6]
German *(language)* (el) alemán[2]; *adj. or noun* alemán, alemana[3]; (he is) a German (es) alemán[3]
get *(to obtain)* conseguir*[22]; *(to take out)* sacar*[24]; get fat engordar[12]; get on the train subir al tren[17]; get some sunshine *or* get out in the sun tomar el sol[15]; get up levantarse[7]; how do you get to . . . ? ¿por dónde se va a . . . ?[19]
girl muchacha[3] *f.,* niña[6] *f.;* little girl niñita[6] *f.*
give dar*[12]; *(donate)* donar[19]
glad: to be glad (that) alegrarse (de que)[22]
glance at *(to leaf through)* hojear[21]
go ir*[b]; go away irse*[23]; go back volver*[7]; go in pasar[23]; go on

an excursion hacer* una excursión[15]; go on a picnic hacer* una jira[15]; go out salir*[7]; go shopping ir* de compras *or* ir* de tiendas[14]; go through recorrer[18]; go to bed acostarse*[7]; go up subir[17]; go with *(to accompany)* acompañar[12]; to be going to *(do something)* ir* a (+ *inf.*)[9]; how goes it? ¿qué tal?[1]
going ida[17] *f.*
good buen, bueno, -a[5]; good morning buenos días[1]; good afternoon buenas tardes[1]; good evening *or* good night buenas noches[1]; to have a good time divertirse*[11]
good-by despedida[1] *f.;* good-by! ¡adiós![1], ¡que usted siga bien![14]; *(so long)* hasta luego *or* hasta la vista[1]; to say good-by to despedirse* de[17]
good-looking guapo, -a[5]; very (quite, extremely) good-looking guapísimo, -a[13]
gradually: to be gradually *(doing something)* ir* (+ *pres. part.*)[20]
grandfather abuelo[6] *m.*
grandmother abuela[6] *f.*
grandparents abuelos[6] *m. pl.*
gray gris[14]
great gran, grande[14]; a great deal *adv.* mucho[4]
green verde[14]
greeting saludo[1] *m.;* greetings *(regards)* recuerdos[1] *m. pl.*
guide, guidebook guía[18] *f.*

H

hairdo peinado[20] *m.*
half *or* a half medio, -a[7]; half past (one) (la una) y media[7]
hall *(large room)* salón[20] *m.*
hand mano[14] *f.;* (he has it in) his hand (lo tiene en) la mano[14]; on the other hand en cambio[14]

handkerchief pañuelo[14] *m.*
handsome guapo, -a[5]
happy feliz[25]; *(contented)* contento, -a[15]
hard *(difficult)* difícil[3]; **harder** más difícil[4]
hardly apenas[25]
hat sombrero[14] *m.;* **(he puts on) his hat** (se pone) el sombrero[14]
Havana la Habana[16]
have tener*[4]; *(in compound tenses)* haber*[18]; *(food or drink)* tomar[7]; *(meals)* tomar *or* hacer*[12]; **have fun** *(or a good time)* divertirse*[11]; **have an interview** entrevistarse[22]; **have just** *(done something)* acabar de (+ *inf.*)[18]; **have (picnic) lunch** *or* **supper** merendar*[15]; **have to** *(do something)* tener* que (+ *inf.*)[11]
he *subj. pron.* él[1] *(used for stress)*
hear oír*[23]
hearty *(meal)* abundante[12]
heat calor[8] *m.*
Helen Elena[2]
hello *(good morning)* buenos días[1]; *(good afternoon)* buenas tardes[1]; *(good evening)* buenas noches[1]; *(answering the telephone)* diga[23]; *(calling on the telephone)* oiga[23]; **hello!** *(hey!, hi!)* ¡hola![1]
her *poss. adj.* su, sus *or* el (la, los, las) . . . de ella[4]; *dir. obj.* la[5]; *ind. obj.* le[5], se[12] *(before lo, la, los, las); obj. of prep.* ella[5], *reflex.* sí[6]; **with her** con ella[5], *reflex.* consigo[6]
here aquí[3]; **here is** *or* **here are** aquí tiene usted *or* tome usted[14]
hers *poss. adj.* suyo, -a, -os, -as *or* de ella[4]; *pron.* el suyo, el de ella[4], *etc.*
herself *reflex. pron., dir. or ind. obj.* se[6]; *obj. of prep.* sí[6]; **with herself** consigo[6]
hey¡ *(hello!)* ¡hola![1]

hi! ¡hola![1]
him *dir. obj.* le, lo[5]; *ind. obj.* le[5], se[12] *(before lo, la, los, las); obj. of prep.* él[5], *reflex.* sí[6]; **with him** con él[5], *reflex.* consigo[6]
himself *reflex. pron., dir. or ind. obj.* se[6]; *obj. of prep.* sí[6]; **with himself** consigo[6]
his *poss. adj.* su, sus *or* el (la, los, las) . . . de él[4], suyo, -a, -os, -as *or* de él[4] *(in stressed position); pron.* el suyo, el de él[4], *etc.*
historical histórico, -a[16]
history (la) historia[4]
home casa[7] *f.;* **at home** en casa[7]; **to arrive home** llegar* a casa[7]; **to leave home** salir* de casa[7]; **to return home** volver* a casa[7]
hope *vb.* esperar[22]; **I hope (so)!** ¡ojalá![22]
hot: to be (very) hot *(referring to persons)* tener* (mucho) calor[8]; *(weather)* hacer* (mucho) calor[8]
hotel hotel[16] *m.*
hour hora[7] *f.*
house casa[7] *f.*
how? ¿cómo?[1]; ¿qué tal?[10]; **how do you get to . . . ?** ¿por dónde se va a . . . ?[19]; **how goes it?** ¿qué tal?[1]; **how is the weather?** ¿qué tiempo hace?[8]; **how many?** ¿cuantos, -as?[4]; **how much?** ¿cuánto, -a?[4]; **how old (is he)?** ¿cuántos años (tiene)?* or* ¿qué edad (tiene)?[6]
how! ¡qué![13]; **how many!** ¡cuántos, -as![4]; **how much!** ¡cuánto, -a![4]
humid: it is (very) humid *(weather)* hay (mucha) humedad[8]
humidity humedad[8] *f.*
hundred, a *(or one)* **hundred** cien, ciento[6]
hungry: to be (very) hungry tener* (mucho) apetito[12]
husband esposo[6] *m.,* marido[21] *m.*

I

I *subj. pron.* yo[1] *(used for stress)*
idea idea[24] *f.*
ideal ideal[8]
if si[15]; **as if** como si[25]; **even if** aunque[13]
imagination imaginación[24] *f.*
impossible imposible[21]
improve mejorar[21]
in en[2]; *(after superlative)* de[13]; **in (the afternoon)** por (la tarde)[7]; **(one o'clock) in (the afternoon)** (la una) de (la tarde)[7]; **in order to** para[10]; **in order that** para que[24]
indeed: yes, indeed! ¡ya lo creo![9]
India la India[16]
inexpensive barato, -a[14]
intend pensar*[9]
interest interesar[9]; **I am interested in (it)** me interesa[9]
interesting interesante[3]
international internacional[21]
intersection *(street)* bocacalle[19] *f.*
interview: **to have an interview** entrevistarse[22]
introduce *(to present)* presentar[23]
invitation invitación[22] *f.*
invite invitar[20]; **to invite to** *(do something)* invitar a (+ *inf.*)[20]
it *subj. pron., not expressed in Spanish; dir. obj.* lo[2], la[5]; *ind. obj.* le[5]; *obj. of prep.* él, ella[5]
Italian *(language)* (el) italiano[2]; *adj.* italiano, -a[19]
its *poss. adj.* su, sus[4]
itself *reflex. pron., dir. or ind. obj.* se[6]; *obj. of prep.* sí[6]; **with itself** consigo[6]

J

January enero[8] *m.*
jealousy celos[21] *m. pl.*

job *(position)* empleo[22] *m.*, colocación[22] *f.*
John Juan[5]; Johnny Juanito[5]
Joseph José[3]
juice jugo[12] *m.*
July julio[8] *m.*
June junio[8] *m.*
just *(merely)* tan sólo[22]; **to have just** *(done something)* acabar de (+ *inf.*)[18]

K

keep *(to take)* quedarse con[14]; **to keep on** *(doing something)* seguir* (+ *pres. part.*)[21]
kill matar[21]
kind *(amiable)* amable[5]
know *(a fact)* saber*[8]; *(to be acquainted with)* conocer*[5]; **I don't know** no (lo) sé[8]

L

lady señora[3] *f.;* **young lady** señorita[3] *f.;* **lady and gentleman** señores[3] *m. pl.*
lake lago[15] *m.*
language lengua[2] *f.*
large grande[14]
last *(latest)* último, -a[18]; *(past)* pasado, -a[11]; **last night** anoche[11]; **at last** por fin[17]; **until** *(or* **for)** **the very last (minute)** para última hora[18]
late *adv.* tarde[23]; **later** más tarde[23], *(afterwards)* después[5]; **see you later** hasta luego[1]
latest *(last)* último, -a[18]
Latin America Latinoamérica[16] *f.*
lawyer abogado[6] *m.*
leaf through hojear[21]
least *adv.* menos[13]; **at least** por lo menos[11], siquiera[18]
leave dejar[18]; *(to go out)* salir* (de)[7]; **to take leave of** despe-

dirse* de[17]; we haven't much time left no nos queda mucho tiempo[18]
left izquierdo, -a[17]; on the left a mano izquierda[19]; to the left a la izquierda[17]
less menos[4]
let: *wish or command form*[23]
letter carta[22] *f.*
library biblioteca[19] *f.*
life vida[7] *f.*
light ligero, -a[12]; *(color)* claro, -a[14]
likable simpático, -a[3]
like: what's (he) like? ¿cómo es?[3]; like that *(thus)* así[5]; *vb., usually expressed by* gustar[9], *to please:* I like (it) me gusta, *etc.*
likely probable[21]
line línea[22] *f.*
list lista[12] *f.*
listen (to) escuchar[9]; *(to hear)* oír*[23]
literature literatura[24] *f.*
little *adj.* poco, -a[19]; *adv.* poco[2]; a little *adv.* algo[2], un poco[2]; a little walk un paseíto[18], una vuelta[25]; a little while un rato[10]
live *vb.* vivir[6]
lively *(animated)* animado, -a[20]
long largo, -a[16]; as long as *(while)* mientras[24]
look (at) mirar[9]; look for buscar*[15]; look over *(to go through)* recorrer[18]; (he) looks swell *(stylish)* está muy elegante[14]
lose perder*[16]
lot: a lot mucho[4]; what a lot (of)! ¡cuánto, -a,- os, -as![4]
Louis Luis[23]
Louise Luisa[1]
love amor[21] *m.*
lovely *(precious)* precioso, -a[19]; *(divine)* divino, -a[20]
loyal *(constant)* constante[24]
luggage equipaje[17] *m.*

lunch (el) almuerzo[12]; *(special lunch)* cubierto[12] *m.;* to eat lunch almorzar*[10]; to have (picnic) lunch merendar*[15]

M

ma'am señora[2]
magnificent magnífico, -a[13]
make hacer*[7]; that makes (twenty dollars) son (veinte dólares)[17]
mamma mamá[16] *f.*
man hombre[16] *m.*
management *(business)* dirección[21] *f.*
manager gerente[22] *m.*
manner *(way)* modo[11] *m.*
many muchos, -as[8]; as many tantos, -as[11]; as many . . . as tantos (-as) . . . como[13]; how many? ¿cuántos, -as?[4]; how many! ¡cuántos, -as![4]; so many tantos, -as[11]
map *(city)* plano[18] *m.*
March marzo[8] *m.*
married casado, -a[6]; to get married casarse[21]
Mary María[1]
masterpiece obra maestra[24] *f.*
mathematics (las) matemáticas[4]
matinee función *(f.)* de la tarde[24]
matter: it's a matter of es cosa de[23]
May mayo[8] *m.*
may *(can)* poder*[9]; may I *(or we)* come in? ¿se puede?[23]
maybe quizá *or* quizás[15]
me *dir. or ind. obj.* me[5]; *obj. of prep.* mí[5]; with me conmigo[5]
meal comida[12] *f.*
meat carne[12] *f.*
meet *(to see each other)* verse*[15]
meeting *(sight, view)* vista[1] *f.*
melon melón[12] *m.*
menu lista[12] *f.*
merely tan sólo[22]
mess: we've made a fine mess of it! ¡buena la hemos hecho![18]

Mexican *adj. or noun* mejicano, -a[3]; (he is) a Mexican (es) mejicano[3]

Mexico Méjico[16] *m.*

Michael Miguel[1]

midnight: to burn the midnight oil quemarse las cejas[25]

milk leche[12] *f.*

million millón[19] *m.;* a million... un millón de...[19]

mine *poss. adj.* mío, -a, -os, -as[4]; *pron.* el mío[4], *etc.*

minute minuto[7] *m.*

Miss señorita[2], (la) señorita *(abbrev.* Srta.)[3]

miss *(to lose)* perder*[16]

model *(style)* modelo[14] *m.*

modern moderno, -a[18]

Monday lunes[9] *m.;* (on) Monday *adv.* el lunes[9], *adj.* del viernes[9]

money dinero[16] *m.*

month mes[6] *m.;* (six) months old de (seis) meses[6]

monument monumento[16] *m.*

more más[4]

moreover además[11]

morning mañana[7] *f.;* (in the) morning por la mañana[7]; (eight o'clock) in the morning (las ocho) de la mañana[7]; good morning buenos días[1]

mortal mortal[25] *m.*

most *adv.* más[9]

mother madre[6] *f.; (mamma)* mamá[16] *f.*

motive motivo[21] *m.*

movie *(picture)* película[9] *f.;* movies *(cinema)* cine[5] *m. sing.*

Mr. (el) señor *(abbrev.* Sr.)[3]; Mr. and Mrs. (los) señores *(abbrev.* Sres.)[3]

Mrs. (la) señora *(abbrev.* Sra.)[3]; Mr. and Mrs. *see* Mr.

much *adv.* mucho[4]; *adj.* mucho, -a[8]; as much *adv.* tanto[13], *adj.* tanto, -a[11]; as much . . . as tanto (-a) . . .

como[13]; how much? ¿cuánto, -a?[24]; how much! ¡cuánto, -a![4]; so much tanto, -a[11]; very much mucho[4]

museum museo[18] *m.*

music música[9] *f.*

musical musical[12]; musical comedy zarzuela[13] *f.*

must *(to be obliged)* deber[16]; one must *(do something)* hay que (+ *inf.*)[17]; must, must have: *often expressed by future or conditional of conjecture*[17]

my *poss. adj.* mi, mis[4]

myself *reflex. pron., dir. or ind. obj.* me[6]; *obj. of prep.* mí[6]; with myself conmigo[6]

N

name: my name is (Philip) me llamo (Felipe)[6]; what is your name? ¿cómo se llama usted?[6]

named llamado, -a[6]; to be named llamarse[6]

nationality nacionalidad[3] *f.*

natural natural[19]

naturally *(of course)* por supuesto[15]

near *adv.* cerca[5]; *prep.* cerca de[5]

nearby *adv.* cerca[5]

necessary preciso, -a[22]; it is necessary to *(do something)* es preciso (+ *inf.*)[22], hay que (+ *inf.*)[17]

neither tampoco[20]; neither . . . nor ni . . . ni[5]

nephew sobrino[6] *m.;* niece(s) and nephew(s) sobrinos[6] *m. pl.*

never nunca[19]

nevertheless sin embargo[25]

new nuevo, -a[11]; what's new? ¿qué hay (de nuevo)?[23]

news *(item)* noticia[21] *f., (items)* noticias[21] *f. pl.*

newspaper periódico[7] *m.,* diario[21] *m.*

next próximo, -a[22]; next (week) la (semana) próxima[22], la (semana) que viene[9]

nice *(likable)* simpático, -a[3]
niece sobrina[6] *f.;* niece(s) and
nephew(s) sobrinos[6] *m. pl.*
night noche[5] *f.;* (at) night por la
noche[7]; good night buenas noches[1]; last night anoche[11]
nine nueve[6]; nine (o'clock) las
nueve[7]; nine hundred novecientos, -as[19]
nineteen diez y nueve[6]
nineteenth *(in dates)* diez y nueve[19]
ninety noventa[6]; ninety-one noventa y un, noventa y uno, -a[6];
ninety-two noventa y dos[6]; *etc.*
ninth noveno, -a[13]; *(in dates)*
nueve[19]
no no[2]; *adj.* ningún, ninguno, -a[24]
nobody nadie[17]
none ningún, ninguno, -a[24]
noon mediodía[12] *m.;* at noon al
mediodía[12]
no one nadie[17]
nor ni[5]
not no[2]; not even ni siquiera[18]; to
believe not *or* to think not creer*
que no[9]
nothing nada[16], (no) . . . nada[16]
novel novela[24] *f.*
November noviembre[8] *m.*
now ahora[8]
number número[15] *m.*

O

objection *(difficulty)* inconveniente[23] *m.*
obliged: to be obliged *(must)* deber[16]
obtain conseguir*[22]
occasion ocasión[16] *f.*
occur ocurrir[25]; an idea occurs to
me se me ocurre una idea[25]
o'clock: at one o'clock (two o'clock,
etc.) a la una (las dos, *etc.)*[7]; it
is one o'clock (it is two o'clock,
etc.) es la una (son las dos, *etc.)*[7]

October octubre[8] *m.*
of de[2]; (a quarter) of (one) (la
una) menos (cuarto)[7]
officer *(policeman)* guardia[19] *m.*
often muchas veces[11]
oh! ¡ah![17], ¡ay![12], ¡oh![23]
oil: to burn the midnight oil quemarse las cejas[25]
old viejo, -a[5]; *(ancient)* antiguo,
-a[19]; to be . . . (years) old, *etc.*
tener*. . . años[6], *etc.;* how old (is
he)? ¿cuántos años (tiene)? *or*
¿qué edad (tiene)?[6]
older *or* oldest mayor[6]
on *(doing something)* al (+ *inf.*)[17];
on (Monday) *adv.* el (lunes)[9],
adj. del (lunes)[9]; on the dot en
punto[7]; on the (right) a mano
(derecha)[19]; to put on *(a play)*
poner*[24], *(clothes)* ponerse*[14]
once una vez[23]
one un, uno, -a[6]; *pron.* uno, -a[16],
se[17]; one another nos, os, se[6];
one (o'clock) la una[7]; one hundred cien, ciento[6]; one must *(do
something)* hay que (+ *inf.*)[17];
which one? ¿cuál?[8]
oneself *reflex. pron., dir. or ind.
obj.* se[6]; *obj. of prep.* sí[6]; with
oneself consigo[6]
one-way *(ticket)* de ida[17]
only *adv.* sólo[2], tan sólo[22]; *adj.*
único, -a[6]
open abierto, -a[18]; *vb.* abrir*[18]
opera ópera[13] *f.*
opportunity *(occasion)* ocasión[16] *f.*
or o[6]; u[6] *(before o- or ho-)*
orange naranja[12] *f.*
orchestra orquesta[9] *f.;* symphony
orchestra orquesta sinfónica[9]; orchestra seat *(theatre)* butaca[24] *f.*
order orden[23] *f.;* in order to para[10];
in order that para que[24]
other otro, -a[4]; *(remaining)* demás[21]; each other nos, os, se[6];
on the other hand en cambio[14]

ought *(to be obliged)* deber[16]
our *poss. adj.* nuestro, -a, -os, -as[4]
ours *poss. adj.* nuestro, -a, -os, -as[4];
pron. el nuestro[4], *etc.*
ourselves *reflex. pron., dir. or ind.*
obj. nos[6]; *obj. of prep.* nosotros,
-as[6]
out: to go out salir*[7]; to take out
sacar*[24]
outing excursión[15] *f.*
over: over there ahí[17]; to look over
(to go through) recorrer[18]
ow! ¡ay![12]
owe deber[16]

P

pack: to pack the suitcase hacer*
la maleta[17]
pain *(trouble)* pena[15] *f.*
painting pintura[19] *f.*
pair par[14] *m.*
papa papá[16] *m.*
Paraguay el Paraguay[16]
pardon me dispense usted[19]
parents padres[6] *m. pl.*
partner: dancing partner pareja[20] *f.*
party *(political)* partido[21] *m.; (fes-*
tival) fiesta[25] *f.*
pass pasar[10]
passenger pasajero[21] *m.*
past pasado[11] *m.;* pasado, -a[11]; (a
quarter) past (one) (la una) y
(cuarto)[7]
pastime diversión[9] *f.*
Paul Pablo[1]
pay (for) pagar*[16]
people gente[20] *f. sing.*
perfectly perfectamente[14]
perform *(a play)* representar[13]
performance función[24] *f.*
perhaps quizá *or* quizás[15]
permission permiso[16] *m.*
permit *vb.* permitir[22]
Peru el Perú[16]
Peter Pedro[6]

Philip Felipe[1]; Phil Felipillo[20]
philosophy (la) filosofía[4] *f.*
phonograph fonógrafo[11] *m.*
physics (la) física[4]
picnic jira[15] *f.;* to go on a picnic
hacer* una jira[15]; to have picnic
lunch *or* supper merendar*[15]
picture cuadro[19] *m.; (film)* película[9] *f.*
pity lástima[22] *f.*
place lugar[15] *m.,* sitio[15] *m.*
plane avión[23] *m.;* by plane en
avión[23]
play comedia[13] *f.; vb. (music)* tocar*[13], *(a game)* jugar*[9]; to play
(football) jugar* al (futbol)[9]
pleasant agradable[8]; *(likable)* simpático, -a[3]
please *(to be pleasing)* gustar[9]; *(as*
a favor) por favor[23]; to please
(do something) hacer* el favor
de (+ *inf.*)[12]; will you please *(do*
something)? ¿(me) hace usted el
favor de (+ *inf.*)?[12]
pleasure gusto[5] *m.*
P.M.: (one) P.M. (la una) de la
tarde[7]; (eight) P.M. (las ocho) de
la noche[7]
poem poesía[24] *f.*
poetry poesía[24] *f.; (poems)* poesías[24]
f. pl.
point punto[7] *m.*
policeman guardia[19] *m.*
political político, -a[21]
poor pobre[8]; poor (John) el pobre
(Juan)[8]; a poor *(needy)* boy un
muchacho pobre[8]
poorly mal[2]
Portuguese *(language)* (el) portugués[2]
position *(job)* empleo[22] *m.,* colocación[22] *f.*
possible posible[21]; as soon as possible cuanto antes[25]
precious precioso, -a[19]
prefer preferir*[9]

preparations preparativos[17] *m. pl.*
present *vb.* presentar[23]
pretty bonito, -a[3], lindo, -a[5]
prevent impedir*[22]
price precio[14] *m.;* **at different prices** de diferentes precios[14]
probable probable[21]
probably: *often expressed by future or conditional of conjecture*[17]
professor (el) profesor[3], (la) profesora[3]; **(he is) a professor** (es) profesor[3]
program programa[9] *m.*
progress *vb.* progresar[22]
prospect perspectiva[25] *f.*
prove probar*[14]; **prove to be** *(to turn out)* resultar[18]
proverbial expression dicho[24] *m.*
purchase compra[10] *f.*
purpose propósito[22] *m.*
put poner*[14]; **to put on** *(a play)* poner*[24], *(clothes)* ponerse*[14]

Q

quarter *(of an hour)* cuarto[7] *m.;* **a quarter to (one)** (la una) menos cuarto[7]; **a quarter past (one)** (la una) y cuarto[7]
quite muy[1]; -ísimo[13]; *(terribly)* soberanamente[25]

R

radio (la) radio[9]
rain lluvia[25] *f.; vb.* llover*[8]
rare raro, -a[19]
rate: at any rate de todos modos[18]
rather *(enough)* bastante[2]
Raymond Ramón[22]
read leer*[7]
ready listo, -a[5]
recall recordar*[11]
receive recibir[22]
record *(phonograph)* disco[11] *m.*
recreation recreo[14] *m.*

redheaded pelirrojo, -a[21]
refreshment(s) refresco[11] *m. sing.*
regards recuerdos[1] *m. pl.*
regret *vb.* sentir*[8]
relate contar*[22]
relative pariente[6] *m.,* parienta[6] *f.*
remain quedar[18]; *(to stay)* quedarse[10]
remaining *(other)* demás[21]
remark *(comment)* comentario[20] *m.*
remember recordar*[11]; **remember me to (everybody)** recuerdos a (todos)[1]
repeat repetir*[22]
request *vb.* pedir*[22]
restaurant restaurán[12] *m.*
result *(to turn out)* resultar[18]
return vuelta[17] *f.; (to go back)* volver*[7]
review revista[12] *f.*
revue revista[12] *f.*
rhythm ritmo[20] *m.*
rich rico, -a[16]
right derecho, -a[19]; *adv.* mismo[23]; **right?** ¿eh?[1]; **right now** ahora mismo[23]; **all right** bien[1]; **if it's all right (with you)** si usted no tiene inconveniente[23]; **on the right** a mano derecha[19]; **to the right** a la derecha[19]
river río[15] *m.*
room *(large room)* sala[17] *f.; (hall, salon)* salón[20] *m.;* **baggage room** sala de equipajes[17]; **waiting room** sala de espera[17]
round-trip *(ticket)* de ida y vuelta[17]
routine: daily routine vida *(f.)* de todos los días[7]
rumba rumba[20] *f.*
Russian *(language)* (el) ruso[2]

S

salad ensalada[12] *f.*
salon salón[20] *m.*
Salvador el Salvador[16]

same mismo, -a[7]; the same (thing) lo mismo[12]

sandwich sandwich[12] *m.*

Saturday sábado[9] *m.;* (on) Saturday *adv.* el sábado[6], *adj.* del sábado[9]

say decir*[4]; say good-by to despedirse* de[17]; I should say so! ¡ya lo creo![9]; let's say *or* we might say *(after negative statement)* que digamos[24]; what do you say? *(what's new?)* ¿qué me cuenta?[23]

saying *(proverbial expression)* dicho[24] *m.*

scarcely *(hardly)* apenas[25]

school year curso[25] *m.*

science (la) ciencia[4]

sculpture escultura[19] *f.*

seat asiento[24] *m.;* *(ticket)* localidad[24] *f.;* orchestra seat butaca[24] *f.*

seated sentado, -a[15]

second segundo, -a[13]; *(in dates)* dos[19]

secure *(to obtain)* conseguir*[22]

see ver*[5]; see you (tomorrow) hasta (mañana)[1]

seem parecer*[9]

September septiembre[8] *m.*

series serie[13] *f.*

serious serio, -a[21]

servant servidor[17] *m.*

serve servir*[12]

service: at your service: servidor (de usted)[17], a sus órdenes[23]

seven siete[6]; seven (o'clock) las siete[7]; seven hundred setecientos, -as[19]

seventeen diez y siete[6]

seventeenth *(in dates)* diez y siete[19]

seventh séptimo, -a[13]; *(in dates)* siete[19]

seventy setenta[6]; seventy-one setenta y un, setenta y uno, -a[6]; seventy-two setenta y dos[6]; *etc.*

several varios, -as[5]

shall: *future tense*[15]

sharp: (one o'clock) sharp (la una) en punto[7]

she *subj. pron.* ella[1] *(used for stress)*

shirt camisa[14] *f.*

shoe zapato[14] *m.*

shop tienda[14] *f.;* to go shopping ir* de compras *or* ir* de tiendas[14]

short corto, -a[16]; *(of stature)* bajo, -a[5]; short time rato[10] *m.*

should *(ought to)* deber[16]; *conditional*[16]; I should say so! ¡ya lo creo![9]

show *(performance)* función[24] *f.*

side lado[17] *m.*

sight vista[1] *f.*

since *(cause)* ya que[16], pues[16]

sincerely yours su afmo. (= afectísimo) amigo[22]

sing cantar[13]

single *(unmarried)* soltero, -a[6]

sir señor[2]

sister hermana[6] *f.;* brother(s) and sister(s) hermanos[6] *m. pl.*

sit down sentarse*[23]

situation situación[21] *f.*

six seis[6]; six (o'clock) las seis[7]; six hundred seiscientos, -as[19]

sixteen diez y seis[6]

sixteenth *(in dates)* diez y seis[19]

sixth sexto, -a[13]; *(in dates)* seis[19]

sixty sesenta[6]; sixty-one sesenta y un, sesenta y uno, -a[6]; sixty-two sesenta y dos[6]; *etc.*

sleep *vb.* dormir*[7]

small pequeño, -a[13]

snow *vb.* nevar*[8]

so tan[4]; *(it)* lo [13]; *(thus)* así[5]; *(therefore)* luego[15]; *(and so)* conque[11], de modo que[11]; *(so that)* para que[24], de modo que[11]; so long *(good-by)* hasta luego[1], hasta la vista[1]; so many tantos, -as[11]; so much tanto, -a[11]; so-so *(fair)* así así[1]; so that para que[24], de modo que[11]; and so conque[11], de modo que[11]; **I should say so!** ¡ya lo creo![9]; **to believe so** or **to think so** creer* que sí[9]

sociology (la) sociología[4]

sole (only) único, -a[6]

so long (good-by) hasta luego[1], hasta la vista[1]

solution solución[21] f.

some adv. algo[2]; adj. algún, alguno, -a[5], pl. unos, -as[3], algunos, -as[5]; pron. algunos, -as[4]

somebody alguien[24]

someone alguno, -a[4], alguien[24]

something algo[17]

sometimes a veces[3]

somewhat algo[2]

son hijo[6] m.

soon pronto[23]; (then) luego[1]; **as soon as** conj. en cuanto[24]; **as soon as possible** cuanto antes[25]

sorry: to be sorry (to regret) sentir*[8]; (to regret it) sentirlo*[8]

so-so (fair) así así[1]

soup sopa[12] f.

Spain España[3] f.

Spaniard español[3] m., española[3] f.; **(he is) a Spaniard** (es) español[3]

Spanish (language) (el) español[2]; adj. español, española[3]

speak hablar[2]; **this is . . . speaking** (at the telephone) ¡al aparato![23]

speed velocidad[21] f.; **speeding** exceso (m.) de velocidad[21]

spend (time) pasar[10]

sport deporte[9] m.

sports adj. deportivo, -a[9]

spot (place) lugar[15] m., sitio[15] m.

spring (season) primavera[8] f.

station estación[17] f.

stay quedarse[10]

still (yet) aún[18]; **to be still** (doing something) seguir* (+ pres. part.)[21]

stock (supply) surtido[14] m.

stop: to stop by for ir* a buscar[15]

store: department store almacén[14] m.

storm tormenta[21] f.

story cuento[24] m.

straight derecho, -a[19]; **straight ahead** todo derecho[19]

street calle[15] f.; **at (40th) Street** en la calle (40)[15]

streetcar tranvía[15] m.

street intersection bocacalle[19] f.

strict (demanding) exigente[4]

strike huelga[21] f.

stroll paseo[15] m.; vb. pasear or pasearse[11]

study vb. estudiar[3]

style (model) modelo[14] m.

stylish elegante[14]

subject (course of study) asignatura[4] f.

success éxito[13] m.

such or **such a** tal[16]

suit (to be becoming) sentar*[14]

suitcase maleta[17] f.; **to pack the suitcase** hacer* la maleta[17]

summer verano[8] m.

sun sol[8] m.; **to get out in the sun** tomar el sol[15]

Sunday domingo[9] m.; **(on) Sunday** adv. el domingo[9], adj. del domingo[9]

sunny: to be sunny (weather) hacer* (or haber*) sol[8]

sunshine sol[8] m.; **to get some sunshine** tomar el sol[15]

supper (la) cena[12]; **to eat supper** cenar[7]; **to have picnic supper** merendar*[15]

supply (stock) surtido[14] m.

suppose suponer*[18]; often expressed by future or conditional of conjecture[17]

sure seguro, -a[21]; **sure!** ¡claro![10], ¡cómo no![22]

suspect vb. sospechar[21]

symphony sinfonía[13] f.; **symphony orchestra** orquesta (f.) sinfónica[9]

T

take tomar[7]; *(to keep)* quedarse con[14]; take leave of despedirse* de[17]; take out sacar*[24]; take a trip hacer* un viaje[16], *(excursion)* hacer* una excursión[15]; take a walk pasear *or* pasearse[11], dar* un paseo[15], dar* una vuelta[25]
talk hablar[2]; *(to chat)* charlar[7]
tall alto, -a[5]
tango tango[20] *m.*
taxi *or* taxicab taxi[18] *m.*
teach enseñar[3]
teacher (el) profesor[3], (la) profesora[3]; (he is) a teacher (es) profesor[3]
team equipo[9] *m.*
telephone teléfono[23] *m.;* on the telephone al teléfono[23]
television televisión[9] *f.*
tell *(to say)* decir*[4]; *(to relate)* contar*[22]
ten diez[6]; ten (o'clock) las diez[7]
tennis (el) tenis[9]
tenth décimo, -a[13]; *(in dates)* diez[19]
terribly *(quite)* soberanamente[25]
test *(to try)* probar*[14]
than que[4]; *(before a numeral)* de[13]
thanks gracias[1] *f. pl.;* thank you gracias[1]
that *conj.* que[4]; *rel. pron.* que[5]; *dem. adj.* ese, esa, *(over there)* aquel, aquella[14]; that (one) *pron.* ése, ésa, aquél, aquélla[14]; that *(idea, fact, etc.) pron.* eso[5], aquello[14]; that of el de, la de[4]; that which lo que[11]; that makes *or* will be (twenty dollars) son (veinte dólares)[17]
the el, la, los, las[1]; el[12] *(f.);* lo[12] *(neut.);* of the del (= de + el), de la, de los, de las[5]; to the al (= a + el), a la, a los, a las[5]
theatre teatro[16] *m.*

their *poss. adj.* su, sus *or* el (la, los, las) . . . de ellos, -as[4]
theirs *poss. adj.* suyo, -a, -os, -as *or* de ellos, -as[4]; *pron.* el suyo, el de ellos[4], *etc.*
them *dir. obj.* los, las[5]; *ind. obj.* les[5], se[12] *(before lo, la, los, las); obj. of prep.* ellos, -as[5], *reflex.* sí[6]; with them con ellos, -as[5], *reflex.* consigo[6]
themselves *reflex. pron., dir. or ind. obj.* se[6]; *obj. of prep.* sí[6]; with themselves consigo[6]
then entonces[11]; *(soon)* luego[1]; well, then pues[14]
there allí[20]; *(over there)* ahí[17]; there is *or* there are hay[8]; there are (five) of us somos (cinco)[6]
therefore luego[15]
these *dem. adj.* estos, estas[4]; *pron.* éstos, éstas[14]
they *subj. pron.* ellos, -as[1] *(used for stress)*
thing cosa[7] *f.;* the same thing lo mismo[12]
think pensar*[9]; *(to believe)* creer*[9]; to think of *or* about pensar* en[10]; to think not creer* que no[9]; to think so creer* que sí[9]
third tercer, tercero, -a[13]; *(in dates)* tres[19]
thirteen trece[6]
thirteenth *(in dates)* trece[19]
thirtieth *(in dates)* treinta[19]
thirty treinta[6]; thirty-one treinta y un, treinta y uno, -a[6]; thirty-two treinta y dos[6]; *etc.;* thirty-first *(in dates)* treinta y uno[19]
this *dem. adj.* este, esta[4]; this (one) *pron.* éste, ésta[14]; this *(idea, fact, etc.) pron.* esto[14]; this is . . . calling *(at the telephone)* aquí . . . [23]; this is . . . speaking *(at the telephone)* ¡al aparato![23]
those *dem. adj.* esos, esas, *(over there)* aquellos, aquellas[14]; *pron.*

ésos, ésas, aquéllos, aquéllas[14]; those of los de, las de[4]

though: even though aunque[13]

thousand, a *(or* one) thousand mil[19]

three tres[5]; three (o'clock) las tres[7]; three hundred trescientos, -as[19]

through por[7]; to go through recorrer[18]; to leaf through hojear[21]; it is a through train el tren es directo[17]

Thursday jueves[9] *m.; (on)* Thursday *adv.* el jueves[9], *adj.* del jueves[9]

thus así[5]

ticket billete[12] *m.; (seat)* localidad[24] *f.;* ticket agent taquillero[17] *m.*

tie corbata[14] *f.*

time *(duration)* tiempo[11] *m.; (sequence)* vez[3] *f.; (hour)* hora[7] *f.;* at times a veces[3]; short time *(little while)* rato[10] *m.;* to have a good time divertirse*[11]

timetable horario[17] *m.*

tired cansado, -a[7]

to a[1]; *(in order to)* para[10]; (a quarter) to (one) (la una) menos (cuarto)[7]; according to según[18]; in order to para[10]

toast tostadas[12] *f. pl.;* piece of toast tostada[12] *f.*

today hoy[8]

tomorrow mañana[1]

too *(also)* también[2]

top balcony galería[24] *f.;* seat in the top balcony asiento *(m.)* de galería[24]

torture suplicio[25] *m.*

tour *(little walk)* paseíto[18] *m.*

toward the beginning of a principios de[19]

town *(business district)* centro[10] *m.;* in town en el centro[10]; to town al centro[10]

train tren[17] *m.;* to change trains cambiar de tren[17]; to get on the

train subir al tren[17]; it is a through train el tren es directo[17]

travel viajar[16]

traveler viajero[17] *m.*

treat tratar[21]; *(to cure)* curar[10]

tree árbol[15] *m.*

trip viaje[16] *m.; (excursion)* excursión[15] *f.;* round-trip *(ticket)* de ida y vuelta[17]; to take *(or* make) a trip hacer* un viaje[16], *(excursion)* hacer* una excursión[15]

trolley (el) tranvía[15]

trouble *(pain)* pena[15] *f.*

true? ¿verdad?[2]

trustworthy *(faithful)* fiel[24]

truth verdad[2] *f.*

try on probar*[14]

Tuesday martes[9] *m.; (on)* Tuesday *adv.* el martes[9], *adj.* del martes[9]

turn vuelta[25] *f.;* to turn (left) doblar (a la izquierda)[19]; to turn out *(to result)* resultar[18]

twelfth *(in dates)* doce[19]

twelve doce[6]; twelve (o'clock) las doce[7]

twentieth *(in dates)* veinte[19]

twenty veinte[6]; twenty-one veintiún, veintiuno, -a[6]; twenty-two veintidós[6]; *etc.;* twenty-first, *etc. (in dates)* veintiuno[19], *etc.*

two dos[3]; two (o'clock) las dos[7]; two hundred doscientos, -as[19]

U

uncle tío[6] *m.;* uncle(s) and aunt(s) tíos[6] *m. pl.*

understand entender*[2]

United: the United States los Estados Unidos[16]

university universidad[3] *f.*

unmarried soltero, -a[6]

unpleasant desagradable[8]

until *prep.* hasta[1]; *conj.* hasta que[24]

up: to fill up with *(to become full of)* llenarse de[20]; to get up levantarse[7]

Uruguay el Uruguay[16]
us *dir. or ind. obj.* nos[5]; *obj. of prep.* nosotros, -as[5]
used to: *expressed by imperfect tense*[11]

V

vacation vacaciones[25] *f. pl.*
value *(worth)* valor[19] *m.*
variety variedad[13] *f.; (vaudeville)* variedades[13] *f. pl.*
vegetable legumbre[12] *f.*
very muy[1]; *(extremely)* -ísimo[13]; *in idiomatic phrases:* mucho, -a (+ *noun)*[8]; **very much** *(a lot)* mucho[4]
view vista[1] *f.*
visit visita[10] *f.; vb.* visitar[16], hacer una visita[10]

W

wait espera[17] *f.; vb.* esperar[25]; **to wait until** esperar a que[25] (+ *clause)*
waiting espera[17] *f.;* **waiting room** sala *(f.)* de espera[17]
walk paseo[15] *m.;* **a little walk** un paseíto[18], una vuelta[25]; **to take a walk** pasear *or* pasearse[11], dar* un paseo[15], dar* una vuelta[25]
waltz vals[20] *m.*
want *vb.* querer*[12]
warm: **to be (very) warm** *(referring to persons)* tener* (mucho) calor[8]; *(weather)* hacer* (mucho) calor[8]
warmth calor[8] *m.*
watch reloj[7] *m.; (to look at)* mirar[9]
water (el) agua[12] *(f.)*
way *(manner)* modo[11] *m.;* **which way is . . . ?** ¿por dónde se va a . . . ?[19]
we *subj. pron.* nosotros, -as[1] *(used for stress)*

wealthy: **very wealthy** millonario, -a[19]
weather tiempo[8] *m.;* **to be (good, bad) weather** hacer* (buen, mal) tiempo[8]; **how is the weather?** ¿qué tiempo hace?[8]; **the weather is fine** hace buen tiempo *or* hace un tiempo muy bueno[8]
wedding boda[21] *f.*
Wednesday miércoles[9] *m.;* **(on) Wednesday** *adv.* el miércoles[9], *adj.* del miércoles[9]
week semana[9] *f.*
weekend fin *(m.)* de semana[16]
welcome: **you're welcome** no hay de qué[19]
well bien[1]; **well . . . bueno . . .**[12]; **well (then) . . . pues . . .**[14]
well-known conocido, -a[13]
what *(that which)* lo que[11]
what? ¿qué?[2]; **what is (he) like?** ¿cómo es?[3]; **what is your name?** ¿cómo se llama usted?[6]; **eh, what?** ¿eh?[1]
what! ¡qué![13]; **what a (pretty girl)!** ¡qué (linda muchacha)! *or* ¡qué (muchacha) tan *or* más (linda)![13]; **what a (collection)!** ¡vaya una colección![19]; **what a lot (of)!** ¡cuánto, -a, -os, -as![4]
when cuando[8]; al[17] (+ *inf.)*
when? ¿cuándo?[7]
where? ¿dónde?[3]; *(to what place?)* ¿adónde?[15]; **where (is he) from?** ¿de dónde (es)?[3]
whether si[25]
which el (la, los, las) que[24]; **that which** lo que[11]
which? *adj.* ¿qué?[2]; **which (one)?** *pron.* ¿cuál?[8]; **which way is . . . ?** ¿por dónde se va a . . . ?[19]
while *(as long as)* mientras[24]; **a (little) while** un rato[10]
white blanco, -a[14]
who *rel. pron.* que[5]
who? ¿quién?, *pl.* ¿quiénes?[3]

whole *(entire)* entero, -a[19]
whom? *obj. of verb* ¿a quién?, *pl.*
¿a quiénes?[5]; *obj. of prep.*
¿quién?, *pl.* ¿quiénes?[5]
whose cuyo, -a[19]
why? ¿por qué?[4]
wife señora[3] *f.*, esposa[6] *f.*
will: *future tense*[15]; **will you please**
(do something)? ¿(me) hace usted
el favor de (+ *inf.*)?[12]; **that will**
be (twenty dollars) son (veinte
dólares)[17]
win ganar[9]
wind viento[8] *m.*
windy: it is (very) windy hace (mucho) viento[8]
winter invierno[8] *m.*
wish *vb.* querer*[12]; *(to desire)* desear[23]
with con[2]; **to fill up with** *(to be-*
come full of) llenarse de[20]
without sin[3]
woman mujer[16] *f.*
wonder: *often expressed by future*
or conditional of conjecture[17]
wonderful magnífico, -a[13]
work trabajo[20] *m.; (literary)* obra[24]
f.; vb. trabajar[11]
worker obrero[21] *m.*, obrera[21] *f.*
world mundo[24] *m.*
worse *or* **worst** peor[10]
worth *(value)* valor[19] *m.;* **to be**
worth valer*[14]
would: *conditional*[16]
wreck *(collision)* choque[21] *m.;* **car**
wreck choque de automóviles[21]
write escribir*[22]

Y

year año[4] *m.;* **school year** curso[25]
m.; **to be . . . years old** tener*. ,.
años[6]

yes sí[2]; **yes (sir)** sí, señor[2]; **yes, in-**
deed! ¡ya lo creo![9]
yesterday ayer[10]
yet aún[18]
you *subj. pron. (fam.)* tú, vosotros,
-as[1], *(polite)* usted, ustedes[1], *(in-*
def.) se[17]; *dir. obj. (fam.)* te, os[5],
(polite) le, lo, la, los, las[5]; *ind.*
obj. (fam.) te, os[5], *(polite)* le, les[5],
se[12] *(before lo, la, los, las); obj. of*
prep. (fam.) ti, vosotros, -as[5], *(po-*
lite) usted, ustedes[5], *reflex.* sí[6];
with you *(fam.)* contigo, con vosotros, -as[5], *(polite)* con usted, con
ustedes[5], *reflex.* consigo[6]
young joven[5]; **young lady** señorita[3] *f.*
younger *or* **youngest** menor[6]
young lady señorita[3] *f.*
your *poss. adj. (fam.)* tu, tus, vuestro, -a, -os, -as[4], *(polite)* su, sus
or el (la, los, las) . . . de usted *or*
de ustedes[4]
yours *poss. adj. (fam.)* tuyo, -a, -os,
-as, vuestro, -a, -os, -as[4], *(polite)*
suyo, -a, -os, -as *or* de usted, de
ustedes[4]; *pron. (fam.)* el tuyo, el
vuestro[4], *etc., (polite)* el suyo, el
de usted[4], *etc.*
yourself, yourselves *reflex. pron.,*
dir. or ind. obj. (fam.) te, os[6],
(polite) se[6]; *obj. of prep. (fam.)*
ti, vosotros, -as[6], *(polite)* sí[6]; **with**
yourself, with yourselves *(fam.)*
contigo, con vosotros, -as[6], *(polite)*
consigo[6]

Z

zoology (la) zoología[4]

Index

(References are to lessons and paragraphs, except when otherwise noted.)

ESPAÑA Y PORTUGAL

Copyright by C.S. HAMMOND & CO., N.Y.

ESCALA

KILÓMETROS
0   50   100   150   200

MILLAS
0   50   100   150   200

Capitales .... ⊛
Límites Internacionales ....

FRANCIA

ANDORRA

CATALUÑA

Barcelona
Tarragona

ISLAS BALEARES

Menorca

Mallorca

Palma

Ibiza

Mar Mediterráneo

Longitud Oeste de Greenwich

Valencia
Cuenca
Alicante
Murcia
Cartagena
Almería
Granada
Río Genil
Córdoba
Río Guadalquivir
Málaga
Gibraltar (Brit.)
Tarifa
Estr. de Gibraltar
Cádiz
Sevilla
Itálica
Badajoz
Río Guadiana
Río Tajo
Toledo
Madrid ⊛
Escorial
Segovia
Avila
Zamora
Salamanca
Valladolid
Burgos
León
Zaragoza
Río Ebro
NAVARRA
ARAGÓN
VIZCAYA
Bilbao
San Sebastián
Covadonga
Oviedo
ASTURIAS
Río Miño
Vigo
Santiago
La Coruña
Cabo Finisterre
GALICIA
Oporto
Río Duero
PORTUGAL
Lisboa
EXTREMADURA
ANDALUCIA
La Mancha
CASTILLA LA NUEVA
CASTILLA LA VIEJA
ESPAÑA

Golfo de Gascuña

Océano Atlántico

40°
36°
8°
4°
0°
4°
8°